FOUNDATION

Series Editor:
John Hopkin

Editor:
Paul Brooker

Authors:

Nicola Arber, Bournville School, Birmingham

Heather Blades, Deepings School, Peterborough

Lisa James, Cockshut Hill School, Birmingham

Sue Lomas, Henbury High School, Macclesfield

Garrett Nagle, St Edward's School, Oxford

Chris Ryan, formerly at Heston Community School, London

Linda Thompson, formerly at Sandbach School, Sandbach

Paul Thompson, Ounsdale High School, Wolverhampton

Heinemann Educational Publishers
Halley Court, Jordan Hill, Oxford, OX2 8EJ
Part of Harcourt Limited
Heinemann is the registered trademark of Harcourt Education Limited

© Nicola Arber, Heather Blades, Lisa James, Sue Lomas, Garrett Nagle, Chris Ryan, Linda Thompson, Paul Thompson, 2001

Copyright notice
All rights reserved. No part of this publication may be reproduced in any material form (including photocopying or storing it in any medium by electronic means and whether or not transiently or incidentally to some other use of this publication) without the prior written permission of the copyright owner, except in accordance with the provisions of the Copyright, Designs and Patents Act 1988 or under the terms of a licence issued by the Copyright Licensing Agency Ltd, 90 Tottenham Court Road, London W1P 0LP. Applications for the copyright owner's written permission to reproduce any part of this publication should be addressed to the publisher.

First published 2001

ISBN: 978 0 435355 26 5

09 08 07
10 9 8 7 6

Designed and illustrated by Gecko Ltd, Bicester, Oxon, Dave Mostyn and Peter Bull
Original illustrations © Heinemann Educational Publishers 2001
Printed and bound in Italy by Printer Trento s.r.l.

Acknowledgements
The authors and publishers would like to thank the following for permission to use copyright material:

Maps and extracts
p.6 Alan Bilham-Boult, People, Places & Themes / ; **p.8 A, 9 B** Maps reproduced from Ordnance Survey maps with the permission of the Controller of Her Majesty's Stationery Office © Crown Copyright; License No. 398020; **p.14 E** Maps reproduced from Ordnance Survey maps with the permission of the Controller of Her Majesty's Stationery Office © Crown Copyright; License No. 398020; **p.26 A** Maps reproduced from Ordnance Survey maps with the permission of the Controller of Her Majesty's Stationery Office © Crown Copyright; License No. 398020; **p.27** www.BBC.co.uk; **p.29, 31, 36 A** Maps reproduced from Ordnance Survey maps with the permission of the Controller of Her Majesty's Stationery Office © Crown Copyright; License No. 398020; **p.47** Philips Modern School Atlas / George Philip Ltd; **p.51** Philips Children's Atlas / George Philips; **p.54** www.bbc.co.uk/weather/worldweather/europe/index; **p.57 F** Philips Foundation Atlas / George Philips; **p.59 B, C** Waugh, The UK and Europe / ; **p.68 C** Philips Atlas / George Philips; **p.69 A** Attica Interactive 1997; **p.69 B** Philips Atlas / George Philips; **p.90 A** Philips Atlas / George Philips; **p.91 C** Collins Longman Student Atlas; **p.97 B** Tony Waltham, Karst and Caves / Yorkshire Dales National Park and the British Cave Research Association; **p.98 D, 99 G, 101 J** Maps reproduced from Ordnance Survey maps with the permission of the Controller of Her Majesty's Stationery Office © Crown Copyright; License No. 398020; **p.108 A** Philips University Atlas / George Philips; **p.120 B** Understanding Global Issues – World Fishing; **p.122 B, 123 D** www.guardianunlimited.co.uk ; **p.136 A, B, 137 C, D** www.thamesvalley.police.uk .

Photographs
4 A Stock Market/Tibor Bognar.; **4 B** SPL/Earth Satellite Corp.; **4 C** Corbis / Robert Holmes; **4 D** Mike Ridout; **4 E** FLPA/Fritz Pölking; **5 F** FLPA/Robin Chittenden; **5 G** PA Photos / Owen Humphreys; **5 H** Stock Market; **5 I** Stock Market; **5 J** Stock Market/John M. Roberts; **6 A** Alan Bilham-Boult; **6 B** Alan Bilham-Boult; **6 C** David Tarn; **7 D** FLPA/Mike J. Thomas; **10** Heather Blades; **11 A** Collections/John & Eliza Forder; **18 A** PA Photos/John Giles; **19 B** John Hopkin; **19 C** John Hopkin; **20 A** FLPA/Mike J. Thomas; **20 B** Stock Market/Jose Fuste Rago; **20 C** Stock Market; **20 D** Stock Market/T Stewart; **20 E** FLPA/P. Moore; **22 A** David Tarn; **22 B** Stock Market; **22 C** FLPA/Peter Reynolds; **22 D** Corbis/John Farmer/Cordaiy PL; **22 E** Sue Lomas; **23 B** Sue Lomas; **24 E** Sue Lomas; **27** Camera Press/Andrew Hasson; **28 A** John Connors Press Associates; PA Photos/Tim Ockenden; **30 A** Katz Pictures; **32 A** Stock Market; **32 B** Courtesy USGS; **33 A** Stock Market; **33 B** Stock Market; **34 A** Stock Market; **34 B** Sue Cunningham; **34 C** The Trafford Centre; **34 D** Stock Market; **34 E** Stock Market; **34 F** Stock Market; **35 G** (l-r) Stock Market; Stock Market/Matthias Kulka; Stock Market; Stock Market/Rob Lewine; Barry Atkinson; Peter Morris; Chris Honeywell; Rupert Horrox; Stock Market/Steve Prezant; Rupert Horrox; Hemera Photo-Objects; Gareth Boden; **36 B** Nicola Arber; **37 C** John Hopkin; **37 D** John Hopkin; **37 E** Nicola Arber; **40 A** Stock Market; **40 B** Collections/Brian Shuel; **40 C** Collections/Liz Stares; **40 D** Stock Market/Charles Gupton; **41** Joan Davies; Joan Davies; **46** University of Dundee; **48 A** Corbis/ Richard Hamilton Smith; **48 B** Stock Market; **48 C** Stock Market; **52 A** University of Dundee; **52 B** Jeremy Krause; **52 E** Jeremy Krause; **52 G** University of Dundee; **52 H** Jeremy Krause; **61 D** John Hopkin; **62** (l-r) Stock Market; Associated Press/Fredrik Funck; James Davis Travel Photography; Corbis/Carl Purcell; Stock Market; FLPA/Mark Newman; **63 C** Stock Market; **63 E** PA Photos/John Giles; **63 F** BBC; **64 A** Corbis / Robert Holmes; **64 B** Sue Cunningham; **65 C** Stock Market; **66 E** Sue Cunningham; **66 F** Sue Cunningham; **67 G** Science Photo Library/Tom van Sant, Geosphere Project/Planetary Visions; **72 C** Sue Cunningham; **73 G** Sue Cunningham; **73 H** Sue Cunningham/Patrick Cunningham; **74 J** Sue Cunningham; **75 L** Oxford Scientific Films/George Bernard; **80 A** Sue Cunningham; **81 C** Sue Cunningham; Sue Cunningham; **83 E** SPL/NASA; **84 G** Sue Cunningham; **88 A** FLPA/W. Broadhurst; **88 B** John Hopkin; **88 C** David Tarn; **88 D** Camera Press/Colin Davey; **89 F** Sam Smith; **89 G** Stock Market; **89 H** FLPA/Keith Rushforth; **89 I** Stock Market; **93 D** SPL/Jon Wilson; **93 E** John Hopkin; **94 B** Sam Smith; **95 C** Sam Smith; **95 D** Corbis/Annie Griffiths Belt; **96 E** David Tarn; **96 F** David Tarn; **96 G** David Tarn; **97 B** David Tarn; **99 E** David Tarn; **100 G** Lisa James; **104** left Corbis/James Skok; **104** right FLPA/Anthony T. Matthews; **106 A** Corbis / Lawson Wood; **106 B** David Tarn; **106 C** FLPA/Derek Hall; **106 D** PA Photos / EPA; **106 E** Oxford Scientific Films/Steve Turner; **110 B** Sue Cunningham; **111 D** Rex Features/SIPA; **113 D** Oxford Scientific Films/ Michael and Patricia Fogden; **113 E** Oxford Scientific Films/Tim Jackson; **113 F** FLPA/W Wisniewski; **113 G** FLPA/W Wisniewski; **113 H** Garden Matters; **116 A** David Tarn; **116 B** FLPA/S Jonasson; **116 C** Corbis / Reuters NewMedia Inc; **116 D** FLPA/Martin Smith; **117 E** Eye Ubiquitous/Lawson Wood; **117 F** Oxford Scientific Films/Doug Allan; **121 D** Eye Ubiquitous/Damian Peters; **121 E** Corbis / Natalie Fobes; **121 F** Corbis / Paul A. Souders; **124 A** Oxford Scientific Films/Scott Winer; **124 B** FLPA/Silvestria; **125 C** FLPA/Minden Pictures; **130 A** Associated Press/Dave Thomson; **130 B** Ronald Grant; **130 C** Associated Press/Itsu Inouye; **130 D** Camera Press/Gus Coral; **130 E, 134 A, 134 B, 134 C, 134 D, 134 E, 134 F, 134 G, 135 H, 138 F, 138 I** Garrett Nagle.

The publishers have made every effort to trace the copyright holders, but if they have inadvertently overlooked any, they will be pleased to make the necessary arrangements at the first opportunity.

Throughout the book these symbols are used with activities that use literacy, numeracy and ICT skills.

Contents

❶ Rivers — 4
How does a river valley change downstream?	6
Where is the river section you are going to study?	8
Investigating rivers: how do rivers change downstream?	10
What information can you collect in the field?	11
What does your data mean?	12
Review and reflect	17

❷ Coastal environments — 18
How is our coastline formed?	19
What is erosion?	20
How do waves shape our coast?	22
How does the sea erode the coast?	23
Conflicts along the coast	26
Why do cliffs collapse?	27
How can the coast be managed?	30
Review and reflect	33

❸ Shopping – past, present and future — 34
Setting the scene	35
Shopping hierarchies	38
What's your rating?	39
How will changes affect different people?	40
How has shopping changed?	41
What is the future of shopping?	43
Review and reflect	45

❹ Weather patterns over Europe — 46
What is Europe like?	47
What are clouds and why does it rain?	48
What causes cloud and rain?	50
What can satellite images tell us about the weather?	52
How can weather information be presented?	54
What types of climate does Europe have?	56
What affects Europe's climate?	58
Review and reflect	63

Websites: On pages where you are asked to go to www.heinemann.co.uk/hotlinks to complete a task or download information, please insert the code **1631P** at the website.

❺ Investigating Brazil — 64
What do you know about Brazil?	65
Location, location, location	68
How big is Brazil?	69
What is Brazil like? What are the main differences within the country?	70
What is a developed country?	76
How developed is Brazil?	78
How successful has development been in Brazil?	80
Review and reflect	86

❻ Limestone landscapes of England — 88
England rocks!	90
Why is limestone so special?	92
What are typical limestone features?	94
What is the limestone like in the Yorkshire Dales?	97
Review and reflect	104

❼ Can the Earth cope? — 106
Where are the Earth's major ecosystems?	108
How are ecosystems linked to human activity?	110
How do ecosystems work?	112
Population and resources	114
The sea as a natural resource	116
Threats to marine ecosystems	118
Marine ecosystems and the global fishing industry	120
Coral reefs: the 'tropical rainforests' of the sea	124
Coral reefs under threat	126
Review and reflect	128

❽ Crime and the local community — 130
What is crime?	131
What do people feel about crime?	132
Where do people expect crime to happen?	134
Mapping crime in Oxford	136
Patterns of crime nationwide	140
Review and reflect	141

Glossary — 142

Index — 144

1 Rivers

A The Niagara Falls in North America

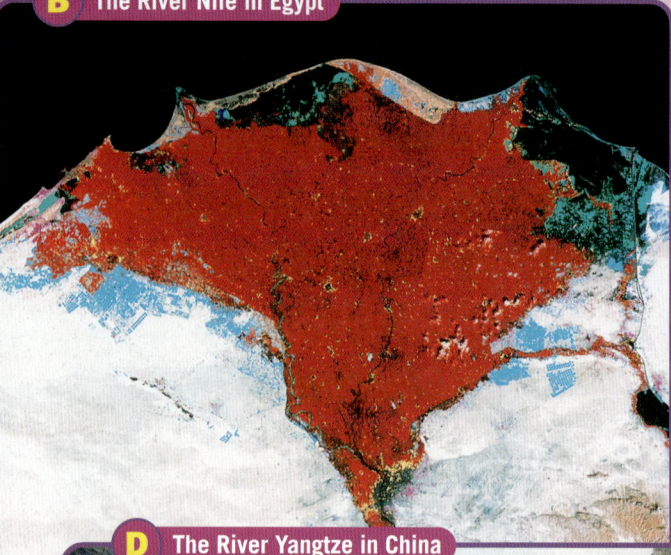

B The River Nile in Egypt

C The Kariba dam in Zimbabwe

D The River Yangtze in China

E River Amazon in Brazil

Learn about

Rivers are important to people because they provide water, are used for transport and can be used to provide power. Rivers constantly change the shape of the landscape, wearing away land in some places and building new land in others. In this unit you will learn about:

- river features and river processes
- how to do a cross-section
- how to investigate rivers.

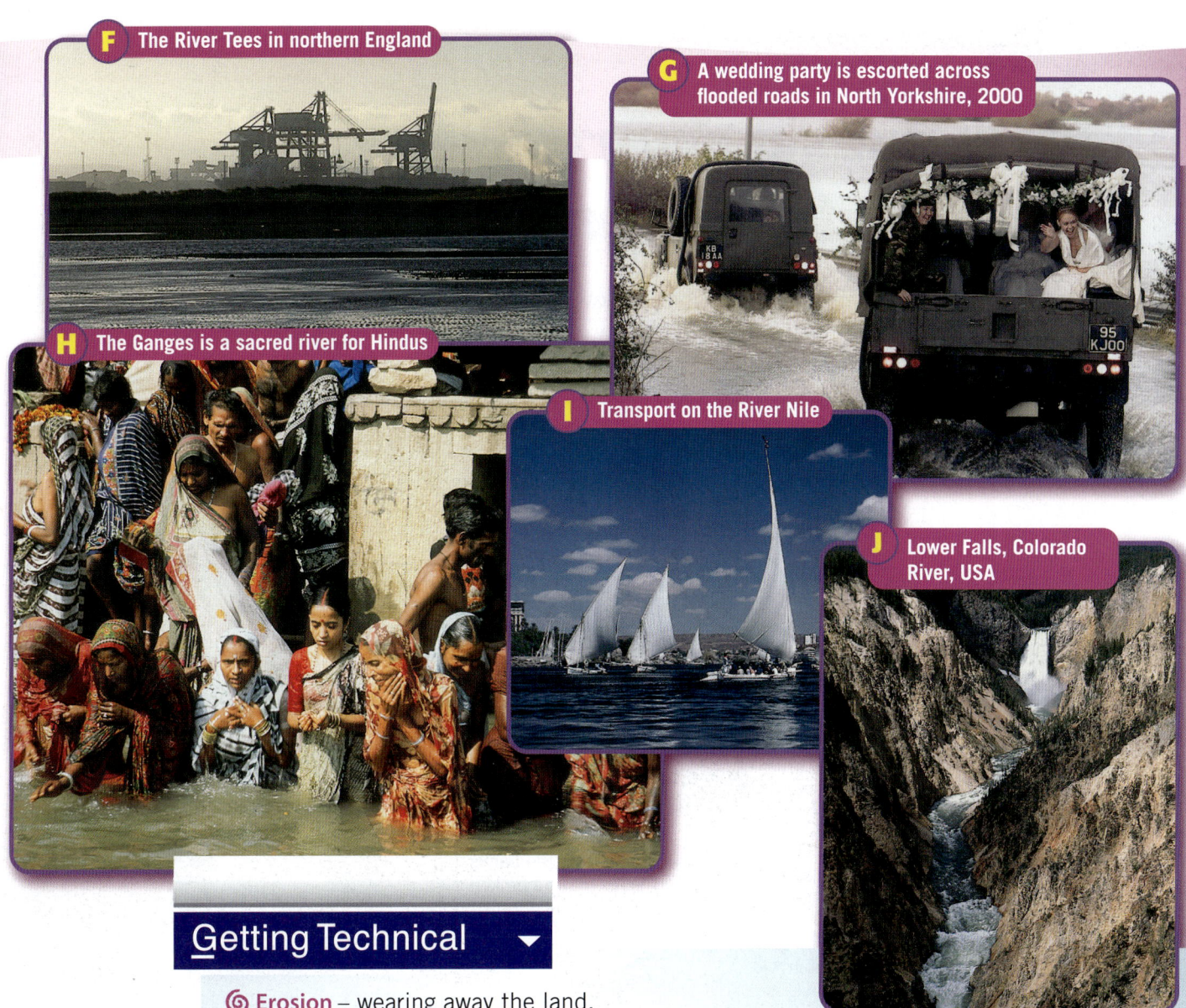

F The River Tees in northern England

G A wedding party is escorted across flooded roads in North Yorkshire, 2000

H The Ganges is a sacred river for Hindus

I Transport on the River Nile

J Lower Falls, Colorado River, USA

Getting Technical

- **Erosion** – wearing away the land.
- **Transportation** – carrying eroded material away.
- **Deposition** – when eroded material is dropped in one place.
- **Weathering** – when rock is exposed to the weather and slowly breaks up.
- **Source** – the start of a river.
- **Gorge** – a steep-sided river valley.
- **Waterfall** – where a river falls down a sheer slope.
- **Meander** – a large looping bend in a river.
- **Delta** – flat land at the mouth of a river, often triangle shaped.
- **Estuary** – where a river widens out in a funnel shape before it reaches the sea.

Activities

1. With a partner, look at all the photographs on these two pages. Pick three photos where people are making use of rivers. Describe what the river is being used for in each photo.

2. **a** Choose the photos which show each of these river landscape features:

   i a meander   ii a waterfall   iii a gorge   iv a delta.

   b In a group, choose any two of these features. Discuss how you think they were formed in that place. Write down your ideas, using diagrams and the words in the Getting Technical box.

Geography Matters

How does a river valley change downstream?

Diagram **A** shows the long profile of a river. It flows from its source in a highland area to its mouth. As a river flows downstream its valley changes shape.

A river's source is often in highland areas where there is usually more rainfall and surface run-off water.

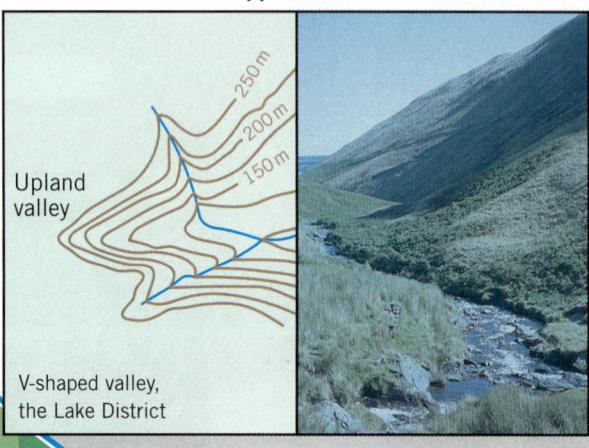

Upper course

V-shaped valley, the Lake District

Rocks and soil from the banks and valley sides may be broken down by weathering.

The river runs downstream from its source, cutting down its valley by **vertical erosion**. Valley sides are steep and there are usually large rocks on the river bed. Waterfalls are often found in this section.

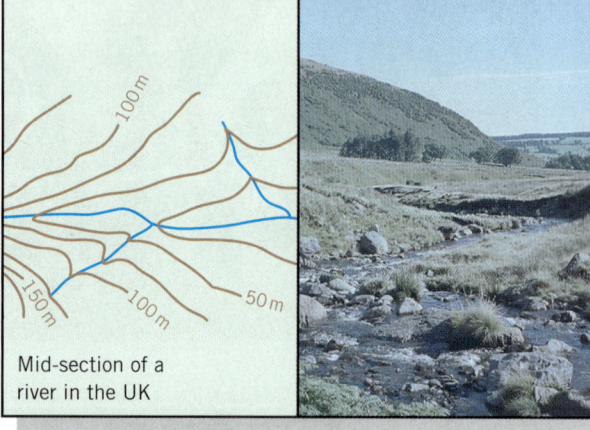

Middle section

Mid-section of a river in the UK

The **gradient** of the river is gentler here and the channel is wider. Tributaries, surface run-off and ground water have increased the volume of the river. There is less vertical erosion and more lateral erosion.

Height (metres above sea level)

Length of river from source to mouth

Gradient or slope decreases

Average speed of the river increases

Size of the river increases

Size of the rocks on the bed of the river decreases

More vertical erosion ⟶ More lateral erosion

Waterfall in Swinner Gill, Swaledale

A The long profile of a river

Rivers

Activities

1 Diagram **B** shows the river valley from source to mouth.

a Make a large copy of this diagram and label the three sections:
- upper course
- middle course
- lower course

b Write these labels on your sketches. Make sure that you label each one in the correct place:
- steep valley sides
- gentle slopes
- waterfall
- small streams
- wide, flat floodplain
- big river channel
- tributary
- source
- mouth

2 Write three sentences to describe how a river valley changes downstream. Use some of the terms from question **1** in your answer.

Lower course or flood plain

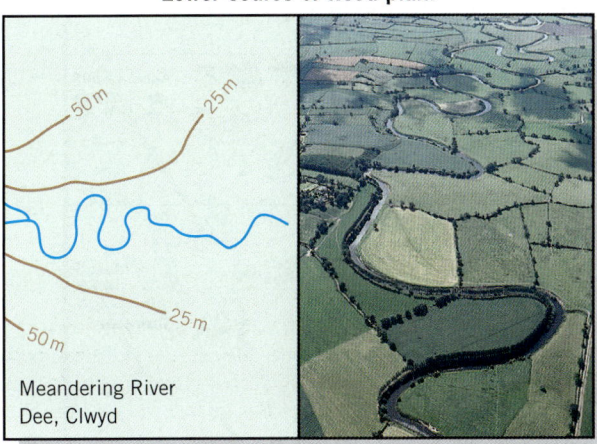

Meandering River Dee, Clwyd

The river is usually wider and deeper here. There is more lateral erosion where the river cuts wide sweeping bends or meanders.

Getting Technical

When water flows fast in a river, it wears away the river banks and river bed. This is called **fluvial erosion**.

B The upper, middle and lower course of a river

Geography Matters

Where is the river section you are going to study?

Using an OS map to identify features in a river valley

Map **A** is an OS map showing two river valleys in Yorkshire: the Wharfe and the Skirfare. Look carefully at the contour patterns. They show the steepness and the shape of the land.

A OS map of Wharfedale, scale 1:50 000

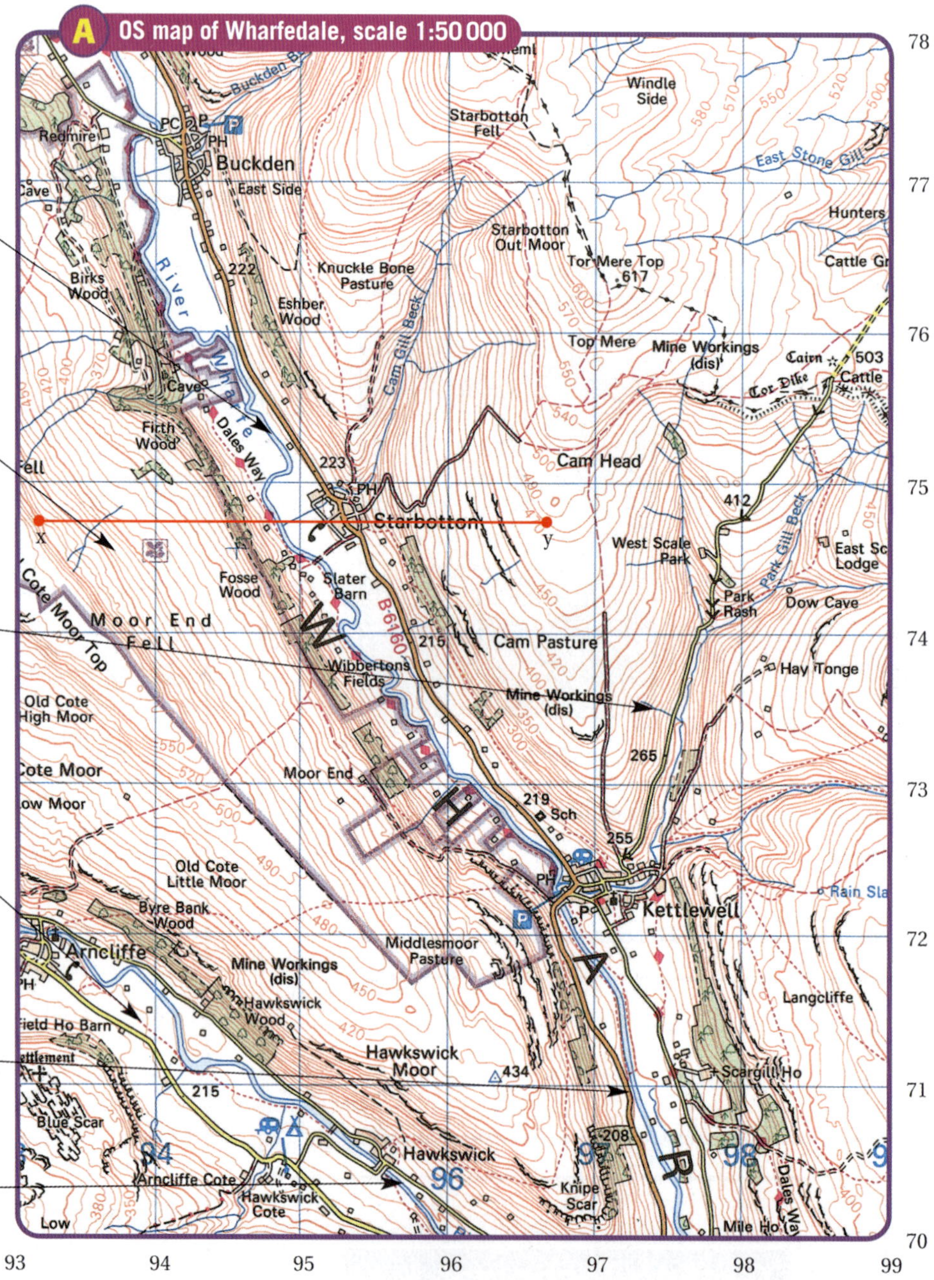

River Wharfe – river meandering in the wide, flat valley floor.

Contour lines are close together, showing a steep slope on the valley sides.

Some smaller streams cut straight across the contour lines. This shows a very steep fall, usually a waterfall.

Contour lines are widely spaced, showing the River Skirfare has a gentle slope.

Road follows the flat land.

River Skirfare

© Crown copyright

Rivers

Drawing cross-sections from contour lines

The contour lines on diagrams **B** and **C** show the shape of the land. A cross-section drawn through the contour lines shows what the landscape looks like.

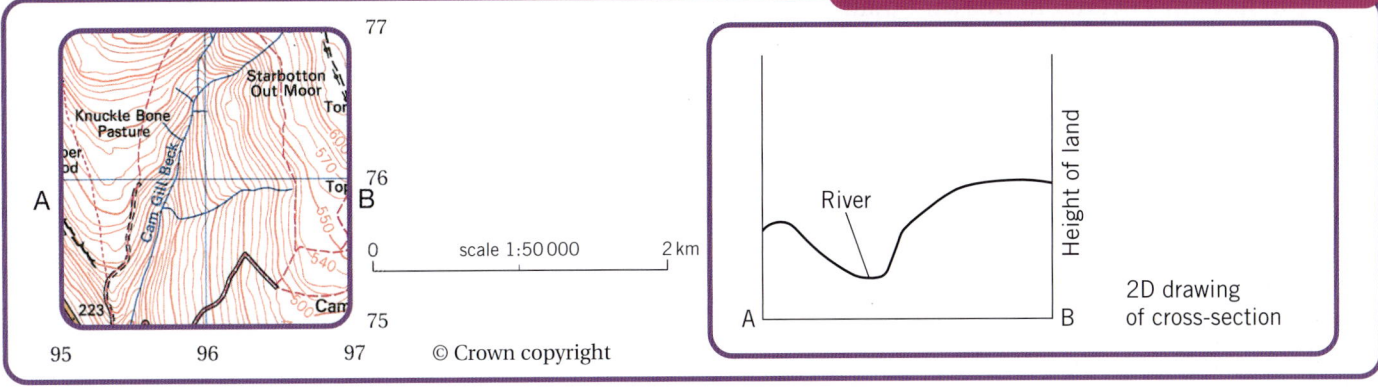

B Contour pattern and cross-section of a steep V-shaped river valley. The cross-section is taken from grid references 950760 to 970760 (A to B)

How to ...

... draw a cross-section

When you draw a cross-section, you imagine cutting a slice through the land down to sea level. Work through these six steps.

1. Choose the place to do your cross-section and place a strip of paper across the contour lines on the map.
2. Mark each point where a contour line crosses the paper. Label the height of each contour on your paper.
3. Now use your paper to draw the bottom axis of your cross-section onto graph paper.
4. The side axis is the height of the land. Draw a scale from 0 (sea level) to the highest point.
5. Then use your strip of paper to plot the heights on the graph paper.
6. Join the dots and label some landscape features onto your cross-section.

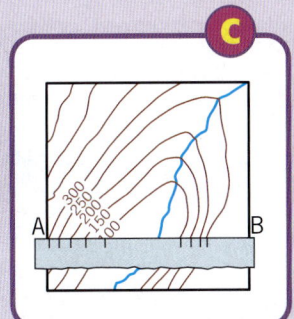

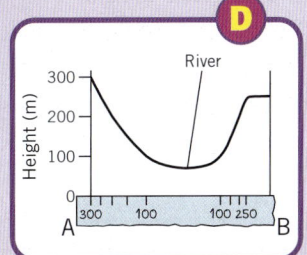

Activities

1
a Copy the diagram on the right. Finish drawing a cross-section between X and Y on Map **A**.

b Label your cross-section with these words:
river road valley side floodplain

c Add a heading and a scale to your cross-section.

2 Extension
Look at your cross-section. Which part of the river valley do you think this is: the **upper** course, **middle** course or **lower** course? Give three reasons for your choice.

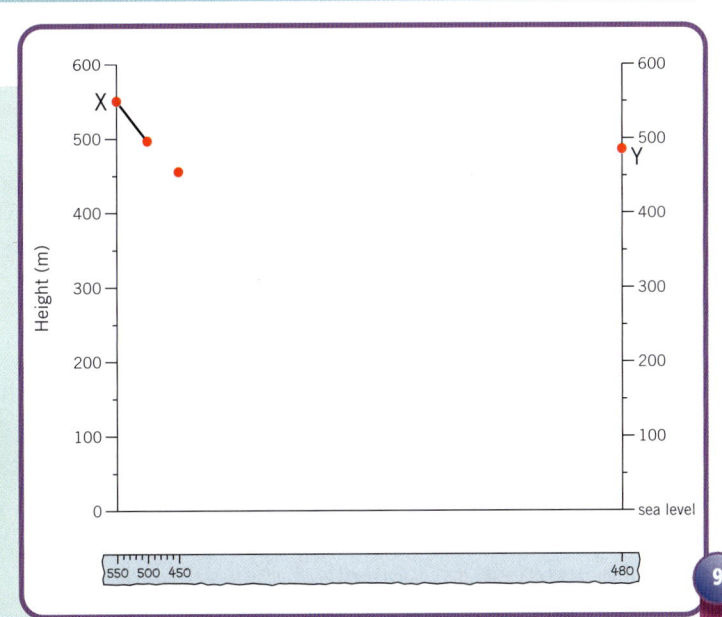

Geography Matters

Investigating rivers: how do rivers change downstream?

You have discovered in this unit that:
- A river changes as it flows from its source to its mouth.
- The river usually gets bigger as more tributaries join the main stream.
- Fluvial erosion changes the shape of the river valley.

A fieldwork investigation would give you the chance find out more about rivers.

Step 1: Asking questions

The first step in an investigation is to ask questions.
What do you want to find out about rivers? Your title for this investigation could be:

How do rivers change downstream?

Here are some questions you could ask.

- Do river valleys become wider further downstream?
- Does a river get bigger downstream?
- Does the size of material in the river bed change as a river moves downstream?
- Does a river flow fastest in the middle of its channel?
- When does a river erode and deposit material?
- Does a river's gradient get steeper downstream?
- How do the shape and size of the river channel change downstream?
- Does a river flow faster when it is steeper?
- Is the deepest part of the river in the middle?
- Does a river flow faster when it is narrow?

Measuring a stream for geography fieldwork

Activity

1. **a** In a group, study the diagram above and decide which questions to investigate.
   b For each question, write a hypothesis. For example: Hypothesis for question 1: 'As a river flows downstream its valley gets wider.'
   c Discuss how you will collect the information.

help!

It is better to work in a group because it makes data collection easier and safer. You must be sure to listen to advice about safety before you collect data in the field.

What information can you collect in the field?

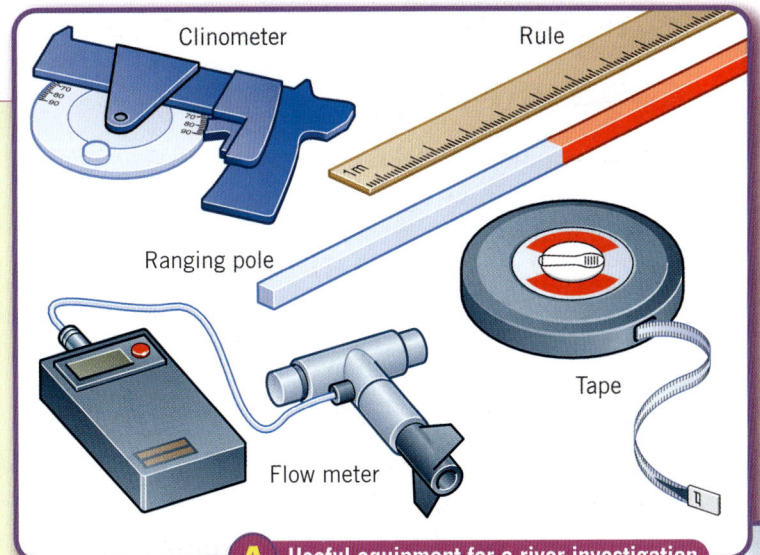

A Useful equipment for a river investigation

Step 2: Collecting information

Make a list of your questions. Decide what equipment you need to measure and record the information. It is important to be accurate.

- Most of your data will be *primary data*. That is data you actually collect yourself by measuring and sketching.
- Some data might be *secondary data*. This is printed information such as an OS map or data from the Environment Agency. Their website address is http:/www.environment–agency.gov.uk.

... record data

Before you set off, you need to design your data collection sheets. Here is an example of a data collection sheet for channel depth. The group decided to compare three different sites downstream. At each site they measured the depth in five places across the channel, so they could calculate the average depth.

Position	Depth of river				
	Readings (cm)				
	1	2	3	4	5
Site 1	12	31	35	12	10
Site 2					
Site 3					

Activity

1. **a** Look at the equipment in source **A**. Make a list of the equipment that you need for each of your investigation questions.
   b Construct a data collection sheet for each investigation question.

1 Geography Matters

What does your data mean?

Step 3: Showing your results

Once you have collected your data, you must decide how to show your results. You could use:

- sketches
- labelled photos
- cross-section drawings
- tables
- graphs
- written work.

Look at the next four pages to get some ideas.

Drawing a field sketch

If you did a field sketch, then you can draw a neat version. Annotate your sketch to show the main features and processes. Diagrams **A** and **B** show two sketches that a student drew as part of her investigation.

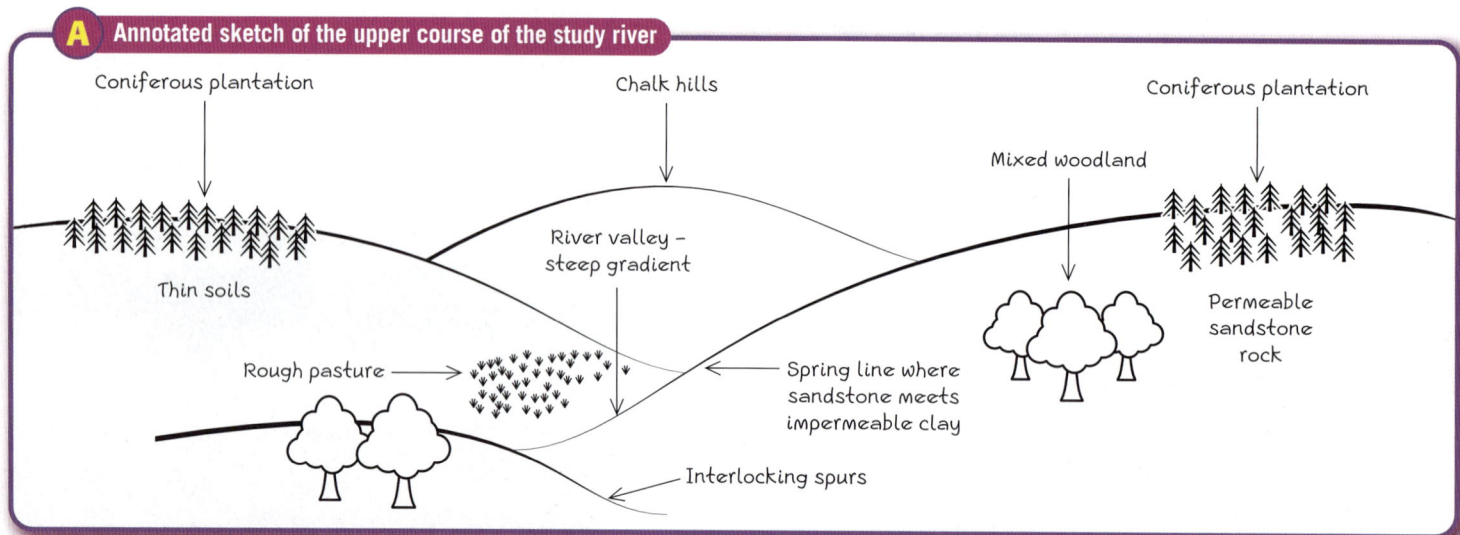

A Annotated sketch of the upper course of the study river

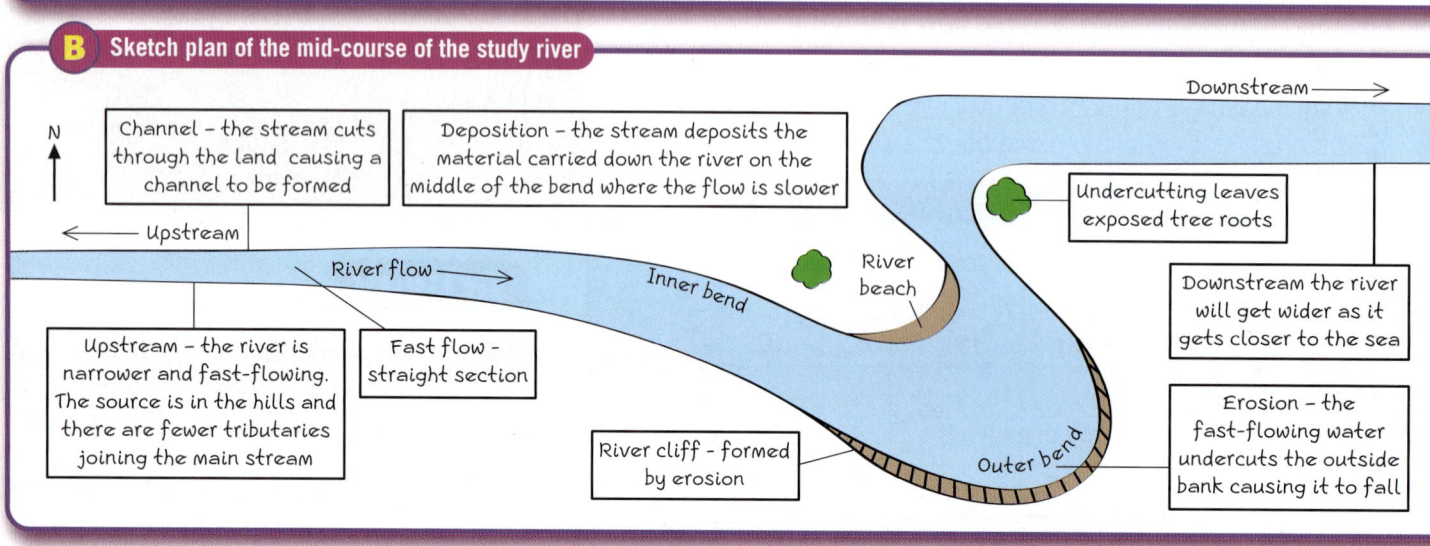

B Sketch plan of the mid-course of the study river

Rivers

Drawing cross-sections

To draw the cross-section of a river, you need measurements of:

- the depth of the river
- the width of the channel
- the width of the river from bank to bank
- the height of the bank above the river.

Activities

1. Cross-section **C** is site 1 on table **D**. Draw a cross-section for site 2.
2. Work out the average depth and the cross-section area at sites 2 and 3. Use the Getting Technical box to help you.

How to ... draw a cross-section of a river

1. Look at the measurements you have collected and decide on a scale that will fit on your paper.
2. Draw the river first. Start with a line for **width** and a line for each **depth**.
3. Mark the height of each bank above the river.
4. Measure the width of the channel bank to bank. Now draw in the banks.
5. Shade your cross-section with colours. Add a scale and a heading.

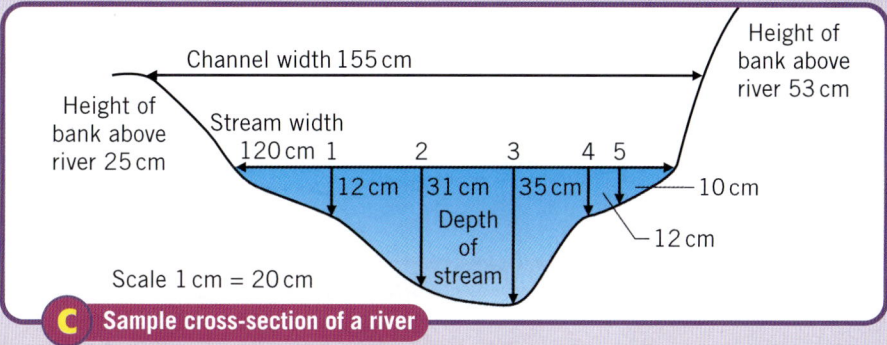

C Sample cross-section of a river

Getting Technical

- The amount of water flowing down a stream is called the **discharge**. You can calculate the discharge with this formula:

  discharge = velocity × cross-section area

- First work out the cross-section area. This is a river's width × depth.

  a Calculate the average depth by adding all the depth readings and divide by the number of readings. In **C** the average would be (12 + 31 + 35 + 12 + 10)/5 = 20.

  b Multiply the average depth by the width of the river to give the area. In **D** the area of site 1 would be 22 × 120 = 2400 cm^2.

	Channel width (bank to bank) (cm)	Height of bank above the river (cm)	River width (cm)	River depth (cm) left bank 1	2	3	4	right bank 5	Average depth (cm)	Cross-section area (cm^2)
Site 1	155	left = 25 right = 53	120	12	31	35	12	10	100 ÷ 5 = 20 cm	2400
Site 2	180	left = 40 right = 50	150	8	26	44	30	12	120 ÷ 5 =	
Site 3	220	left = 56 right = 66	195	10	20	48	46	12		

D River measurements

Geography Matters

Graphs and proportional lines

Once you have collected your data, set it out neatly in a results table, like table **D** on page 13. Some of your measurements can then be shown on graphs and diagrams. For each site that you collected data on, you can show:

- the speed of the river (velocity)
- the size of bed material found in the river
- how velocity varies across the channel.

Look at **E** to see how data can be shown in two different ways.

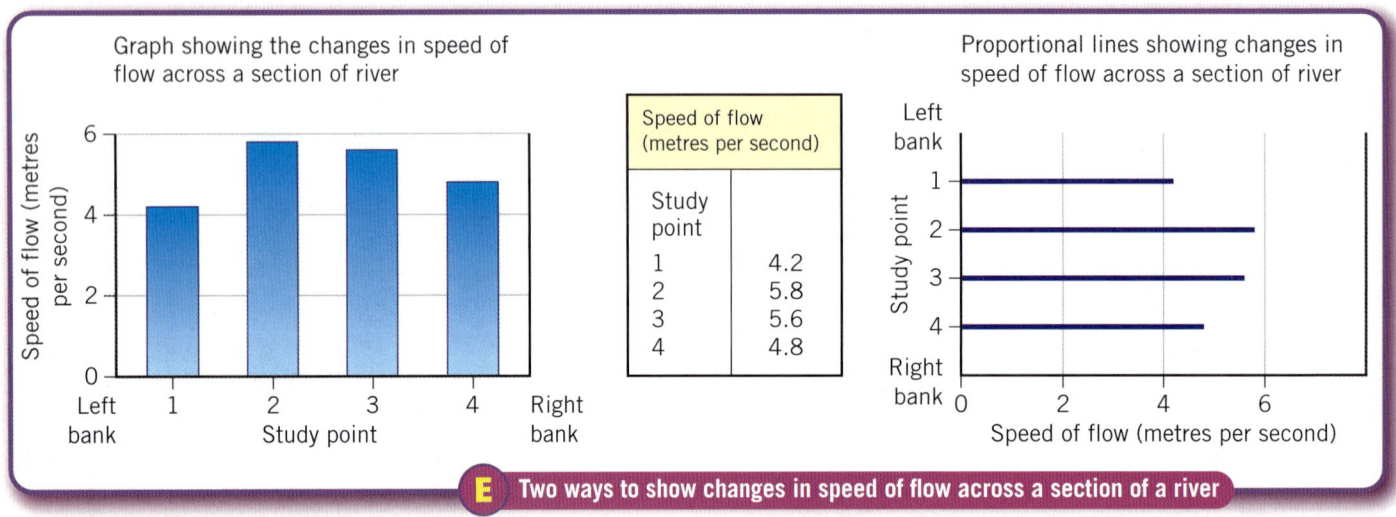

E Two ways to show changes in speed of flow across a section of a river

	Speed (m/sec)				Average speed (m/sec)	Steepness (°)				Average steepness (°)	Size of material (mm)				Average size of material (mm)
	1	2	3	4		1	2	3	4		1	2	3	4	
Site A	0.1	0.7	0.4	0.1	1.3 ÷ 4 = 0.3	15	34	12	30	91 ÷ 4 = 23	28	14	68	32	35.5
Site B	0.2	0.5	0.4	0.3		6	33	15	20		30	62	10	28	32.5
Site C	0.2	0.9	0.8	0.7		8	35	6	48		26	16	18	12	18
Site D	0.5	0.8	1.5	0.1		22	25	17	9		19	21	18	10	17

F Results of an investigation on the River Caldew

Rivers

Activity

3
a Some students collected data for a small river in the Lake District to investigate changes downstream. The four survey sites are shown on map **G**. The students' results are shown in table **F**. Make a copy of the results table and use a calculator to fill in the gaps. 123

b Use these results to draw some graphs. You could use a spreadsheet package. 123 ICT

c Look at the graphs that you have drawn and decide what they prove. Try to give some reasons for your findings. You can use this writing frame to get you started:

The fastest flowing section of the river was at site … , with an average speed of … metres/sec. The slowest section was at site … where the average speed was … metres/sec.

This shows that, as the river flows downstream its speed gets … . This is probably because … .

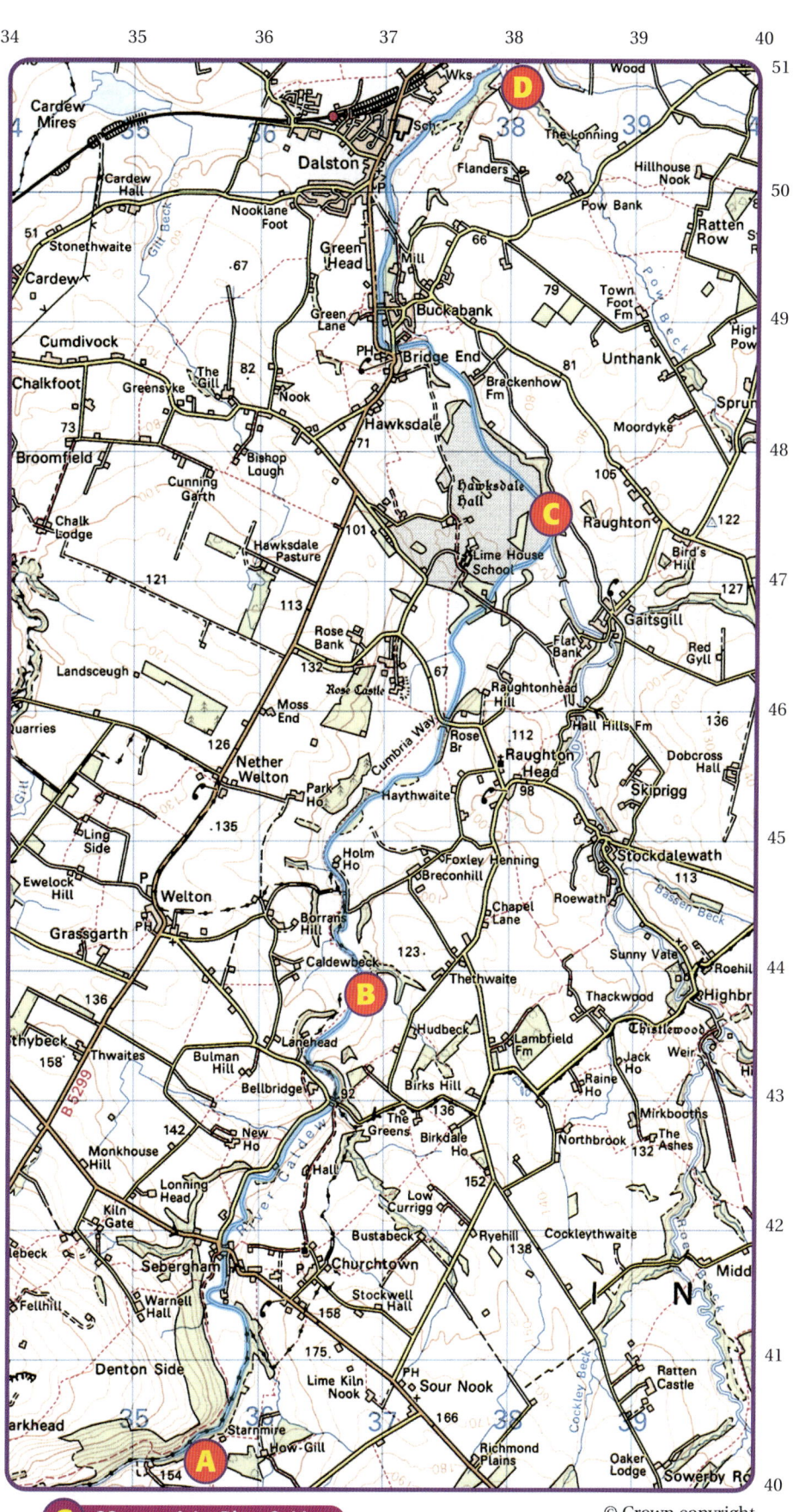

G OS map of the River Caldew

© Crown copyright

Geography Matters

Step 4: Drawing conclusions

Once you have collected enough data and displayed the results using a range of techniques, you must now draw some conclusions about your investigation and evaluate your work. The more data you collect, the more reliable your conclusions will be.

help!

A conclusion:
- looks at all the work you have done
- links the results to the questions you asked in the beginning.

An evaluation:
- evaluates the strengths and the weaknesses of the work as a whole
- makes suggestions about further investigations you might carry out.

Conclusion

The main enquiry question was:

How do landscapes and processes change in a river valley?

The first part of your conclusion should give a general statement about what you found from your investigations. You could start your conclusion by writing:

> From my study of the different sections of the river ... I found that the river did change as it moved downstream. The main changes were ...

Now give details including figures and refer to the diagrams, maps and graphs you have drawn.

Evaluation

Your evaluation should finish off your enquiry. It refers to the whole piece of work and you should make a note of the strengths and weaknesses of the project. You should mention what went well and what didn't go so well. Go on to suggest how it could be improved next time. You also need to suggest ideas for further investigation of the same topic.

You could start your evaluation by writing:

> I learned a lot about rivers from doing this enquiry.
> I also learned how important it was to ...

You could then go on to say:

> We had some difficulty collecting the information because ...

and finally give suggestions of how you could extend your investigations:

> It would be good to go and do some further study on ...

Activity

4. Now that you have learned to collect primary data, used different methods of presenting your data, drawn conclusions and evaluated your work, you can write an investigation using secondary data. You could, for example, use data from the Environment Agency's website at http:/www.heinemann.co.uk/hotlinks (insert code 1631P). You should try to get information for a complete stretch of river rather than just the two or three sections that you studied in your fieldwork.

Review and reflect

Activities

1 a In this unit you have learned about rivers and the features of a river valley. You have also learned about fieldwork investigation. Copy and complete the spider diagram below adding facts and details that you have covered in this unit.

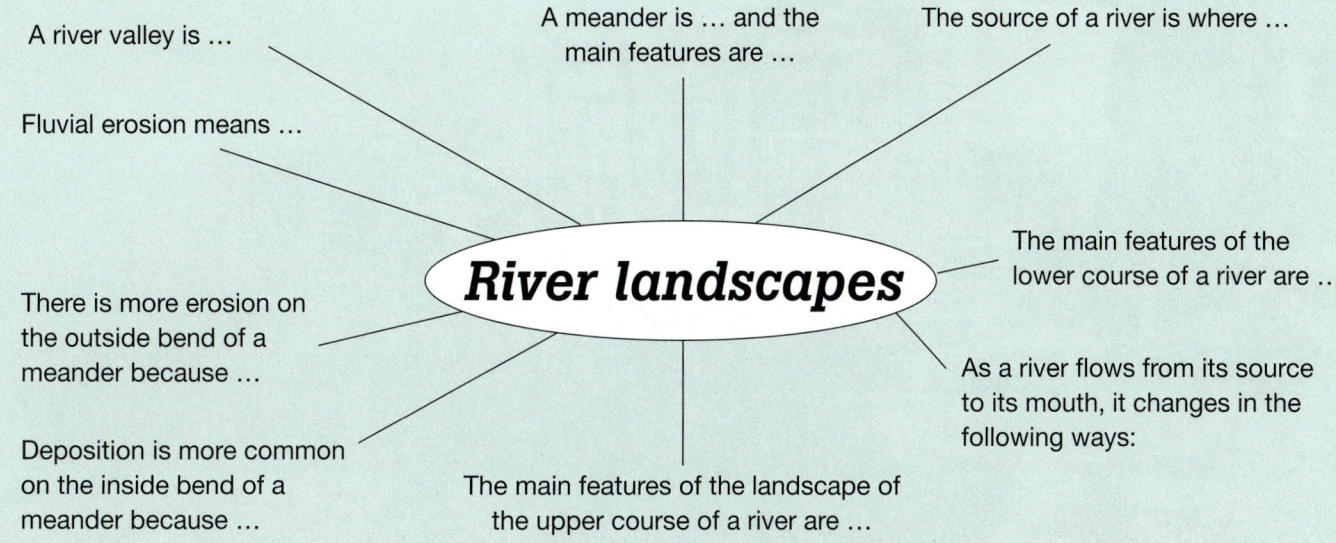

- A river valley is …
- Fluvial erosion means …
- There is more erosion on the outside bend of a meander because …
- Deposition is more common on the inside bend of a meander because …
- A meander is … and the main features are …
- The main features of the landscape of the upper course of a river are …
- The source of a river is where …
- The main features of the lower course of a river are …
- As a river flows from its source to its mouth, it changes in the following ways:

2 Now you have learned to carry out a fieldwork enquiry on a river landscape you will be able to apply the same skills to any other enquiry by using these steps:

- **Deciding on a title** – this is often in the form of a question, which may start with the words:

  What is …? Where are …? How …? Who …? Why …?

  It may also state a **hypothesis** (a theory or statement) which you set out to prove or disprove through your investigation.

- **Collecting information** – you must decide what information you need and where you can get it, and design data collection sheets. Look back at page 11 to remind you.

- **Showing results** – you can use many different methods to show your results: maps, graphs, sketches, photographs, written work. You can see examples on pages 12–15.

- **Drawing conclusions and evaluating** – you must reflect back to the original title of your study and attempt to answer it using evidence from the data you have collected. Look back at page 16.

Position	Depth of river					
	Readings (cm)					
	1	2	3	4	5	6
Site 1	3.5	8	8.5	10	4	2.5
Site 2						

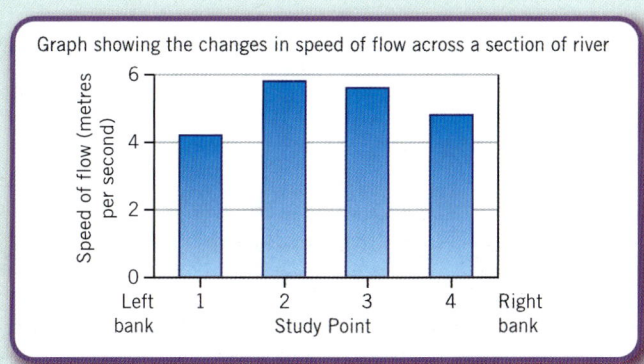

Graph showing the changes in speed of flow across a section of river

2 Coastal environments

A Cliff erosion in Great Cowden near Hornsea

Learn about

Different processes constantly shape the Earth's landscape. Sometimes this causes problems along the coast. In this unit you will learn:
- how weathering and erosion affect coastlines
- how waves shape the coast
- why cliffs collapse
- how people try to protect the coast.

Activity

1. Write down five geographical questions you could ask about photograph **A**. Use words like *why*, *where*, *what* and *how* in your questions.

How is our coastline formed?

The UK's coastline stretches for over 10 000 kilometres around the country. Coasts change rapidly. **Weathering** and **erosion** attack the rocks all the time and shape the coast into bays, beaches and headlands that people like to visit. How does this happen?

What is weathering?

Over time, the weather can break down even the hardest rocks. Sun, frost, rainwater and plants slowly break rock into smaller pieces. This process is called **weathering**. There are three main types of weathering.

Mechanical weathering is caused by changes in temperature. In freeze–thaw weathering, water gets into cracks in a rock and freezes. As it freezes it expands. Repeated freezing and melting eventually cause the rock to split.

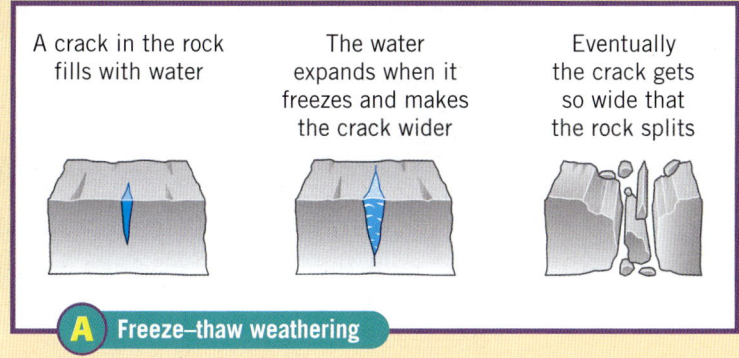

A crack in the rock fills with water | The water expands when it freezes and makes the crack wider | Eventually the crack gets so wide that the rock splits

A Freeze–thaw weathering

Biological weathering is caused by the action of plants on rocks. Plants can grow in cracks in rocks. As their roots develop they can force the cracks to widen and the rocks to fall apart. Lichens and mosses can also grow on rocks. They make the rock surface slowly crumble.

C Biological weathering in Majorca

Chemical weathering is caused by chemicals in rainwater or salts in the sea. Acids in rainwater can slowly dissolve some rocks. You can find more about chemical weathering of limestone on page 93.

B The cracks in this limestone pavement are caused by chemical weathering

Activities

1. Copy and complete this table:

	Type of weathering
ice in a rock	mechanical
acid rain	
the roots of a plant	
high temperatures	

2. Draw a set of diagrams like those in **A** to show how **biological weathering** occurs. These words might help: *grow, develop, force, crumble*.

3. Where might you find weathering? Study your school to find out where the building is being weathered. Record:
   - the location, e.g. sports hall wall
   - what material, e.g. concrete, tarmac, brick
   - the evidence, e.g. crumbling surface
   - the height, e.g. at ground level
   - the aspect, e.g. facing south.

2 Geography Matters

What is erosion?

Getting Technical

Weathering is a process that weakens and breaks up rocks. The wearing away of the rocks and the removal of the weathered material is called **erosion**. The material can be carried away by rivers, wind, the sea, glaciers – or by people. The work of these **agents of erosion** is explained below.

Rivers are constantly wearing away tiny pieces of rock from their banks and their beds. These particles are carried away by the river. When a river is flowing fast it can carry huge boulders.

A River erosion on the River Clwyd

B The Mittens in Arizona, USA

If you walk along a beach when there is a strong **wind**, you will feel the sand blowing against your face. The particles carried by the wind blast away the rocks in their path, sometimes forming weird and wonderful shapes like this.

C Waves erode the cliffs on the Oregon coast

Waves constantly batter our shores and wear away the cliffs. Waves carry away the eroded material and deposit it on the beach.

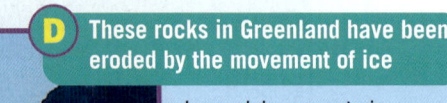
D These rocks in Greenland have been eroded by the movement of ice

In cold mountain areas, huge rivers of **ice** called **glaciers** flow slowly down valleys. As the ice moves, it picks up rocks and stones. The glacier is like sandpaper. The stones wear away at the ground surface below.

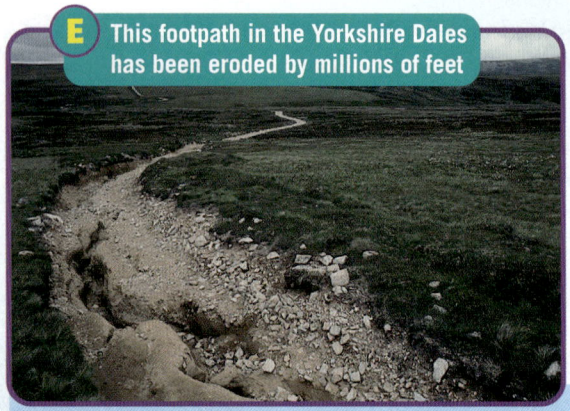
E This footpath in the Yorkshire Dales has been eroded by millions of feet

People cause erosion in many different ways. Bulldozers can be used to dig out large amounts of soil. People can wear away a surface just by walking over it. They can also remove trees and other plants which hold the soil together, allowing water and wind to remove the soil more easily.

Coastal environments

Washing the dishes is like erosion. The force of the water and the scrubbing you do remove the dirt from the plates. Throwing the water away **transports** the waste material down the drain to another place, where it is **deposited**. On a larger scale, mountains, valleys and coasts are shaped and changed by water, wind and ice. Erosion wears away the land; the loose material is transported to another place where it may be deposited to make new landforms.

Activities

1. Match each word with its definition. Write out the correct sentences.

weathering	is when loose material is dropped
transportation	is when rocks are broken down by weather processes or plants
erosion	is when weathered material is carried along by wind, ice or water
deposition	is when ice, wind or water wears away the rock surface

2. **Odd one out**

1	Freeze–thaw	5	Sea	9	River
2	Weathering	6	Mechanical	10	People
3	Biological	7	Deposition	11	Tree roots
4	Wind	8	Erosion	12	Glacier

For each set below, decide which is the odd one out, and give a reason for your choice.

Set A	1	4	9	12	Set D	2	3	7	11
Set B	1	3	5	6	Set E	2	4	7	9
Set C	4	9	11	12	Set F	1	5	8	10

3. Make your own scale of hardness using things you can find at home. Test five materials by trying to scratch them with a nail file or emery board. You could include glass, steel, concrete or wax. Complete a table of your results.

Scale of hardness	Material
Hardest 1	
2	
3	
4	
Softest 5	

Hard and soft rocks

Some rocks are soft – they crumble easily in your hands. Rocks like **clay** and **chalk** are washed away very easily. Other rocks such as **granite** and **marble** are very resistant to erosion. They are made of very hard crystals which are well cemented together.

2 Geography Matters

How do waves shape our coast?

Waves erode the land and transport material all day and all night. But most erosion happens on stormy days when strong winds drive large waves against the shore. These storm waves have such force that they can break off bits of rocks from cliffs and move vast amounts of sand and shingle, before depositing it along the shore. Erosion and deposition create coastal landforms such as cliffs and beaches.

A Runswick Bay, North Yorkshire

B Vertical cliffs of the Seven Sisters, East Sussex

C Country Park, East Lothian showing saltmarsh, sandflats and spits

D Aerial view of Chesil Beach, Dorset

E Mount Cliff, Beaumaris

Activity

1 a With a partner, look at photographs **A–E**. Put them into pairs and look for connections between them. For example, **A** and **B** both show cliffs. There is more than one correct answer – your answer is right as long as you have found a good connection.

b Copy the table below. Write down the letters for each of your pairs with a short explanation of the connection.

Pair	Connection
A and B	Both show cliffs

Coastal environments

How does the sea erode the coast?

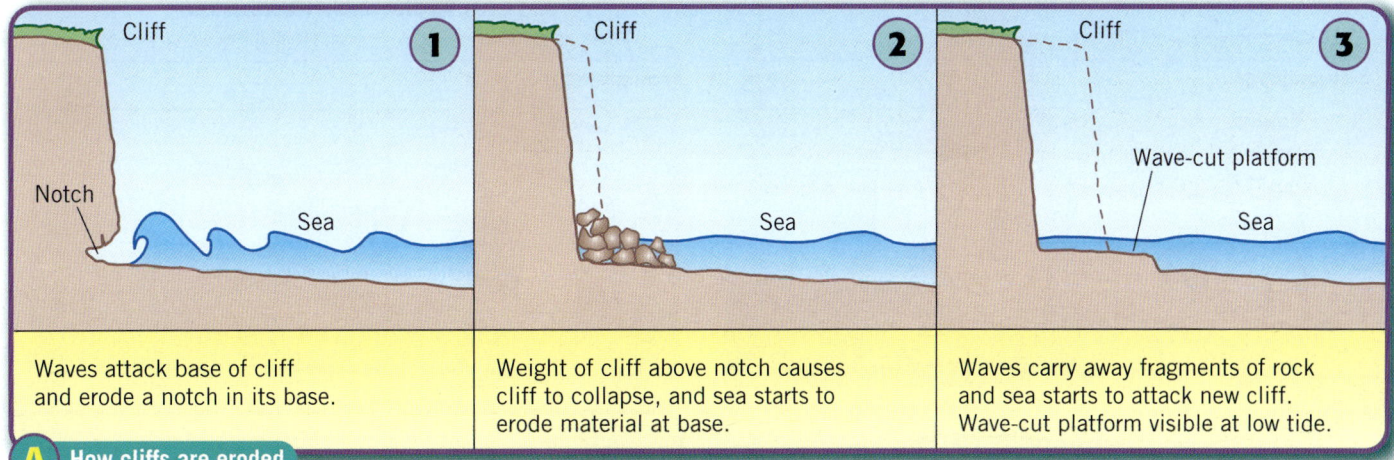

A How cliffs are eroded

Erosion occurs in different ways along the coast when powerful waves crash against the foot of a cliff.

- The waves hurl sand and shingle against the cliff. This slowly chips at the rock.
- Waves also trap air in the cracks in the rock, and the pressure created causes large pieces of rock to break off.

Softer rocks are eroded more easily and wear away more quickly to form bays. Harder rocks stand out as headlands. Photograph **B** shows what happens when bands of hard and soft rock reach the coast.

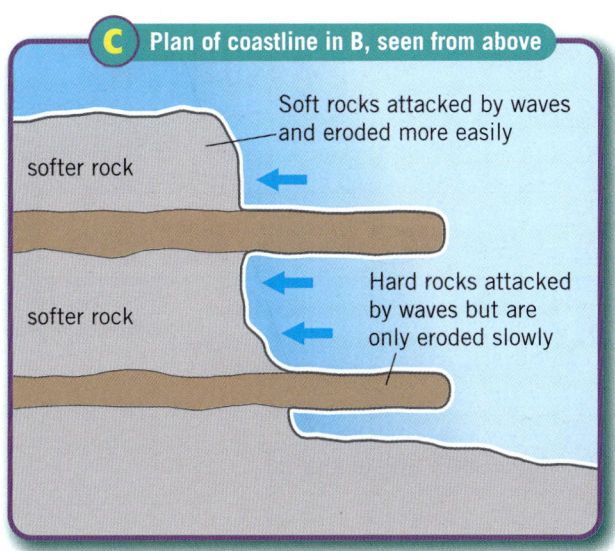

C Plan of coastline in B, seen from above

How to ...

... describe a photograph of a coastline

1 Begin with a general statement, e.g. *The picture shows a coast with bays and headlands.*
2 Go on to give greater detail about the type of rock you can see, the colours and the shapes that they make.
3 Mention whether the rock is bare or covered in vegetation. Is there any sign of people or their activities?
4 Try to find something in the picture to give you a scale and try to give sizes to what you are describing.

B This coastline in Pembrokeshire is formed of hard and soft bands of rock

Activities

1 Create a word list to help you describe the coast in **B**.
2 Use your word list and the How to ... box to help you write a description of the coast in the photograph.
3 Using the sentences below, explain how the headlands and bays in **B** were formed.

> Some parts of the coast stand out as headlands because the rocks are ... In other places bays develop because the rocks are ... , so they are ...

2 Geography Matters

Features of coastal erosion

D Erosion of a headland

E A cave, an arch and a stack at Elegug

Activities

4 The three diagrams in **D** show how the sea erodes cliffs to develop other landforms (see **E**). Make a sketch of the photo and then use the labels below to annotate your diagrams.
- The sea attacks small cracks and opens them.
- The cracks get larger and develop into a small **cave**.
- When the cave wears right through the headland, an **arch** forms.
- More erosion causes the arch to collapse. This leaves a pillar of rock called a **stack** in the sea.

5 Map **F** shows that the area is made up of several different types of rocks, which are shown in the key.
   a Trace or draw a sketch map of the coast.
   b Label the bays and headlands.
   c Shade the rock types.

6 a Which type of rock forms the headlands?
   b Which type of rock forms the bays? Why?

7 Add the words *cliff*, *headland*, *bay*, *arch* and *stack* to your word bank and explain what they mean.

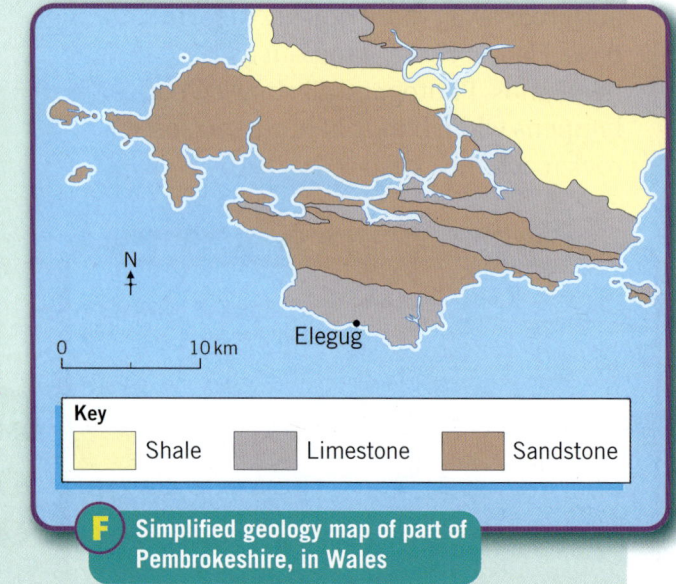

F Simplified geology map of part of Pembrokeshire, in Wales

Key: Shale, Limestone, Sandstone

Features of coastal deposition

Material that has been eroded by the sea is carried along the coast by a process known as **longshore drift** (see **G**).

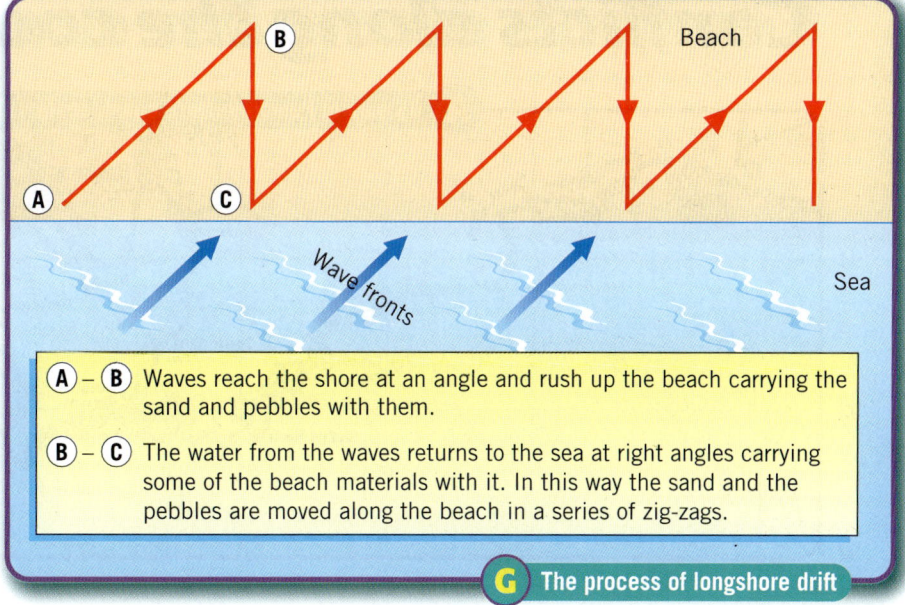

Ⓐ–Ⓑ Waves reach the shore at an angle and rush up the beach carrying the sand and pebbles with them.

Ⓑ–Ⓒ The water from the waves returns to the sea at right angles carrying some of the beach materials with it. In this way the sand and the pebbles are moved along the beach in a series of zig-zags.

G The process of longshore drift

Where there is a curve in the coastline, longshore drift stops, and the waves dump the material. This is called **deposition**. Over many years a long finger of sand and shingle grows. This is called a **spit**. You can see a photograph of a spit in **C** on page 22.

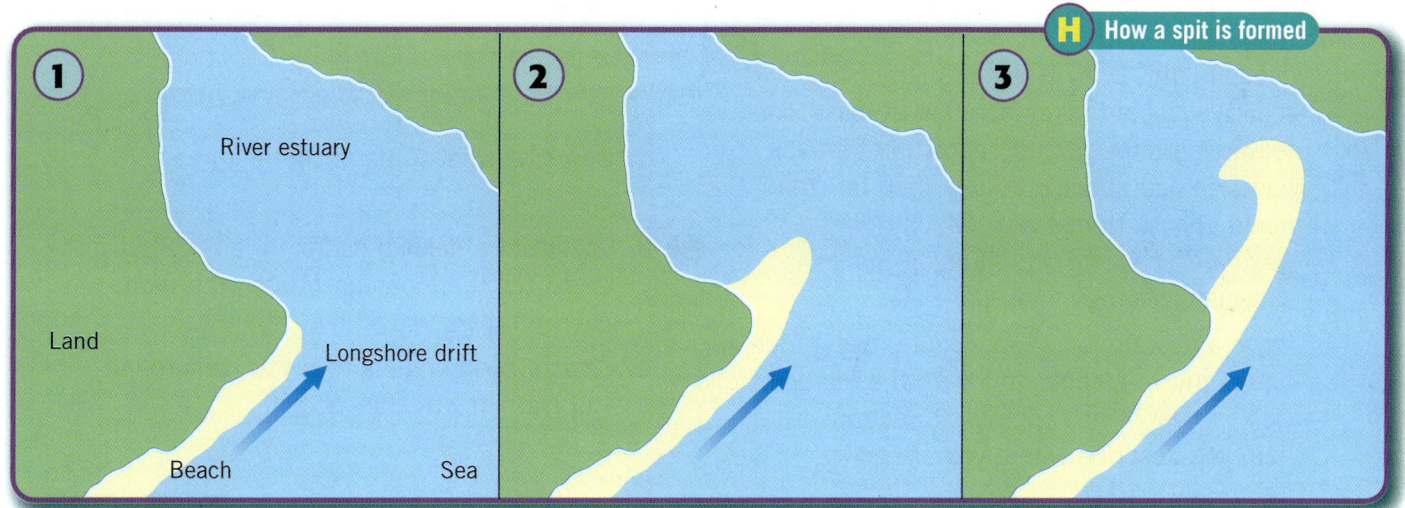

H How a spit is formed

Activity

8 Copy the diagrams in **H**. Annotate them and give them a title like you did for question 4. Use these words in your annotations: *wind direction, longshore drift, deposition, beach*. You could scan your drawings and annotate them using a computer. **ICT**

2 Geography Matters

Conflicts along the coast

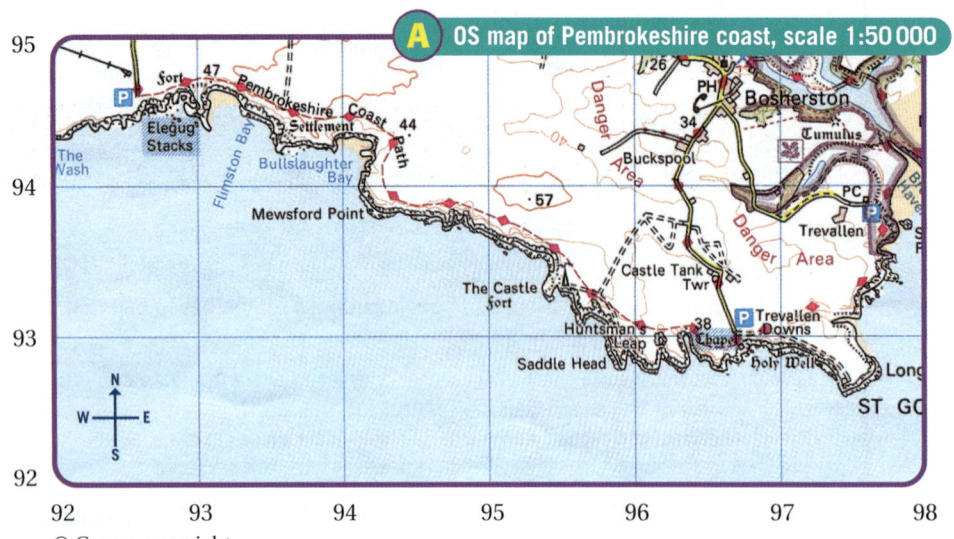

A OS map of Pembrokeshire coast, scale 1:50 000

© Crown copyright

Coastal areas are popular for lots of different activities, but some land uses **conflict** with each other. On the area shown on **A** the army shooting range (Danger Area) conflicts with tourism because people want to walk along the spectacular coastal path.

Activities

1 OS map **A** shows an area of the coast in Pembrokeshire.

  a Imagine you are taking a walk along the coastal path. Draw a sketch map of the route you would take, labelling at least four features of erosion and deposition that you have learned about in this unit so far. You could choose from *stack, beach, cliff, headland, bay* and *arch*. Elegug Stacks is shown on photograph **E**, page 24.

  b Write a description of your route, using four-figure grid references to locate the features. Don't forget to use compass directions to help you describe where you are going.

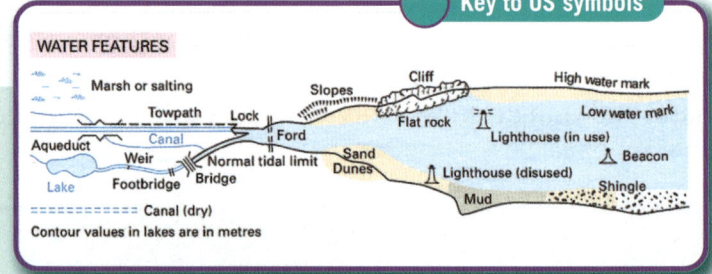

Key to OS symbols

  c Describe what three of the features look like.

2 a Construct a **conflict matrix** for all the coastal land uses that you can find on the map. Then fill it in.

  b Choose two conflicts that you have found and explain why they occur.

How to...

... construct a conflict matrix

Copy the table opposite. Choose four more groups who use the coast and write them in the green user group boxes. Complete the unshaded boxes in the matrix by thinking about where there is conflict between two users.

- If there is a conflict, put a cross.
- If groups can exist without interfering with one another, put a tick.
- If neither, put zero.

1 homes	2 sheep farm	3 bird watching	4	5	6
1 homes					
	2 sheep farm				
		3 bird watching			
			4		
				5	
					6

26

Coastal environments

Why do cliffs collapse?

BBC HOMEPAGE | WORLD SERVICE | EDUCATION

BBC NEWS — UPDATED EVERY MINUTE OF EVERY DAY

Front Page — 12 January, 1999, 08.00 GMT
World — Beachy Head collapse
UK — More news soon…

UK Politics
Business
Sci/Tech
Health
Education
Entertainment
Talking Point
In Depth
Audio Video

BBC SPORT>>

Search BBC News Online [ ] GO

Beachy Head collapse

A huge chunk of the famous cliff at Beachy Head near Eastbourne in Sussex crashed into the sea in a massive landslide over the weekend.

The rockfall, which can be seen from 5 km out to sea, has been blamed on climate change by some people. Ray Kent, a spokesman for the Environment Agency, said: 'This was a massive fall, hundreds of thousands of tonnes have fallen away from the cliff face. It has caused very significant damage to Beachy Head. It is basically down to climate change. The level of the sea is rising, so bigger waves are hitting against the cliff base, causing bigger vibrations to reverberate up the cliff.

'This was combined with twelve days of extremely wet weather during the Christmas period. The chalk was absolutely sodden so the combination has caused the rock to fall away. Unfortunately, it could be the shape of things to come.'

Freezing temperatures are believed to have expanded the water which seeped into the chalk, causing it to crumble and sheer off.

© **BBC** ^^ Back to top

Activities

1 Read the Internet page above. It reports the cliff collapse at Beachy Head.

a Copy and complete this fact file:

location of cliff collapse	
rock type	
size of rock fall	
date of rock fall	

b Choose two of these factors. Explain how each one caused the rock fall:

　⊙ rainfall　　⊙ ice　　⊙ waves

c Do you think that the rock fall was due to **erosion** or **weathering**? Explain your answer carefully.

27

2 Geography Matters

Case Study
Save our homes!

The tiny settlement of Birling Gap near Beachy Head is teetering on the edge of the cliffs. The sea has been creeping closer for thousands of years, eroding away at the soft chalk. If nothing is done, the houses will fall into the sea in the near future. The residents want sea defences built to protect the cliff. English Nature, the government's wildlife adviser, is against the idea. Here is what different people think:

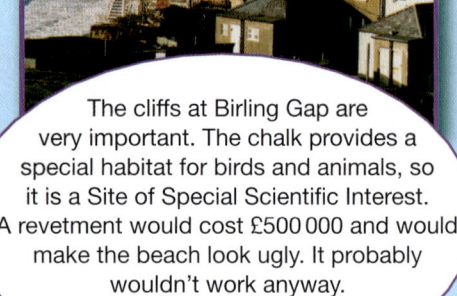

A Birling Gap in 1900 and 1999

Joan Hammond

There are three houses still lived in and a lovely pub in our hamlet. We want a small wall, or revetment, to be built at the base of the cliff so that the waves will stop undercutting the cliff. The sea defence would NOT spoil the famous view of the Seven Sisters cliffs and the beach would be safer!
Birling Gap resident

The cliffs at Birling Gap are very important. The chalk provides a special habitat for birds and animals, so it is a Site of Special Scientific Interest. A revetment would cost £500 000 and would make the beach look ugly. It probably wouldn't work anyway.
Spokesperson for English Nature

Louise MacDonald

Peter Forster (National Trust)

We own the land and three of the cottages at Birling Gap. The National Trust accepts that we will have to lose land because it is not worth protecting. We have even offered to buy the three other cottages.
Spokesperson for National Trust

Guy Walker (English Nature)

The sea cannot be held back forever. The cottages will eventually fall into the sea because the sea will erode any protection that we put there. However, a small revetment will hold back the sea for the next 15–20 years and would be cheap to build.
Civil engineer

Activity

1. Read what each person says. Decide which people are **for** building a sea wall and who is **against**.

   - Joan Hammond — for/against
   - Louise MacDonald — for/against
   - Guy Walker (English Nature) — for/against
   - Peter Forster (National Trust) — for/against

B Some views on the future of Birling Gap

C OS map showing the Birling Gap area, scale 1 : 50 000

© Crown copyright

Key to OS symbols

- National Trust-always open
- Lighthouse (in use)
- Lighthouse (not in use)
- Youth hostel / Auberge de jeunesse / Jugendherberge
- Viewpoint / Point de vue / Aussichtspunkt
- P Parking / Parking / Parkplatz

Activities

2 Imagine you are a reporter for a Sunday newspaper. You have been asked to interview people about the Birling Gap story.

  a Read the details of each person, and use this information to locate their homes on the map.

  b Work out the best route to visit all the homes, and draw a sketch map of your journey. How far will you need to travel?

○ Alice Richards is just 10 and loves to go down to the beach in the bay when the tide is out. She and her mother take a picnic down from their house perched on top of the cliff.

○ Bill and Anna Humphreys are proprietors of the Birling Gap Hotel, a large faded Victorian building. Being close to the sea, it attracts visitors from busy cities.

○ Paul Taylor has spent years building up his collection of rare breeds of sheep. He is about to buy more land on Went Hill so he can graze them more easily.

Melanie Brown lives in a farm not far from the cliffs. She has watched the road to Beachy Head get busier and busier: on a hot Sunday afternoon the car parks along the road to her farm are overflowing.

Mark and Louise Roberts live in the most unusual place on the map. They have just spent thousands of pounds moving their lighthouse back from the cliff edge.

Karen Banks is warden at the Youth Hostel. It is handy for the South Downs Way and only a short walk from the old town.

3 Should the cliff at Birling Gap be protected by a new revetment? In groups, look at the four people in **B**. Each person must choose a role and prepare a short speech on the question.

2 Geography Matters

How can the coast be managed?

It is not only cliffs that are attacked by the sea. Some lowland areas of the coast are constantly at risk from flooding. The local council must protect these areas, but sea defences cost a lot of money.

Case Study: Protecting Towyn from the sea

In the winter of 1990 the little town of Towyn on the North Wales coast was flooded when the sea broke through the sea wall. After the flood the Council looked at four different ways to protect the town from future flooding events.

A Flooding in Towyn in 1990

B Towyn, North Wales

Technical report

The embankments along the coast at Towyn have protected the low-lying land for over 200 years. A sea wall was built to protect the land from high tides.

On 26 February 1990 a deep depression brought very strong winds (up to 160 km/hour) and high waves. The sea wall was 5 m above sea level but it could not stop the waves flooding over.

Any land less than 5 m above sea level was flooded.

Activities

Use map **C** and other information from these pages to answer the following questions.

1 a Lay a piece of tracing paper over the map. Shade in the area that would have been covered by the floods if the waves were 5 m above sea level when they broke through the old wall. Use the How to ... box to help you.

b On your tracing, label four different land uses that would have been flooded.

How to ...

... use contour lines to help you estimate

- On your tracing, draw in the coastline.
- Find the 5 m contour line and trace along that.
- Shade in the area inside your lines and use the grid lines to estimate the area that the flood would have covered. Remember: each grid square is one kilometre square.

C OS map of Towyn, scale 1:25 000

A sea wall costs £5000 per metre to build

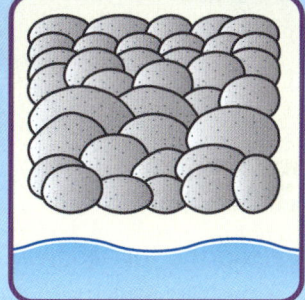
Rock armour costs £1000 per metre

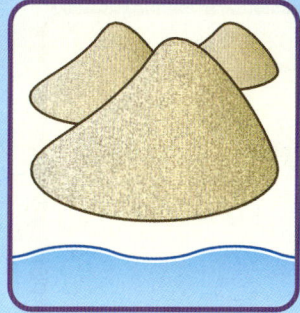
Beach nourishment is cheap – sand is added to the beach to make it higher

These groynes cost £10 000 each to build.

D

2 Look at figures **C** and **D**. Use the information to copy and complete this table:

Type of defence	length/number	cost	Total cost
Beach nourishment	1000 tonnes per year	£20 a tonne	£20 000 per year
Sea wall	… metres	£… per metre	£…
Groynes	ten new groynes	£… each	£…
Rock armour in front of the sea wall	… metres	£… per metre	£…

3 Which of the four defences stop waves reaching the sea wall? Explain your answer.

4 Explain why beach nourishment needs to be replaced every year.

5 **Extension**
Explain why people living along the coast to the east might be worried about the new groynes at Towyn.

2 Geography Matters

Case Study

Managing the beaches in Florida, USA

Beaches are important in Florida because:

- Millions of holidaymakers enjoy the white sandy beaches and bring billions of dollars to the local economy.
- The beaches protect the coast from wave erosion.

But if groynes in one place trap the sand, then the next beach down the coast loses its sand. To make matters worse, hurricane storms remove thousands of tonnes of sand every year. There are three solutions to the problem:

1. Let the coastline erode naturally – this is called '**managed retreat**'.
2. Dump fresh sand on the beaches every year – this is called '**beach nourishment**'.
3. Construct groynes and sea walls – this is called '**hard engineering**'.

A Sarasota beach in Florida

B A beach in Florida (a) before and (b) after beach nourishment

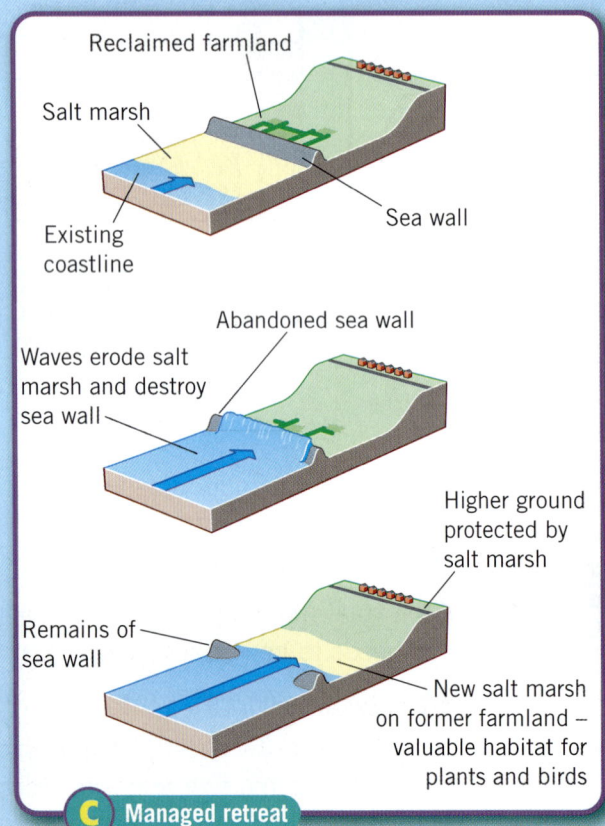

C Managed retreat

Activities

1. Read the text above. Discuss the solutions with a partner and try to agree:
   - Which solution costs the most money?
   - Which solution is cheapest?
   - Which solution is most ugly?

2. Different people will have different opinions. Can you imagine which solution each of these people would prefer?
   - Local hotel owner
   - British tourist
   - Resident who lives in a block of flats on the coast
   - Resident from inland who pays taxes to the council.

   Choose two people and explain why they would disagree.

Coastal environments

Review and reflect

A Sand and shingle beach in Eastbourne

B Chalk cliffs at Selwicks Bay, Humberside

Activities

1. Look at the two photographs. Make a copy of the table below. If the statement is true, then put a ✓. If it is false then put a ✗.

	Photograph A	Photograph B
1 There are cliffs	✗	✓
2 The sea might flood the land during storms		
3 Mechanical weathering occurs here		
4 Chemical weathering occurs here		
5 Longshore drift occurs here		
6 The coast has been protected with sea defences		
7 Waves attack the cliffs		
8 People come here on holiday		
9 The sea deposits material here		
10 The rock is very resistant to erosion		

2. Write down all the things you have learned to do in this unit. You can find some ideas in the help box – but not all of them are right!

help!

- Research
- Using an atlas
- Annotating diagrams
- Working with others

3. Look again at the five geographical questions you asked at the beginning of this unit. Are they the same as any given below? Can you answer them all now?

- What is weathering?
- What is erosion?
- How do waves shape the coast?
- How does the sea erode the coast?
- What features are found around the coast?
- Why do cliffs collapse?
- How can we manage our coasts?

3 Shopping – past, present and future

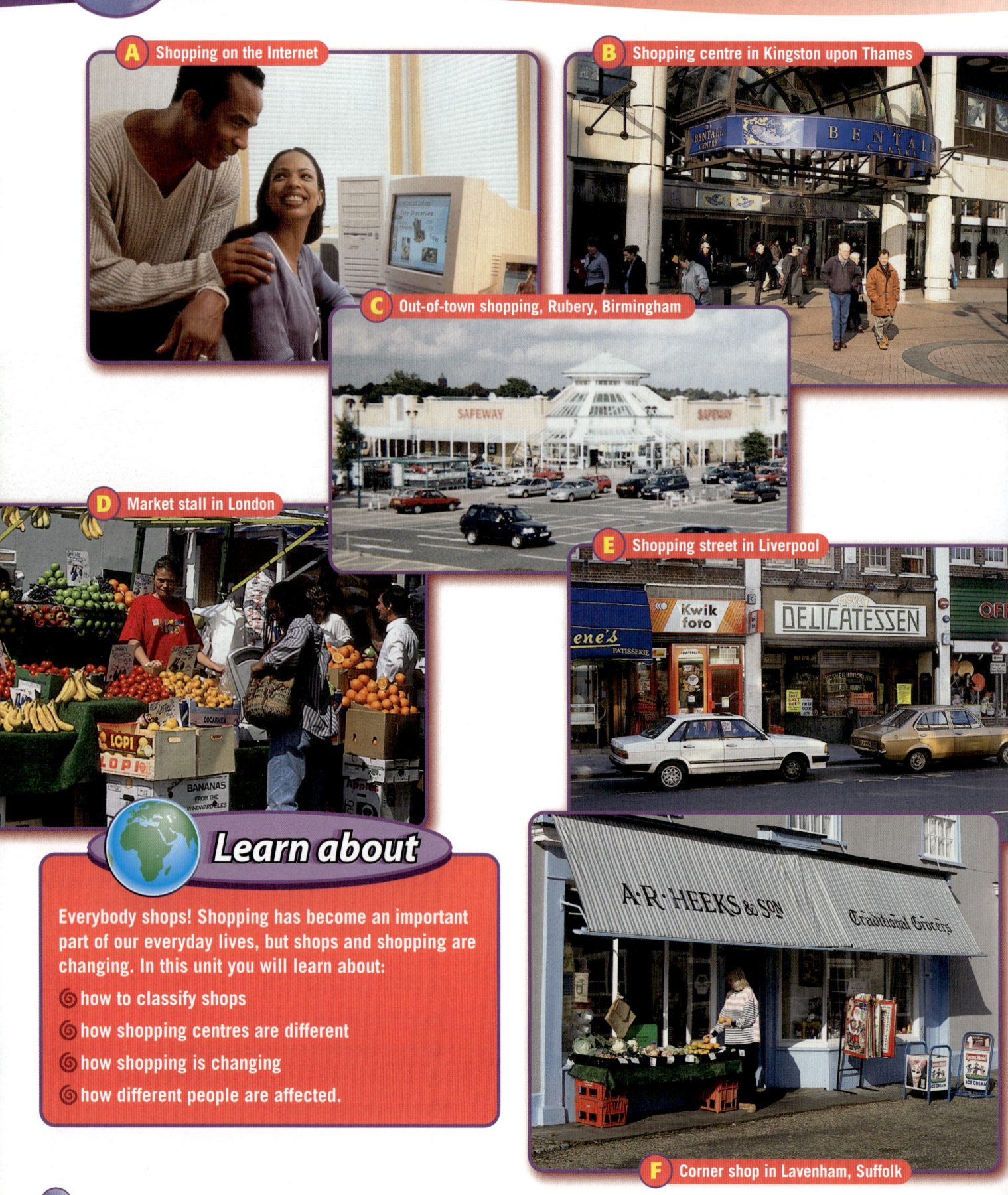

A Shopping on the Internet
B Shopping centre in Kingston upon Thames
C Out-of-town shopping, Rubery, Birmingham
D Market stall in London
E Shopping street in Liverpool
F Corner shop in Lavenham, Suffolk

Learn about

Everybody shops! Shopping has become an important part of our everyday lives, but shops and shopping are changing. In this unit you will learn about:

- how to classify shops
- how shopping centres are different
- how shopping is changing
- how different people are affected.

Setting the scene

Activities

1 a Study collage **G** above. Classify the goods you see into the categories *Necessities* (things people need) and *Luxuries* (things people want but do not need). Write them in a table like this:

Necessities	Luxuries
Potatoes	CDs

b Were all the goods easy to classify? If not, explain why some were difficult.

2 Make a copy of the table below.

Age	How busy it is	How attractive it is
1 oldest =	1 busiest =	1 most attractive =
2	2	2
3	3	3
4	4	4
5	5	5
6 newest =	6 quietest =	6 least attractive =

a Study the six types of shopping in **A–F** and then decide which is the oldest. Put the correct letter at the top of column 1, and then fill in the rest of the table.

b Compare your three lists with a partner. Try to agree on which is the best shopping environment. Write three things that make one shopping environment better than another.

3 a Copy the spider diagram below and add at least three more places to the diagram:

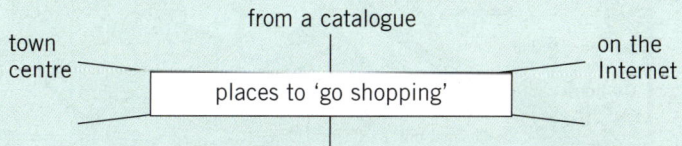

b Look again at your spider diagram. Which of the places did not exist 100 years ago? Highlight these on your diagram with a different colour.

3 Geography Matters

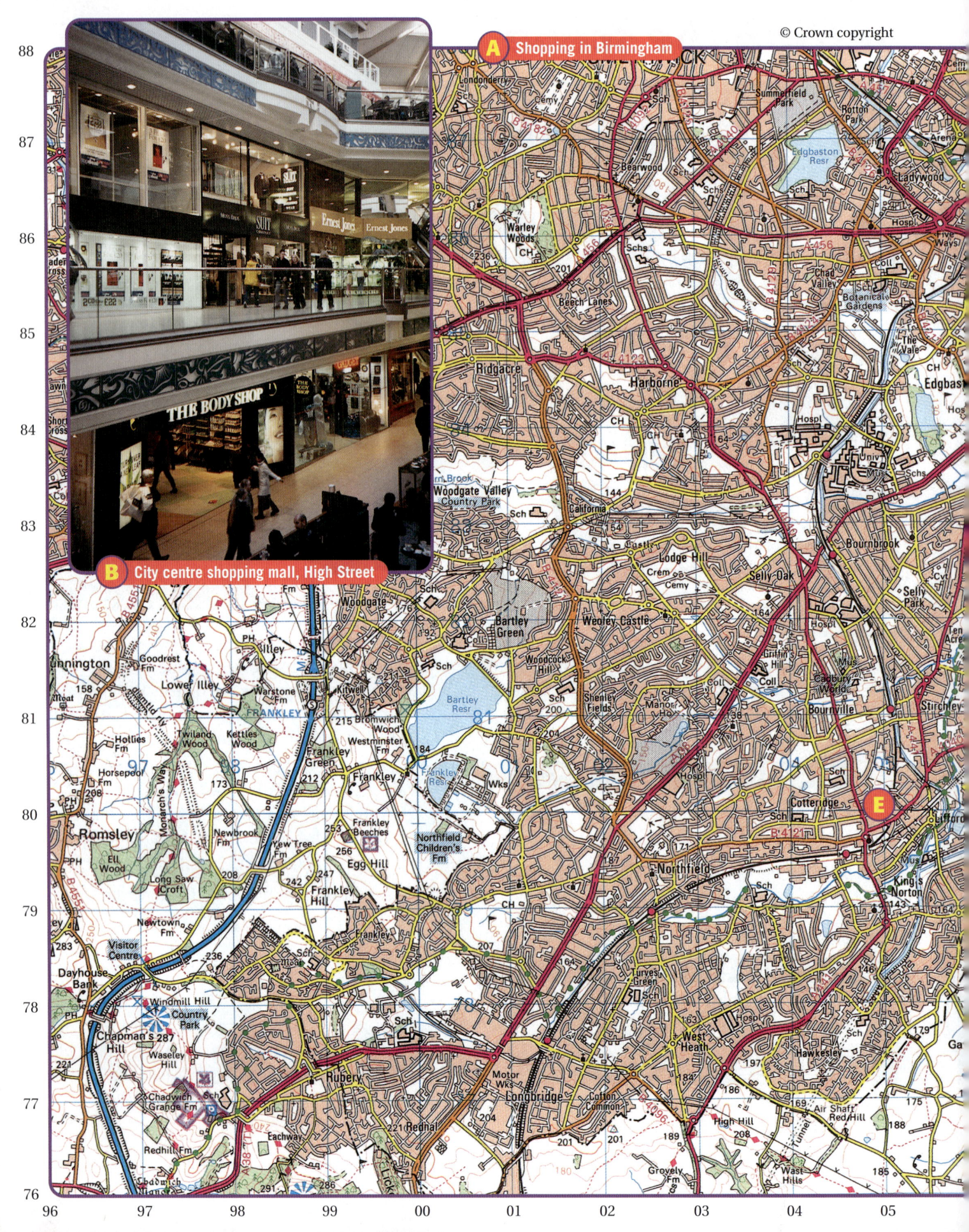

A Shopping in Birmingham

B City centre shopping mall, High Street

© Crown copyright

C City centre shopping street: New Street

Shopping – past, present and future

Birmingham has lots of different shopping areas. The city centre is the biggest, but there are also hundreds of small corner shops that sell everyday **convenience goods**.

People in Birmingham spend an average of £2500 a year each on their shopping. Half of this is spent in local shops, but people are now spending more on luxury goods from **comparison** shops.

D Suburban shopping street: King's Heath

E Suburban corner shop: Cotteridge

Getting Technical

- **Convenience goods:** Goods that are needed every day, such as bread, milk and newspapers. They are often regarded as necessities.

- **Comparison goods:** Goods that are regarded as luxuries, such as furniture, televisions, stereos and clothes. You might go to several shops to compare goods before you decide what to buy.

- **Sphere of influence:** The distance people are prepared to travel to use a shopping centre.

Activities

1 a In pairs, look at the photos on these two pages. Choose one shop and imagine that you visit it. Describe what it is like inside. Mention all these things:

- When I first went in I could see …
- There was the smell of …
- I could hear …
- I felt quite …

b Now read your description to someone else, and see if they can work out which photo you chose.

2 Copy and complete the table below for each of the photos **B–E**.

Shopping area	Location	Goods sold	Advantages	Disadvantages
Shopping mall	City centre	Comparison goods	Indoors, so you keep dry	You have to travel into town

3 Geography Matters

Shopping hierarchies

Shopping centres can be grouped into different types. This classification is based on what they sell or how big they are. When we put this into a diagram it makes a **hierarchy**.

Getting Technical

> **Shopping hierarchy:** When shops are put into an order based upon size or the type of good or service they provide.

Type of shopping area	Frequency of visit	Type of goods/service	Sphere of influence
City centre shopping mall	Weekly/monthly	Specialist goods, mainly comparison, e.g. furniture, televisions	Up to 80 km
Out-of-town shopping centre	Weekly/monthly	Bulk buying, convenience/comparison, e.g. bulk buying of food from a supermarket	Up to 30 km
Suburban shopping street	Two/three times a week	Mainly convenience, e.g. fruit and vegetables	Local area
Corner shop	Daily	Mainly convenience, e.g. milk or newspapers	Neighbouring streets

A A shopping hierarchy

Activities

1. **a** Copy the shopping hierarchy in **A**. Complete the diagram by adding the names of different places in Birmingham.
   b By looking at shopping hierarchy **A**, try to explain *why* people may think shopping malls are 'most important'.
   c Now look at your own shopping hierarchy. Explain why the shopping area you have put at the bottom of your hierarchy is the least important.

2. A shopping centre at the top of the hierarchy is different from a corner shop at the bottom. Use the comparison writing frame below to describe five differences:
   - **size** — City centre shops are usually much ... than
   - **goods** — Corner shops usually sell ... whereas ...
   - **location** — City centre shops are in the middle of town, but ...
   - **shoppers** — Thousands of shoppers ...
   - **frequency** — People go shopping to their corner shop nearly every ...

Shopping – past, present and future

What's your rating?

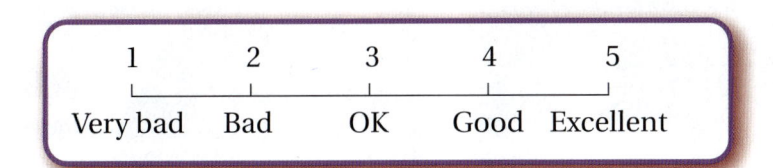

```
1       2       3       4       5
Very bad  Bad    OK     Good  Excellent
```

Performance standards are an important part of evaluation. Schools, hospitals and railways are measured against performance standards to show how well they do. You are going to use a performance standard to rate shopping centres near you.

Activities

1 a Here are ten factors to rate shopping centres:
   In pairs, discuss the meaning and importance of each factor.

- Accessibility – how easy is it to get to?
- Choice of shops – can you compare prices?
- Facilities for children – e.g. crèche
- Restaurants – are there any?
- Seating areas – are there any?
- Parking – is there enough?
- Range of goods – is there much choice?
- Toilets – are there any?
- Facilities for disabled people
- Cleanliness – is there any litter?

b Copy the table below. Think of an example for each of the four shopping centres in your area. Give each place a score for each of the ten factors listed.

c Which shopping centre gets the highest score? Explain why it is the best.

Shopping area type	Name	Access-ibility	Parking	Choice	Toilets	Restaurants	Children	Disabled	Seating	Cleanliness
Corner shop										
Shopping street										
City centre shopping mall										
Out-of-town shopping centre										

2 a What makes one shopping centre better than another? Choose the three most important factors and discuss your choice with a partner.

b Other people might think that another factor is more important. Give one reason why someone else might disagree with you.

3 Geography Matters

How will changes affect different people?

A **B** **C**

Different shoppers have different needs

D

Changes that take place are called **trends**.

The two main trends in shopping are:

1 Big new shopping centres have opened:
   - they are often on the edge of towns and cities, but sometimes in the centre
   - they are usually 'indoors'
   - we must travel further to get to them, usually by car.

2 Most goods can be bought over the Internet or telephone:
   - we have to use credit cards, rather than cash, to buy goods
   - goods are delivered to our homes.

How to ...

... summarise the effects

Your explanation should be split into three sections:

1 **Benefits:** start with any advantages for you
2 **Problems:** outline all the difficulties that you now face
3 **Summary:** decide, on balance, whether the changes have been good for you, or bad. Then write your conclusion.

Activity

1 a Changes affect groups of people in different ways. Choose one group of people from the list below and give six ways that shopping trends affect them.
   - young people
   - elderly people
   - parents with young children
   - people without a car.

b Imagine you are one of these people. Summarise all the benefits and problems that Internet shopping and new shopping centres have had for you. Use the 'How to' box.

Shopping – past, present and future

How has shopping changed?

Case Study: Poplar Road, King's Heath, Birmingham

1904

4	George Atkins	Glass and china dealer
6	Miss Selina Clark	Sweets
8	Joseph Findon	Fried fish
10	Arthur Taylor	Musical instruments
12	Charles Cooper	Tailor
14	Charles Parkes	Hairdresser
16	Robert Guest	Plumber
20	Frederick Gel	Furniture maker
28	Thomas Farren	Butcher
30	Richard Allen	Painter
34	Albert Gell	Furniture maker
36	William Armishaw	Painter and Decorator
38	William Philpott	Laundry owner
40	Albert Spiers	Cycle dealer
42	Henry Humphreys	Ironmonger, glass and china
44	John Barclay	Manager, Cooperative Society
46	John Bluck	China and glass dealer

A From *Kelly's Directory of Birmingham*, 1904

Poplar Road in 1904

B Shops in Poplar Road, 1992

4	**Off Limits** Compact Discs	32	**Poplar Restaurant** Restaurant	
6	**Lady Di** Shoes	34	**Delta** Stationery	
8	**Sarah's** Delicatessen	36	**Poplar Café** Teas and Snacks	
10	**Childsplay** Toys	38	**Clive Mark** School uniform	
12	**Valerie Rudd** Handbags	40	Empty	
14	**Pollyannas** Lace	42	**Smart Gear** Clothes	
16	**AA Jewellery** Jewellery and Giftware	44	Empty	
18–30	**Safeway** Supermarket and car park			

1992

C Shops and businesses in Poplar Road, 2001

4	**The Glory Hole** Catalogue clearance	16	**Jewellers and Repairs** Jewellery and giftware	
6	**AJ's** Hairdresser	18–30	**Safeway** Supermarket and car park	
8	Empty	32	**Los Caracores** Mediterranean restaurant	
10	**Childsplay** Toys	34	**Gas Line** Cookers, fires, fridges	
12	**Caribbean Sam** Caribbean food	36	Empty	
14	**Armadillo** Clothes and gifts	38–40	**Clive Mark** School uniform	
		42	**Mann & Co** Solicitors	
		44	Empty	

2001

Poplar Road in 2001

3 Geography Matters

Activities

1 Look at the photographs and information on Poplar Road. Decide in which year people were most likely to:

  a buy a glass vase
  b hire a decorator
  c get a cup of tea
  d do the weekly food shopping
  e get a violin mended

2 Make a copy of the tally chart below. Use one colour to 'tally' the different shops in 1904, then use different colours for 1992 and 2000.

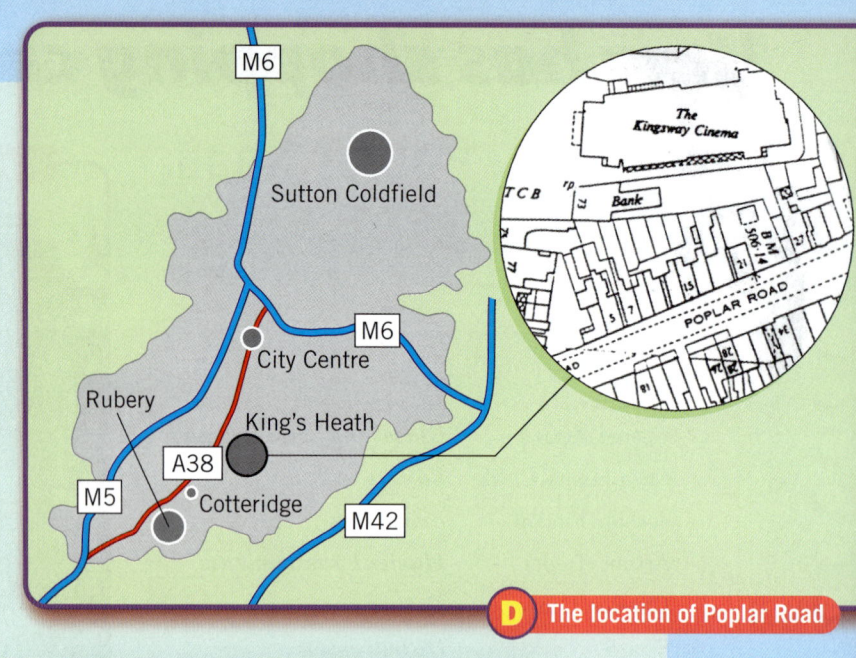

D The location of Poplar Road

	Food shops	Shops selling other goods	Cafes or restaurants	Other services (not selling goods)
1904				
1992				
2000				

3 Look at your tally chart and the sentences below. Write out the statements that are true, and correct the ones that are wrong:

- There are now more food shops in Poplar Road.
- There are now more services.
- There are now more cafés and restaurants.
- There are now more empty premises.

4 In pairs, choose two of the statements in question **3** and try to explain why this has happened. Here are some clues to help you.

out-of-town shopping centres   **cars**   **weekly shopping**   **freezers**

Compare your ideas with others.

5 **Extension**

Write 300 words to describe *how and why* the shops in Poplar Road have changed in the last 100 years.

You could start your *description* like this:

> The types of shops on Poplar Road have changed over the past hundred years. In 1904 …

Your *explanation* could start:

> People's shopping habits have changed since 1904 because … This means that in Poplar Road …

Shopping – past, present and future

What is the future of shopping?

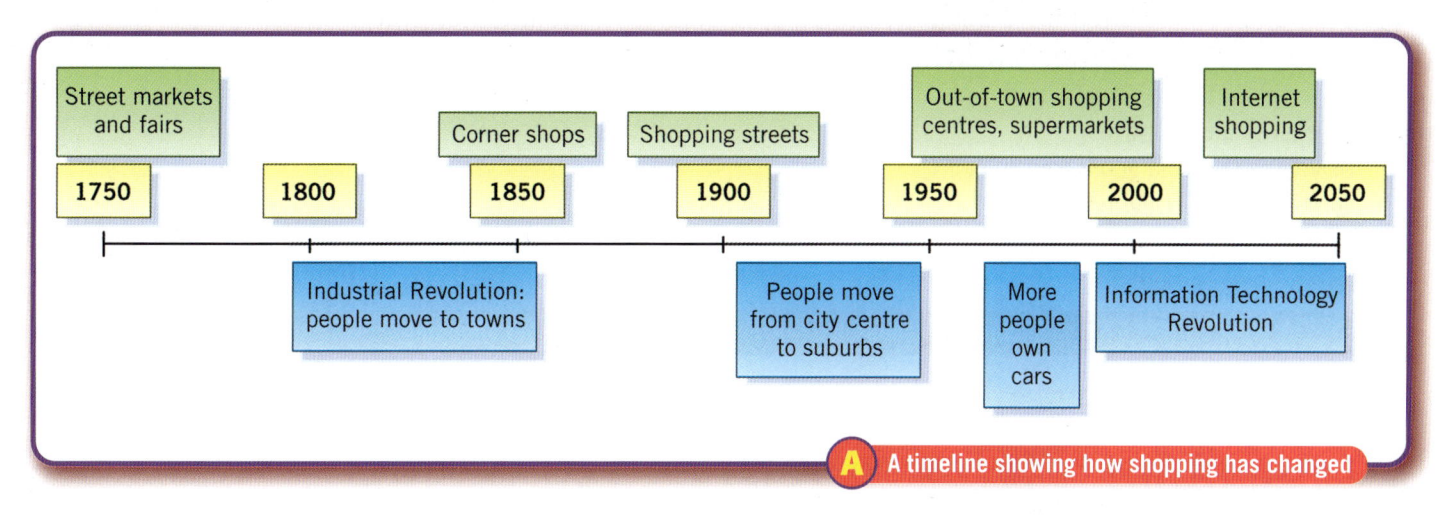

A timeline:

- 1750 — Street markets and fairs
- 1800 — Industrial Revolution: people move to towns
- 1850 — Corner shops
- 1900 — Shopping streets; People move from city centre to suburbs
- 1950 — Out-of-town shopping centres, supermarkets; More people own cars
- 2000 — Information Technology Revolution
- 2050 — Internet shopping

A A timeline showing how shopping has changed

When British towns grew in the 1800s, people needed to be able to walk to their local shops to buy food and other goods. Shopping is now completely different. Most people in the UK can travel much further to go shopping. We don't always use cash to buy goods, and we can even stay at home and buy goods over the telephone or on the Internet. How do you think that shopping will change in the future?

Activity

1 a Which of these goods can you buy on the Internet?
- CDs
- food
- clothes
- a holiday

b Find three websites that sell goods or services that you can also buy in a shop. You can find web addresses in newspaper advertisements or by using a search engine. **ICT**

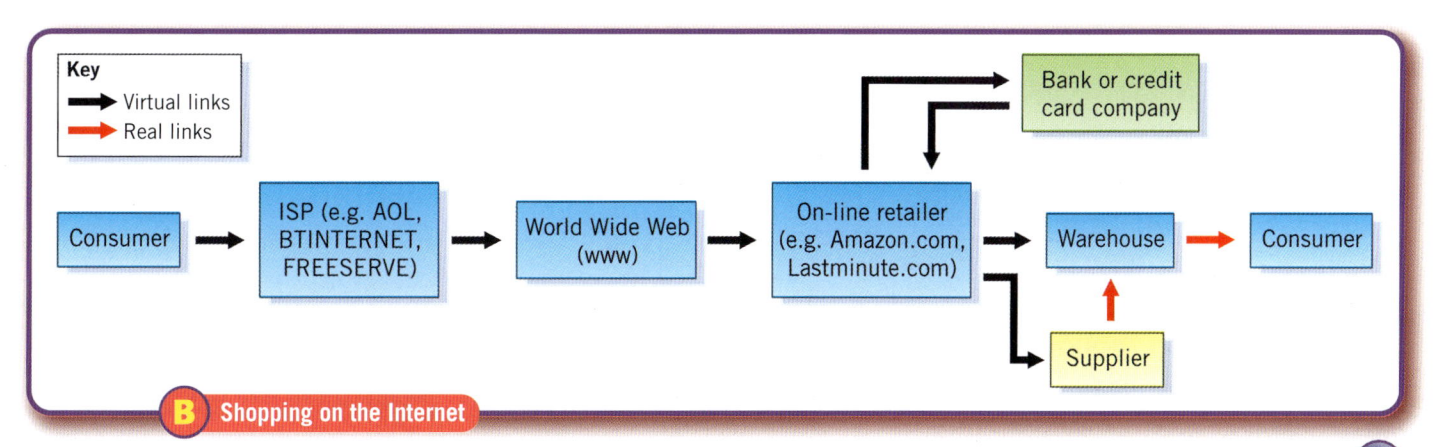

Key
- → Virtual links
- → Real links

Consumer → ISP (e.g. AOL, BTINTERNET, FREESERVE) → World Wide Web (www) → On-line retailer (e.g. Amazon.com, Lastminute.com) → Warehouse → Consumer

On-line retailer ↔ Bank or credit card company
On-line retailer → Supplier → Warehouse

B Shopping on the Internet

3 Geography Matters

Activities

2 Copy and complete the table below. It compares shopping on the Internet with shops. Here are some ideas to get you started:
- you have to use a credit card
- it takes time to travel
- you can see the goods for yourself
- there is less traffic pollution
- there are fewer jobs for shop assistants
- shopping is more fun.

	Shopping in shops	Internet shopping
good points		
bad points		

3 Look again at Poplar Road in 2000. If everyone used the Internet to do their shopping, then which shops would still be there in the year 2050? Explain your answer.

4 Draw and annotate a cartoon or picture of how you think people will shop in 2050.

5 Imagine you are responsible for marketing a product on the Internet.

   a Design a web page advertising the product you have chosen. You could use a desktop publishing package to help you.

   b You have been asked to make a presentation to your company to explain how you are marketing the product. Use the prompts in the help box to structure your presentation.

6 Think about the changes in shopping identified in this unit. Write an account titled: *How and why has shopping changed? How is it likely to change in the future?*

Your account should have three sections:
- **Situation**: the background to changes in shopping
- **Events**: more detail on the changes in shopping
- **Outcome**: closing statement to sum up and predict the future.

help!

Remember to consider all aspects of marketing your product:

- **Product** – what is it?
  – what is it made of?
  – does it have any special features?
- **Promotion** – where is it going to be advertised?
  – any special offers?
- **Price** – how much can you charge? Your price must be low enough to make people want to buy, but remember: you need to make a profit!
- **Place** – where is your product made or stored?
  – how will it reach the customer?

Shopping – past, present and future

Review and reflect

A question of shopping

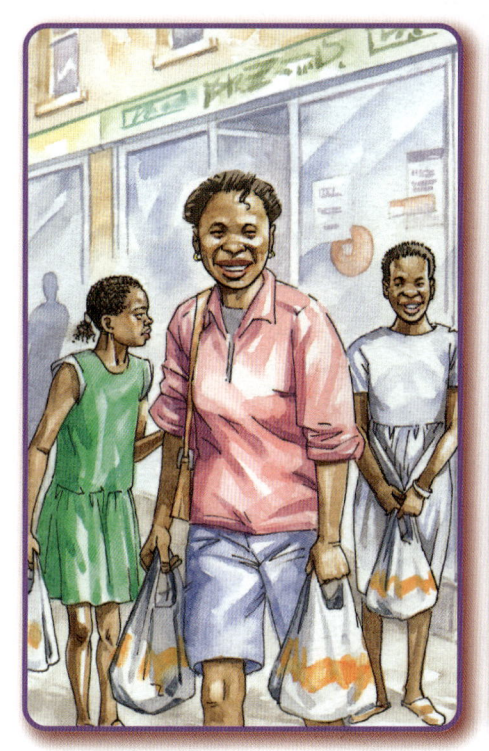

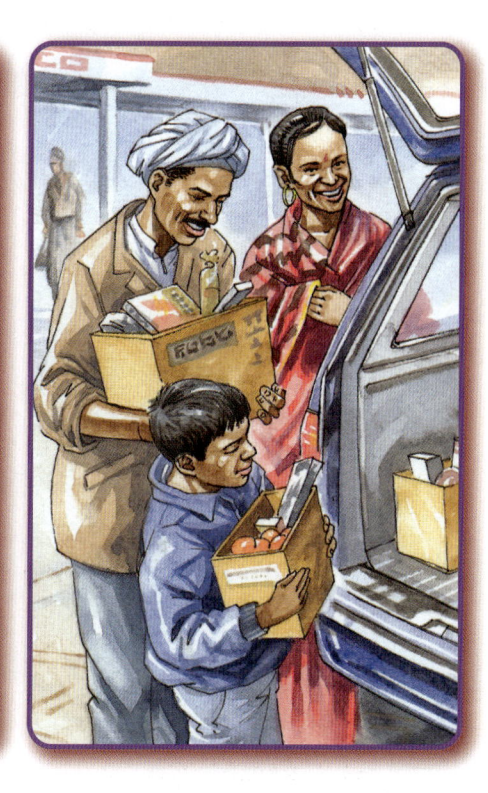

Activities

1 Below is a list of words connected with this unit:

1 bread	4 restaurant	7 shoe shop
2 bookshop	5 sweets	8 café
3 newspaper	6 bar	9 bike shop

Work out which is the odd one out from these sets of numbers, and why. The first has been done for you:

a)   1   3   5   7   **answer:** number 7; the others are all convenience goods

b)   1   2   7   9

c)   2   4   6   8

2 **Extension**

Imagine that you are a Victorian person who travels to the present. Describe what you think of the shops that you see. Mention all these things:

- shops, e.g. type, location, size and appearance
- technology, e.g. computers, tills and telephones
- money and prices.

4 Weather patterns over Europe

A Satellite image of Europe, 18 July 1999

Learn about

Weather is the condition of the atmosphere. It affects most people's lives every day. Many people need to understand the weather to do their jobs. In this unit you will learn about:

- weather and climate in Europe
- reading weather maps and satellite images
- how to forecast the weather
- the difference between weather and climate
- drawing and reading climate graphs
- how to choose a holiday destination with a climate that suits your family.

What is Europe like?

B A political map of Europe

help!

- A **political map** shows countries and their main cities, including the capital.
- A **physical map** shows information about the natural features on the Earth's surface, such as rivers, mountains and oceans.

Activities

1. Maps use words, colours, lines and symbols to show information about places. Look at **B**, which is a **political map** of Europe. There are lots of different lines on this map.

   a Identify an area of coastline. Which country does it belong to?

   b Find a country which does not have a coastline.

   c Identify a line which shows the border between two countries. Name the countries.

2. Find a **physical map** of Europe. It uses colours, lines, symbols and words to show different features. Copy and complete the table with the information that the map shows.

Colours	Lines	Symbols	Words
the sea			

3. Now look at the satellite image **A** of Europe on the opposite page.

   a Is image **A** more like a political map or a physical map? Explain your answer.

   b What information is shown that would not appear on an atlas map?

   c Why is this type of information not shown on atlas maps?

47

4 Geography Matters

What are clouds and why does it rain?

Clouds are made up of tiny water droplets. These are so small that they 'float' in the **atmosphere**. Clouds form when air cools causing **condensation**. This is when **water vapour** in the air turns into water droplets. There are four main cloud types.

- **Cirrus clouds** are made of ice crystals because they form high up in the atmosphere where temperatures are below freezing point.
- **Stratus clouds** form in a layer or 'sheet' across the sky and tend to be much lower in the atmosphere. They are called fog when they are at ground level.
- **Cumulus clouds** have 'bumpy' tops because of the rising air currents that create them.
- Sometimes **cumulonimbus clouds** form when air rises very quickly.

Some cloud types, such as cirrus, never cause precipitation (rain, hail or snow). Others, like cumulonimbus, bring rain or hail with thunder and lightning. Clouds are an important part of the **hydrological cycle** (**D**).

A Stratus clouds

B Cirrus clouds

C Cumulus clouds

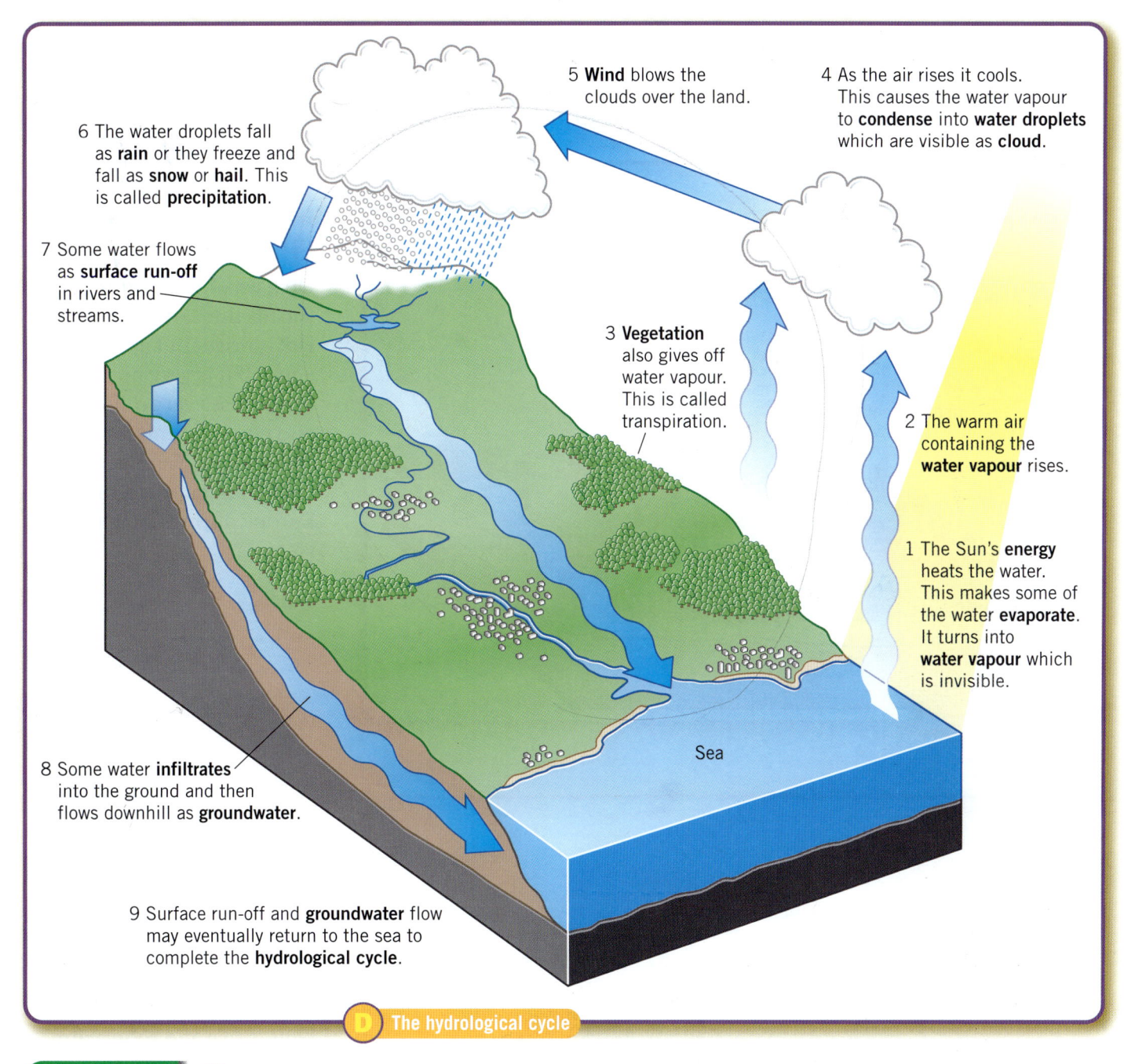

Weather patterns over Europe

The hydrological cycle

The hydrological cycle diagram (D):

1. The Sun's **energy** heats the water. This makes some of the water **evaporate**. It turns into **water vapour** which is invisible.
2. The warm air containing the **water vapour** rises.
3. **Vegetation** also gives off water vapour. This is called **transpiration**.
4. As the air rises it cools. This causes the water vapour to **condense** into **water droplets** which are visible as **cloud**.
5. **Wind** blows the clouds over the land.
6. The water droplets fall as **rain** or they freeze and fall as **snow** or **hail**. This is called **precipitation**.
7. Some water flows as **surface run-off** in rivers and streams.
8. Some water **infiltrates** into the ground and then flows downhill as **groundwater**.
9. Surface run-off and **groundwater** flow may eventually return to the sea to complete the **hydrological cycle**.

D The hydrological cycle

Activities

1. Create a word bank for all the terms in **bold** print on pages 48 and 49, including those in diagram **D** above. You may remember some of them from *Geography Matters 1*.

2. Write a story about a water molecule called H₂O travelling around the hydrological cycle. Try to use most of the geographical vocabulary in your word bank. Use the numbers for each annotation on diagram **D** to help you sequence your story correctly. You could begin your story like this …

> One day H₂O, a water molecule, was warming himself in the heat of the midday Sun when he began to disappear. Suddenly he saw the sea below him and realised he must have <u>evaporated</u> and turned into …

4 Geography Matters

What causes cloud and rain?

When air rises it cools. This causes condensation as water vapour turns into clouds of water droplets. If the air is forced to rise, the droplets get bigger and too heavy to float in the air. Then they fall as rain or other types of **precipitation**. Air can be forced up in three ways to give three types of rainfall.

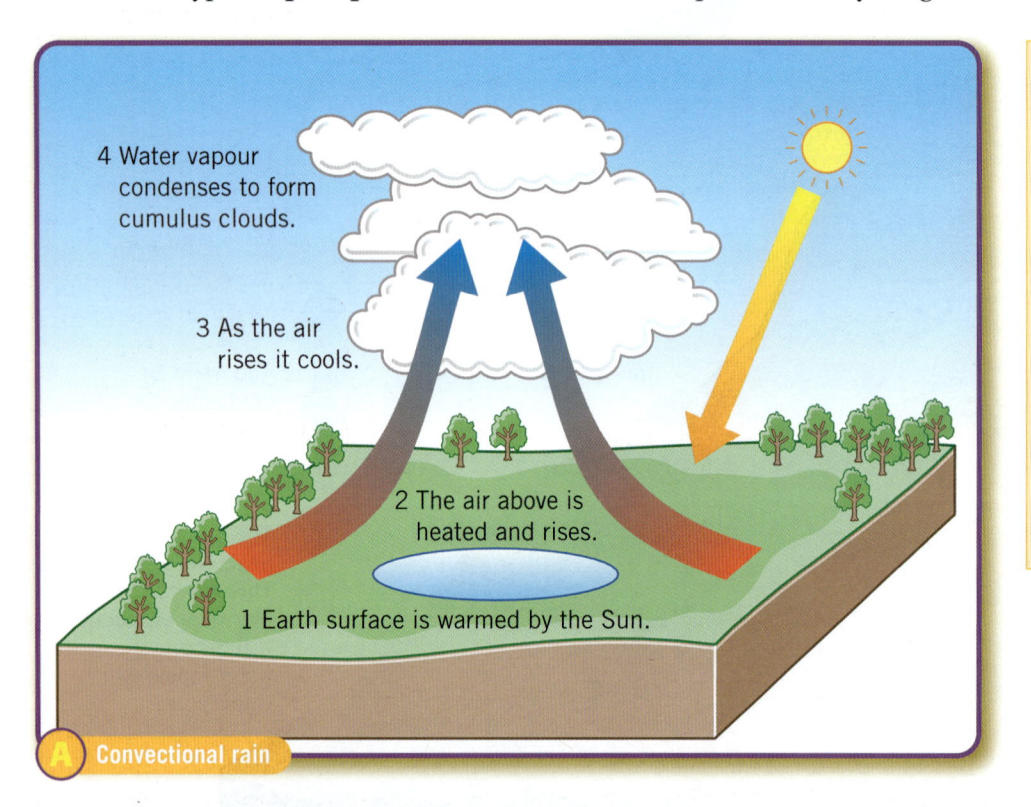

4 Water vapour condenses to form cumulus clouds.

3 As the air rises it cools.

2 The air above is heated and rises.

1 Earth surface is warmed by the Sun.

A Convectional rain

Convectional rain – when air is forced up by heat

On a very hot day the Sun warms the Earth's surface. Hot air rises but as it rises it cools. If it is very hot then the air rises very quickly and cumulonimbus storm clouds form. **Convectional rain** often happens in Europe during hot summer weather.

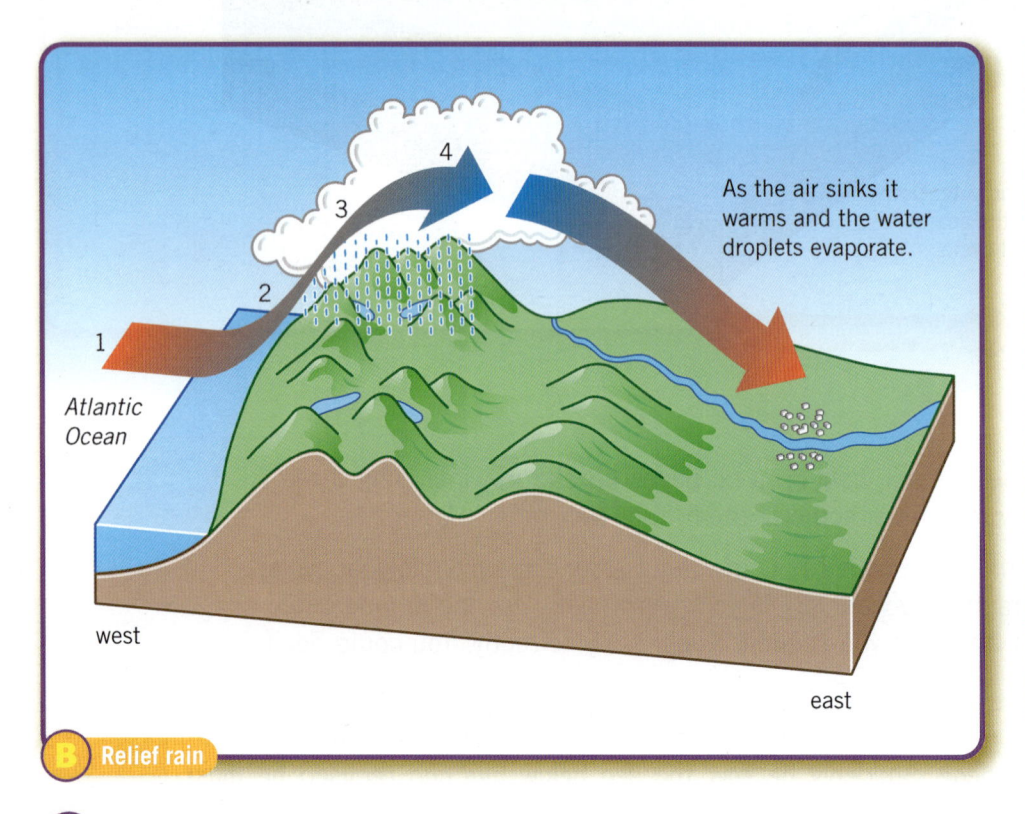

As the air sinks it warms and the water droplets evaporate.

Atlantic Ocean

west

east

B Relief rain

Relief rain – when air is forced up by hills

Relief means the shape of the land. When winds blow inland the air is forced to rise over mountains. The air cools to form clouds, the clouds rise and **relief rain** falls on the mountains. In Europe the winds from the Atlantic Ocean bring rain to the mountains of western Europe. By the time the winds reach eastern Europe the clouds have lost a lot of their moisture so the weather is drier.

Weather patterns over Europe

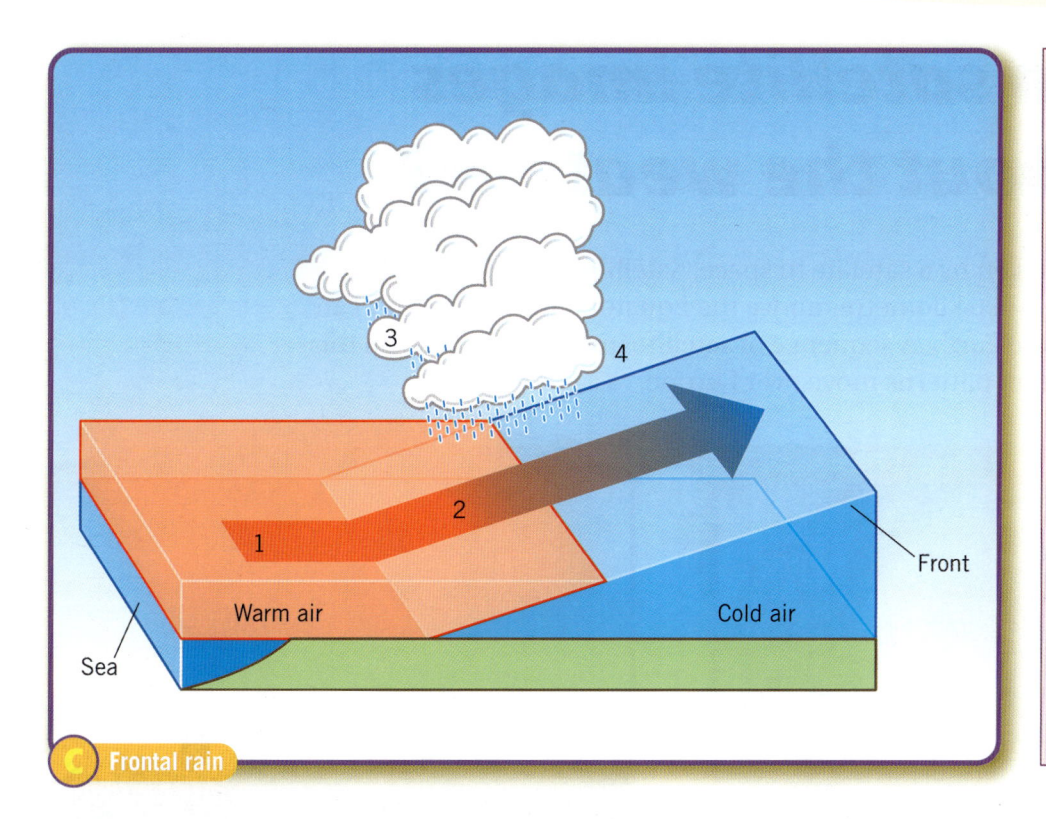

Frontal rain – when warm air is forced up over cold air

A **front** is where warm air meets cold air. Warm air from the tropics is lighter than cold air from the polar regions. When the two meet, the warmer air rises over the colder, heavier air. As the warm air is forced to rise it cools to form clouds. Fronts can bring rain to any part of Europe. On a weather map a cold front looks like this: ▲▲▲ and a warm front like this: ●●● .

C Frontal rain

Activities

1. Make a copy of diagram **A**, to show how convectional rain forms. Add all the labels.

2. Make a copy of diagram **B**: **relief rain**. Each sentence matches a number on diagram B. Write these sentences in the correct place on your diagram:
   - Air rises and cools. Water vapour condenses into clouds.
   - Clouds rise and rain falls.
   - Moist air blows in from the Atlantic Ocean.
   - The air hits the mountains of western Europe and is forced to rise.

3. Now make a copy of diagram **C** and give it a title. Each sentence below matches a number on diagram **C**. Write these sentences in the correct place on your diagram.
   - lighter air rises over cold air
   - clouds develop
   - warm air holds moisture
   - clouds cool to form rain

4. Which type of rainfall is most likely for each of these situations? Give a reason for each answer.
   - A windy day in the English Lake District.
   - A cold windy day in the Netherlands.
   - A hot day in the south of France.

4 Geography Matters

What can satellite images tell us about the weather?

Images **A**, **D** and **G** were taken by a satellite in space. Satellites like METEOSAT orbit the Earth at about 35 000 kilometres above the Equator. From there they can photograph almost half the Earth. A sequence of satellite images like those on this page can show how weather patterns move over Europe.

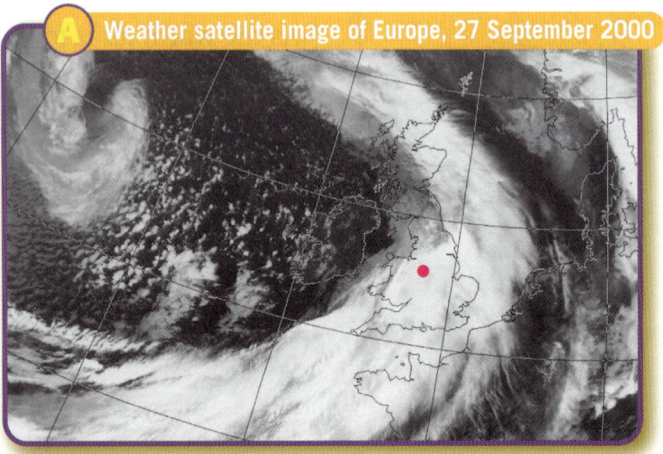

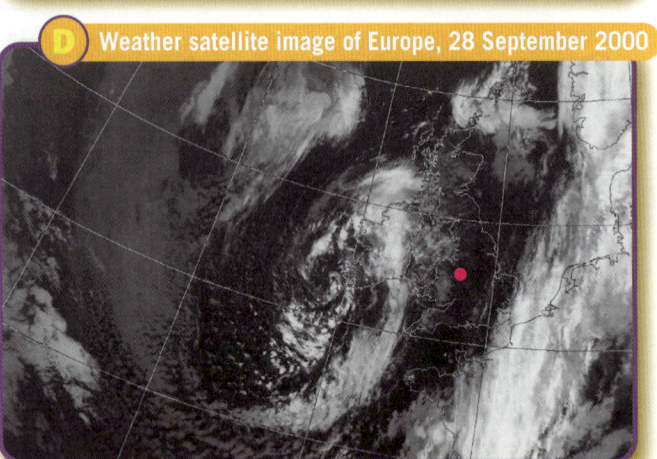

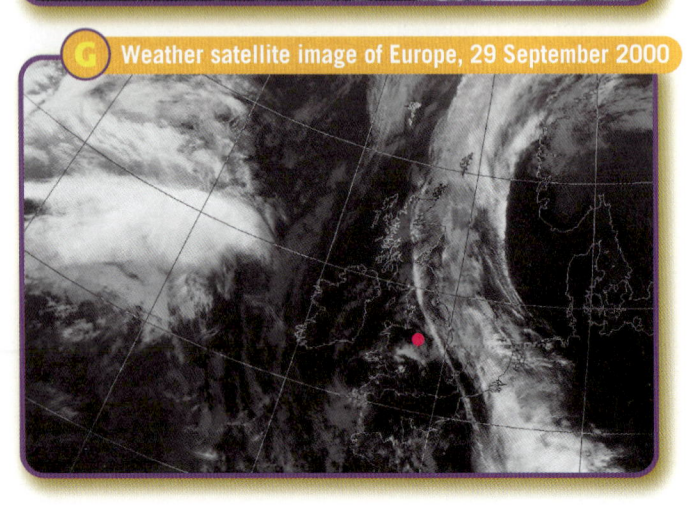

A Weather satellite image of Europe, 27 September 2000

B Weather over Chester, 27 September 2000

D Weather satellite image of Europe, 28 September 2000

E Weather over Chester, 28 September 2000

G Weather satellite image of Europe, 29 September 2000

H Weather over Chester, 29 September 2000

Key
● Location of Chester

52

Weather patterns over Europe

Satellite images give weather forecasters essential information. For example, they can be used to track storms and warn people about strong winds and heavy rain. Many people, such as workers on oil rigs and in power stations, farmers and ferry operators, need to know about the weather.

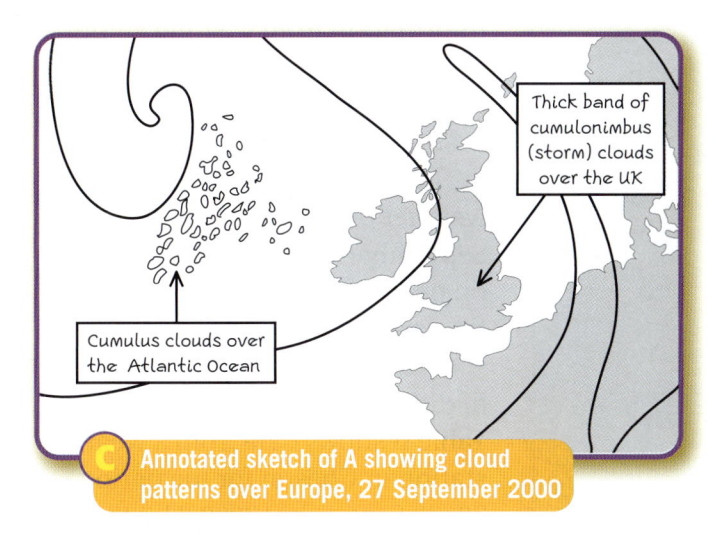

C Annotated sketch of A showing cloud patterns over Europe, 27 September 2000

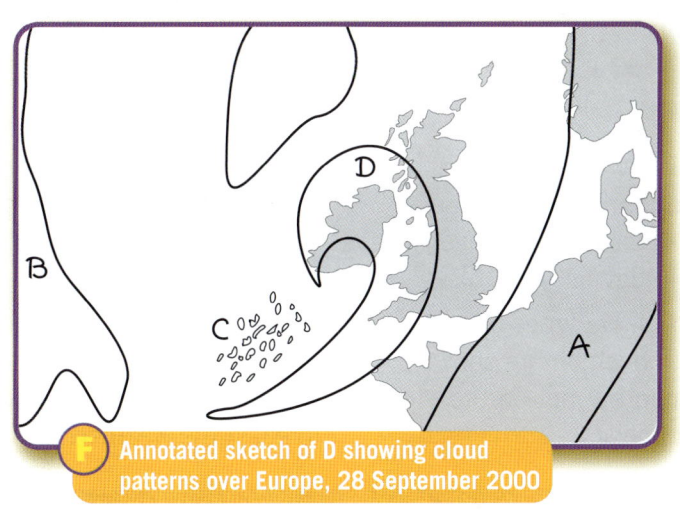

F Annotated sketch of D showing cloud patterns over Europe, 28 September 2000

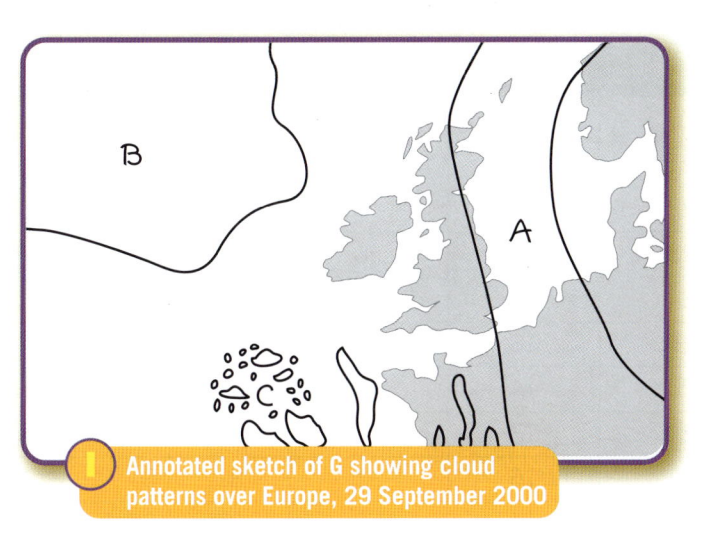

I Annotated sketch of G showing cloud patterns over Europe, 29 September 2000

Activities

Figure **C** is an annotated sketch of satellite image **A**. The annotations describe the cloud patterns and their locations over Europe. Use it as a guide to help you do activities **1** and **2**. You can see the different cloud types on page 48.

1. Match the annotations below to letters **A–D** on sketch **F**.
   - Cumulus clouds to the south-west of Ireland.
   - Thin stratus cloud over the Atlantic Ocean.
   - A band of cumulonimbus cloud over France and Scandinavia.
   - A 'swirl' of thick cloud to the west of the British Isles and France.

2. Now write annotations of your own for letters **A–C** on sketch **I**. For each one, mention a place, like those in activity **1**.

3. Europe's weather usually comes from one main direction. Look at the sequence of weather patterns shown in images **A**, **D** and **G** and suggest which direction this is.

4. **Extension** ICT
   a. Download satellite images for the last three days from http://www.heinemann.co.uk/hotlinks (insert code 1631P).
   b. Draw a sequence of dated sketch maps, like **C**, **F** and **I**, showing the weather patterns. Annotate the cloud patterns.

4 Geography Matters

How can weather information be presented?

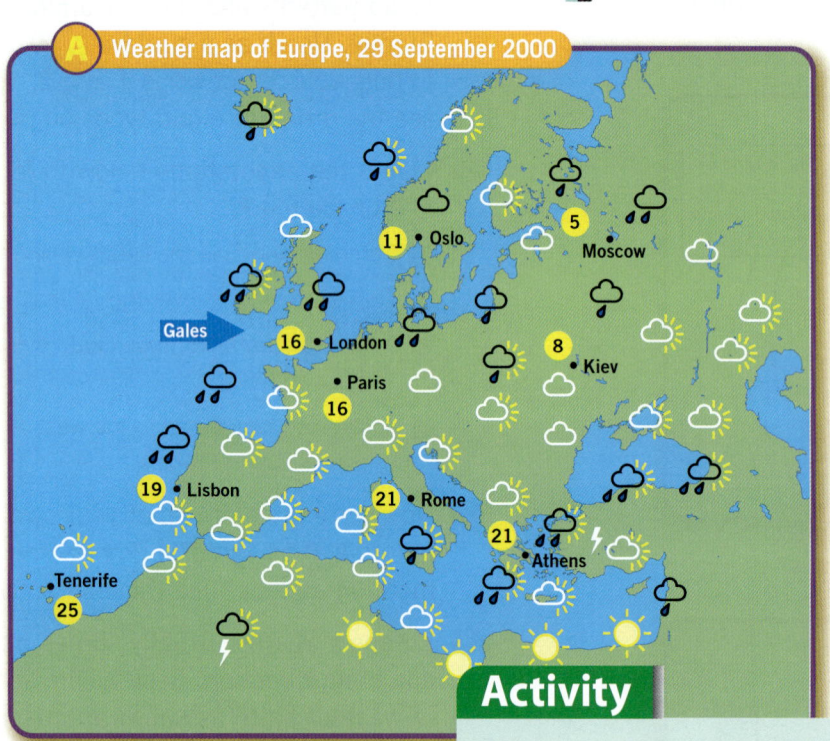

A Weather map of Europe, 29 September 2000

Meteorologists are people who use information from weather stations and satellite images to study the weather. They use computer models to **forecast** the weather.

Map **A** shows the pattern of weather over Europe on 29 September 2000. Satellite image **G** on page 52 shows information for the same day.

Weather stations record a range of different aspects of the weather. Table **B** shows data from a weather station in Chester for the period 20–29 September 2000. Use the Getting Technical box to help you to understand the data shown.

Getting Technical

Humidity: the amount of water vapour held in the air, measured as a percentage. If the air has 100 per cent humidity, then it is foggy and full of moisture.

Wind direction: the compass direction *from* which the wind blows.

Activity

1. Work in pairs to compare the weather map for 29 September 2000 with the satellite image for the same day on page 52.

   a Write down five types of information which are shown on the map but not on the satellite image.

   b Write down three types of information which are shown on the satellite image but not on the map.

   c How can a sequence of weather maps and satellite images, for a number of days, help people to forecast the weather?

Date	Average temperature (°C)	Rainfall (mm)	Humidity (%)	Wind direction
September 20	12	6	89	SE
September 21	17	0	78	S
September 22	17	0	77	S
September 23	18	0	78	S
September 24	12	11	89	SE
September 25	13	8	86	SE
September 26	14	7	88	SE
September 27	13	5	86	SE
September 28	16	1	81	S
September 29	14	2	83	SE

B Weather data for Chester for 20–29 September 2000

Weather patterns over Europe

Geographical enquiry: How do different aspects of the weather affect each other?

Activities

1 Asking geographical questions

To get started with such a big enquiry question, you need to begin with smaller questions. Start by looking at the links between temperature, rainfall and humidity on table **B**.

- What is the link between temperature and humidity? Are warm days more humid?
- What is the link between rainfall and humidity? Are humid days wetter?
- What is the link between the rainfall and the temperature? Are warmer days drier?

Look at the questions above and use the information in table **B** to find links.

> **ICT idea** Enter the data in table **B** into a computer spreadsheet and then carry out the enquiry.

2 Presenting data

a You can use a scattergraph to see if there really is a link (correlation) between two factors. For example, in figure **C** temperature and humidity have been plotted to see if there is a link. It shows that the days with higher temperatures have lower humidity.

b Plot two more scattergraphs for:
- rainfall and humidity
- rainfall and temperature.

3 Analysing data

a What do your graphs prove? Write a sentence about each one.

b Is this what you would expect? Give a reason.

4 Explaining results and making conclusions

a Look at the column about wind direction. Is the weather better when the wind blows from the south or south east?

b Give two reasons to explain your answer.

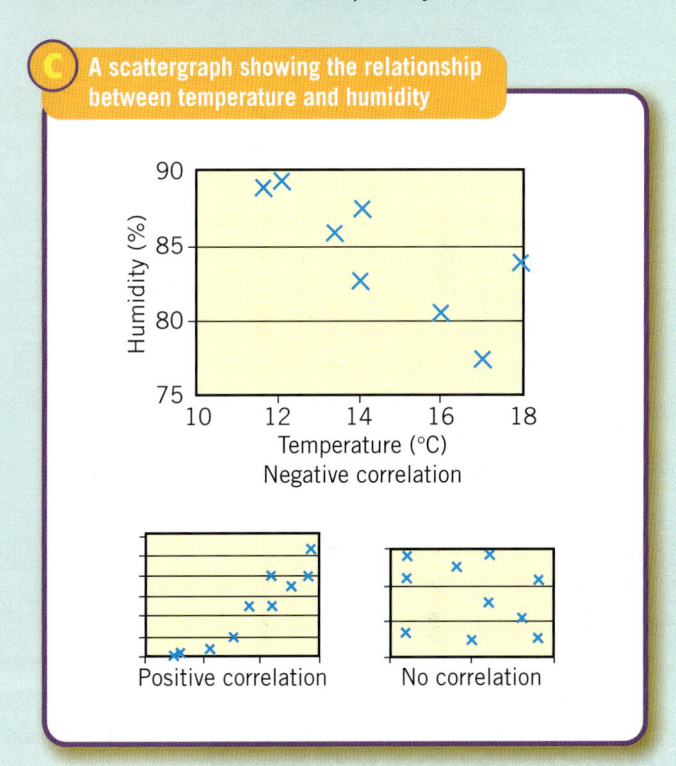

C A scattergraph showing the relationship between temperature and humidity

Negative correlation

Positive correlation   No correlation

4 Geography Matters

What types of climate does Europe have?

So far this unit has looked at weather. **Weather** is the temperature, precipitation and wind on a particular day. **Climate**, on the other hand, is the average weather of a place, taken over many years (usually 30). Europe has lots of different types of climate (see **F** opposite).

A **climate graph** shows the average temperature and precipitation for a place. Graph **A** shows information for Valencia, Ireland. The red line is the average temperature for each month, in degrees Celsius on the left axis. The blue bars show average rainfall or precipitation for each month, measured in millimetres on the right axis.

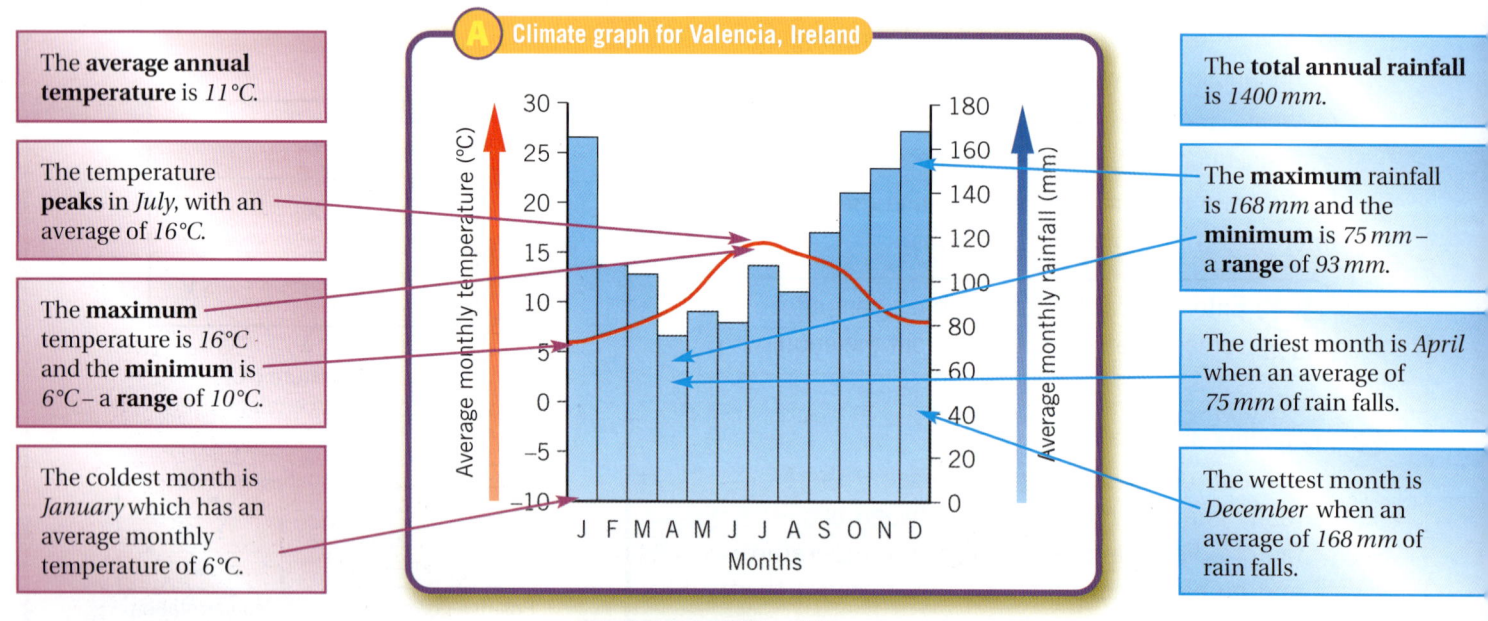

A Climate graph for Valencia, Ireland

The **average annual temperature** is *11°C*.

The temperature **peaks** in *July*, with an average of *16°C*.

The **maximum** temperature is *16°C* and the **minimum** is *6°C* – a **range** of *10°C*.

The coldest month is *January* which has an average monthly temperature of *6°C*.

The **total annual rainfall** is *1400 mm*.

The **maximum** rainfall is *168 mm* and the **minimum** is *75 mm* – a **range** of *93 mm*.

The driest month is *April* when an average of *75 mm* of rain falls.

The wettest month is *December* when an average of *168 mm* of rain falls.

Getting Technical

- **Annual** – yearly
- **Total annual rainfall** – to calculate this, add up rainfall over all 12 months
- **Average annual temperature** – to calculate this, add up each monthly temperature and divide by 12 (months)
- **Maximum** – the highest amount
- **Minimum** – the lowest amount
- **Peak** – the highest point in a graph or trend line
- **Range** – the difference between the lowest and the highest amounts

Activities

1. Table **B** shows the climate data for Lisbon in Portugal. Draw a climate graph, using the one in **A** to help you.

	J	F	M	A	M	J	J	A	S	O	N	D
Average monthly temperature (°C)	11	12	14	16	17	20	22	23	21	18	14	12
Average monthly rainfall (mm)	111	76	109	54	44	16	3	4	33	62	93	103

B Climate data for Lisbon

2. Annotate your climate graph with boxes of text, using **A** to guide you. In most cases you will only need to change the *data* or the *month* – you can use the same wording. Look at the Getting Technical box if you need help.

3. Shade in the annotation boxes that describe the rainfall in blue, and those that describe the temperature in red.

Weather patterns over Europe

C Climate graph for Tromso, Norway

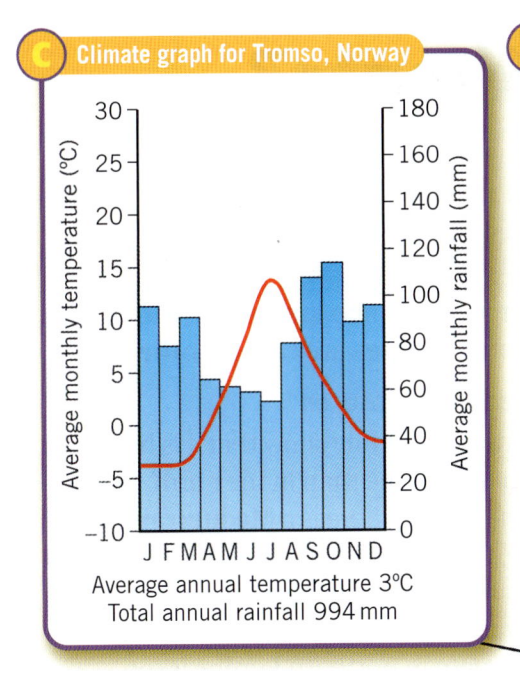

Average annual temperature 3°C
Total annual rainfall 994 mm

D Climate graph for Moscow, Russia

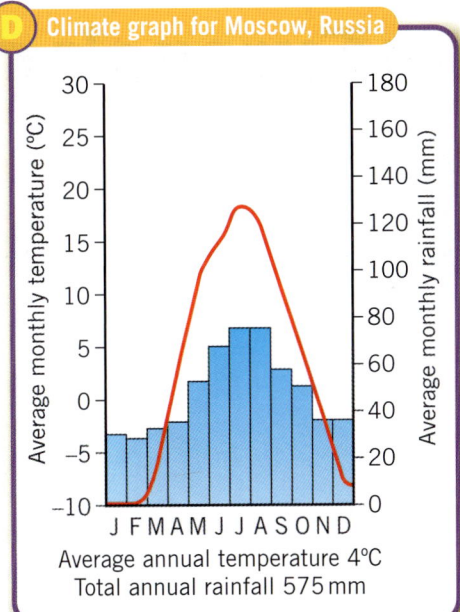

Average annual temperature 4°C
Total annual rainfall 575 mm

E Climate graph for Athens, Greece

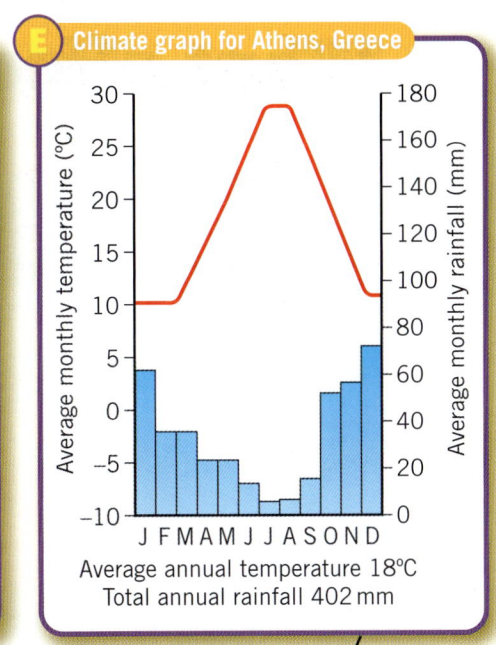

Average annual temperature 18°C
Total annual rainfall 402 mm

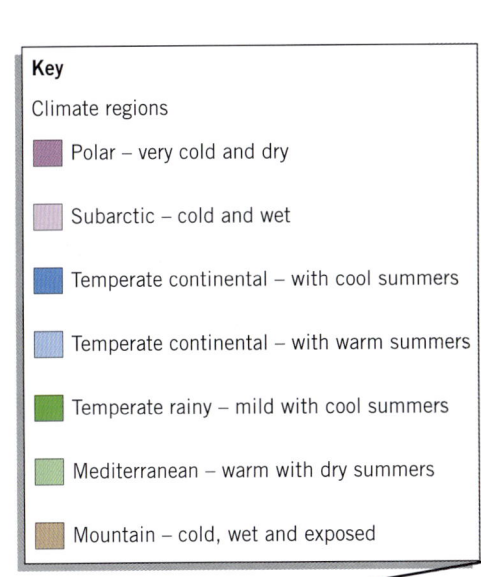

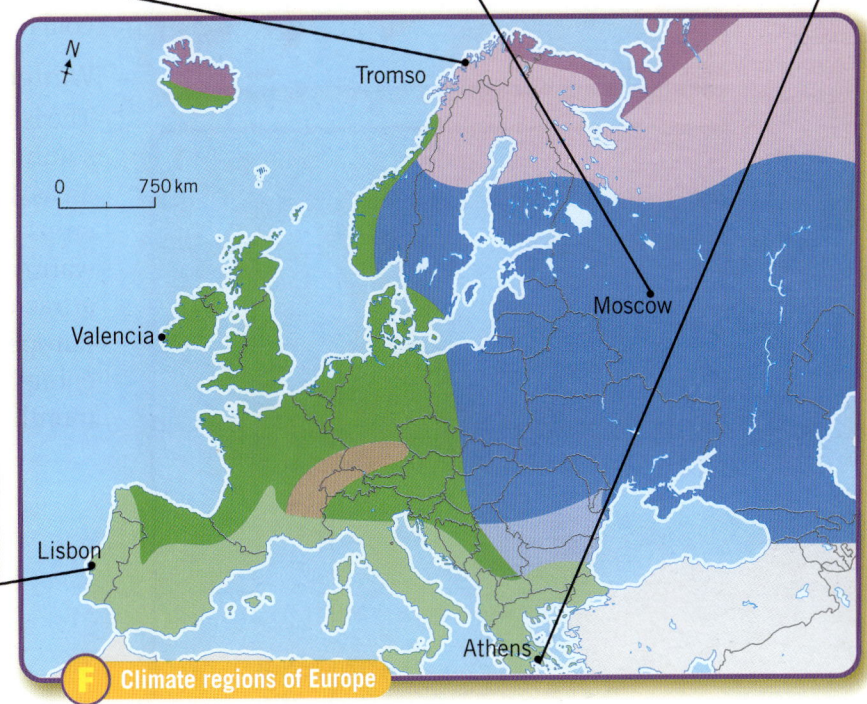

Key

Climate regions
- Polar – very cold and dry
- Subarctic – cold and wet
- Temperate continental – with cool summers
- Temperate continental – with warm summers
- Temperate rainy – mild with cool summers
- Mediterranean – warm with dry summers
- Mountain – cold, wet and exposed

F Climate regions of Europe

Activities

1. For each of the five places marked on **F**, name the climate region in which it is located.

Total annual rainfall	Average annual temperature	Temperature range
wettest =	warmest =	biggest range =
driest =	coldest =	smallest range =

2. Make a large copy of the table. Rank the five places by their total rainfall, average annual temperature and temperature range.

3. Look at map **F** and your rankings. Are these statements true or false?
   - In general, there is more rainfall as you go east across Europe.
   - In general, temperatures are colder as you go north in Europe.
   - In general, temperature range increases as you go east across Europe.

4 Geography Matters

What affects Europe's climate?

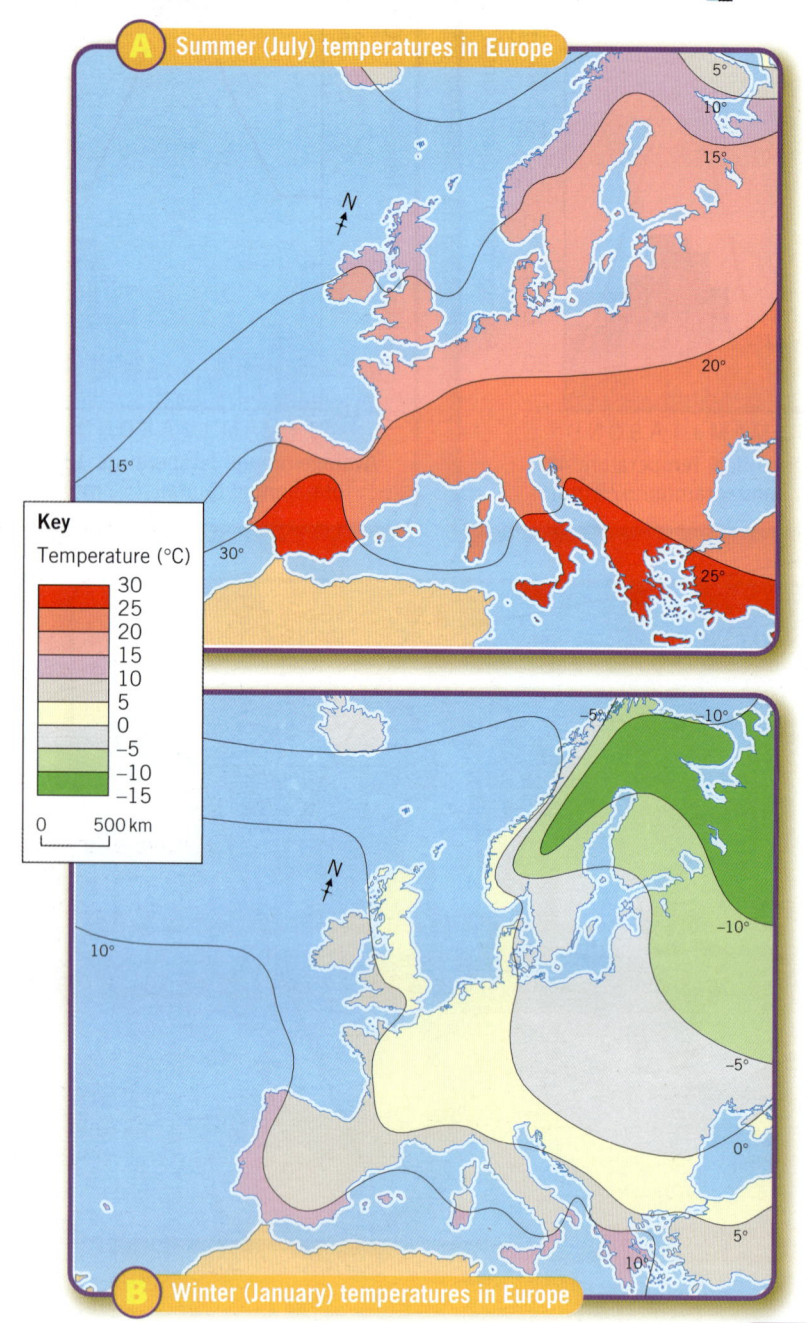

A Summer (July) temperatures in Europe

Key
Temperature (°C)
30
25
20
15
10
5
0
−5
−10
−15

0   500 km

B Winter (January) temperatures in Europe

Temperatures in Europe

Lines on maps which join places with equal temperatures are called **isotherms**.

Summer temperatures

The isotherms for July show that it is hotter in southern Europe than in the north. In southern Europe there is a **Mediterranean climate**, so crops such as olives, grapes and oranges grow well. The high temperatures also attract large numbers of tourists. The **polar climate** in northern Europe is too cold for many crops to grow well.

Winter temperatures

The isotherms for January show that the south and west of Europe are the warmest areas. In southern Spain, Italy and Greece crops will grow even in winter, and it is warm enough for tourists. Tourists are also attracted to the cold mountainous areas of Europe for a different reason. There is enough snow on the ground for many months of skiing and winter sports.

Factors that affect temperature

Altitude

Temperatures decrease by about 1°C for every 100 metres increase in height above sea level. Many parts of the Alps are over 4000 metres above sea level, which means they are about 40°C colder than the coastal area to the south.

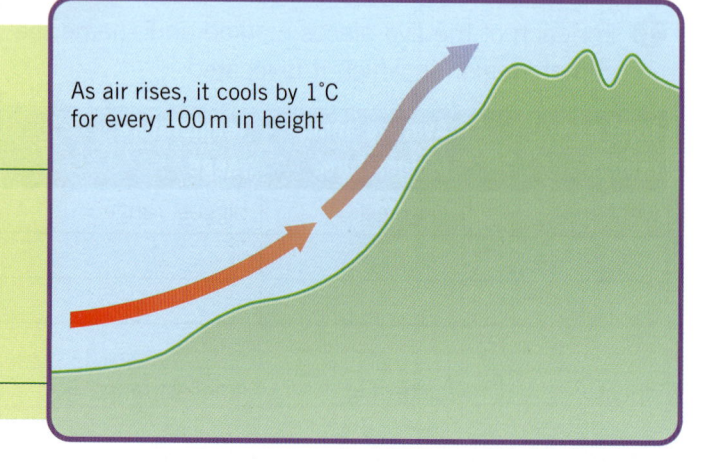

As air rises, it cools by 1°C for every 100 m in height

Weather patterns over Europe

Latitude

Places near the Equator are warmer than places near the poles. This is because the Earth's surface is curved. In northern Europe, the Sun's rays are spread over a larger area so that temperatures are lower. In southern Europe, the Sun's rays are more concentrated so temperatures are higher.

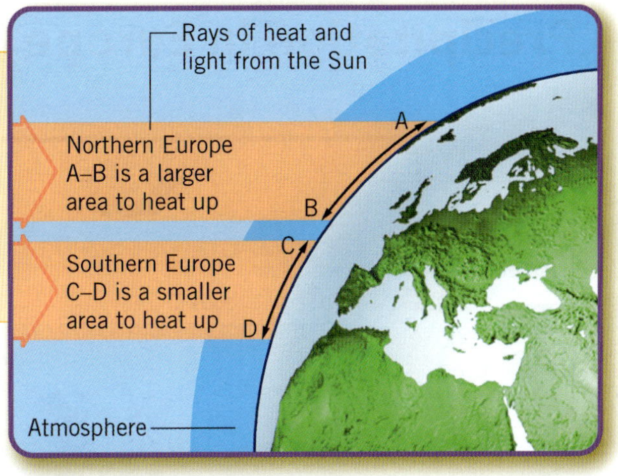

Distance from the sea

In summer the land heats quickly but the sea is slow to warm up. Places inland get hot, but places near the coast are kept cool.

In winter the opposite happens: the land cools down quickly so inland places can be bitterly cold. The sea is slower to cool down and keeps the coasts quite warm in winter.

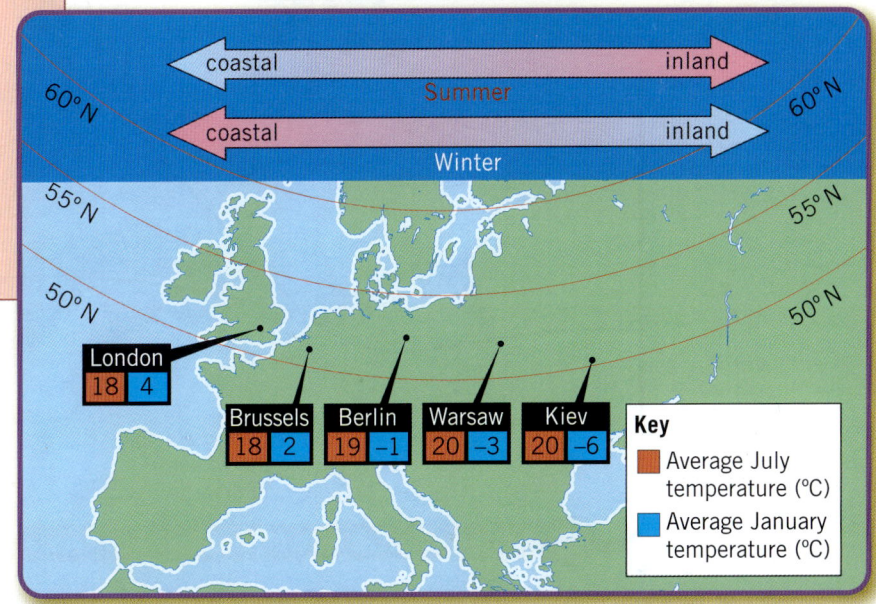

Ocean currents

The North Atlantic Drift is a warm current of water that flows across the Atlantic Ocean from the Gulf of Mexico. It keeps the coasts of western Europe much warmer than areas inland.

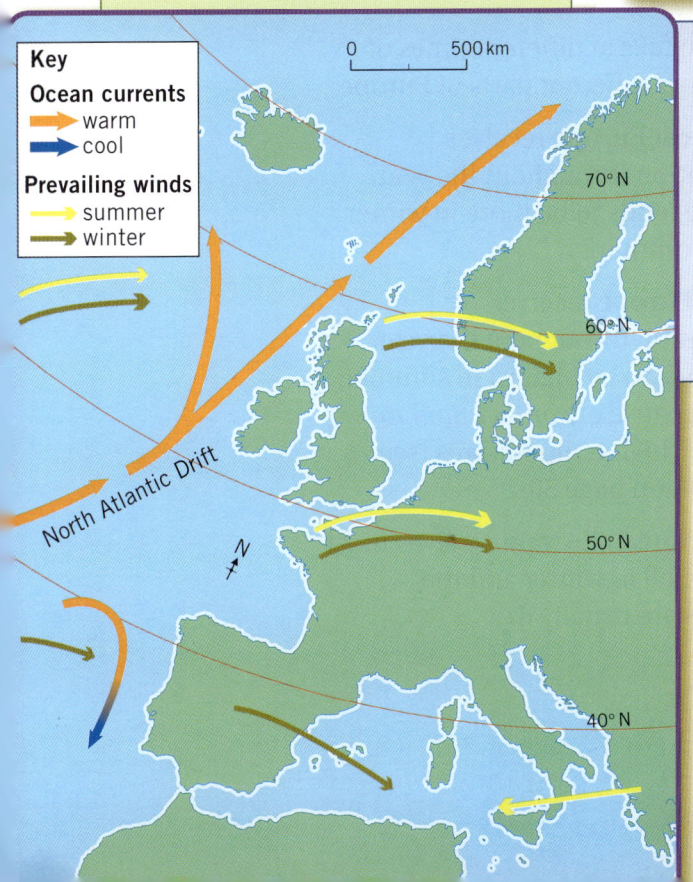

Average July and January temperatures (°C):
- London: 18 / 4
- Brussels: 18 / 2
- Berlin: 19 / −1
- Warsaw: 20 / −3
- Kiev: 20 / −6

Prevailing winds

A warm day can change suddenly if the wind changes direction. Wind brings air from a different place which may be warm, cold, wet or dry. A dominant wind that blows from one direction for much of the year is called a **prevailing wind**.

- Winds from the sea often bring rain.
- Winds from the south are usually warm.
- Winds from inland can be warm or cold, depending on the time of year.

Activities

1. Look at the information about altitude, latitude, sea, ocean currents and winds. Complete the statements below.
   - Tromso is colder than Athens because …
   - In summer, Moscow is warmer than Tromso because …
   - Most of the year Valencia is kept warm by …

2. Use an atlas to find the names of three places in Europe that are cold because of their altitude.

Precipitation in Europe

Key
Annual precipitation (mm)
- 2000
- 1500
- 1000
- 750
- 500
- 250
- 0

Rainfall all year – but most falls during the winter

Rainfall all year – but most falls during the summer

Rainfall occurs mainly during the winter – summers dry

C Average annual amounts of precipitation for Europe

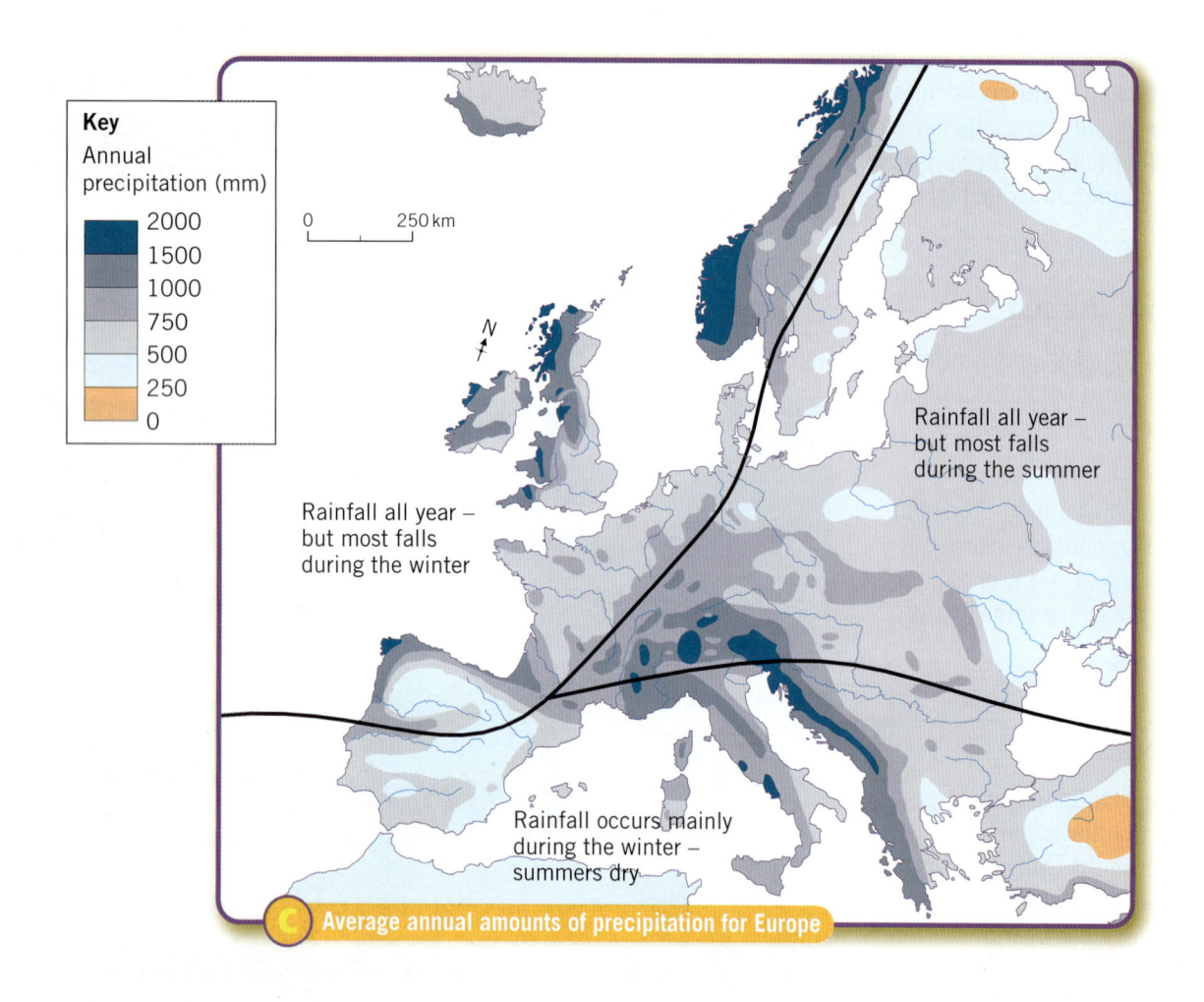

Map **C** shows the average annual amounts of precipitation for Europe. It shows two main patterns:

1. Precipitation is higher where there are mountains, such as the Alps and the Apennines in Italy. This is due to *relief rainfall* (see diagram **B** on on page 50).

2. As you go east across Europe there is generally less precipitation. This is because **prevailing winds** bring moist air from the Atlantic Ocean. As clouds blow inland they lose moisture as *frontal rainfall* (see diagram **C** on page 50), or *relief rainfall*, so there is less to fall inland.

Precipitation falls at different times of the year across different parts of Europe.

- **North-west Europe** receives precipitation throughout the year, but there tends to be more in winter than in summer.

- **Eastern Europe** receives precipitation throughout the year, but it tends to be highest in summer. This is because of *convectional rain* caused by high temperatures (see diagram A on page 50).

- **Mediterranean Europe** receives most of its rainfall in winter and the summers are usually dry.

Weather patterns over Europe

Precipitation and human activities

Dry summers in the Mediterranean can be good and bad. Thousands of tourists go on holiday knowing that they will get good weather. They spend millions of pounds in places like Greece and Portugal. On the other hand, drought is bad for farmers and for local people who need a steady water supply.

In other parts of Europe, precipitation actually attracts tourists. Millions of visitors go to the Alps and Pyrenees seeking snow for winter sports. Too much snow can be a problem for some activities such as farming, communications and industry.

D Soil erosion in Andalucia, Spain

Activities

1 Copy table **E** below, which includes all the places marked on map **F** on page 62. Use the information in the maps on pages 47 (countries), 57 (climate types), 58 (temperatures in July and January) and 60 (rainfall) to complete the table. The information for Zermatt has been filled in for you.

Place	Country	Climate type	Average January temperature	Average July temperature	Average precipitation
Zermatt	Switzerland	mountain	0–5 °C	20–25 °C	1000–1500 mm
Bergen					
Odessa					
Moscow					
Kiruna					
Costa del Sol					

E

2 Answer the following questions about the places in table **E**.
   a Which places have the coldest January temperatures?
   b Which place has the hottest July temperature?
   c Which place has the coldest July temperature?
   d Name the place with the most rainfall.
   e Where is the warmest climate?
   f Where is the coldest climate?

4 Geography Matters

Where shall we go on holiday?

Sail from Bergen and cruise along the coast, down spectacular fjords and to the land of the Midnight Sun.

Stay in the Ice Hotel, Kiruna – built with 10 000 tonnes of crystal-clear ice.

Visit Moscow's famous Red Square and go to see the Bolshoi Ballet.

Ski in the shadow of the Matterhorn. Sample the *après-ski* as you relax by an open fire.

F Europe

Laze on the sandy beaches of Costa del Sol, shop till you drop then club all night long. Any energy left? ... Try paragliding or windsurfing!

The Crimea coastline has many beautiful resorts, splendid palaces and health spas.

Activity

3 Figure **F** shows the locations of the places named in table **E** on page 61, together with a brief description of the type of holiday you could have there.

a Look back at the climate details for each of the six places and then at **F**. Choose the place where you would most like to go on holiday. At which time of year would you go? Give your reasons why.

b Choose a different holiday location on this page for a family member or a friend. At which time of year should they go? Why?

Weather patterns over Europe

Review and reflect

A

C High cumulus clouds at sunset

B Annual average temperature range

D Evidence for global warming in Europe

- If air pollution goes on growing at present rate
- If there are big cuts made in air pollution

E Flooding in Bishopsthorpe near York in 2000

F

G Temperature and rainfall in London

H Average number of snow-covered days per year

Key
- more than 50
- 20-50
- 15-20
- 10-15
- 5-10
- less than 5

Activity

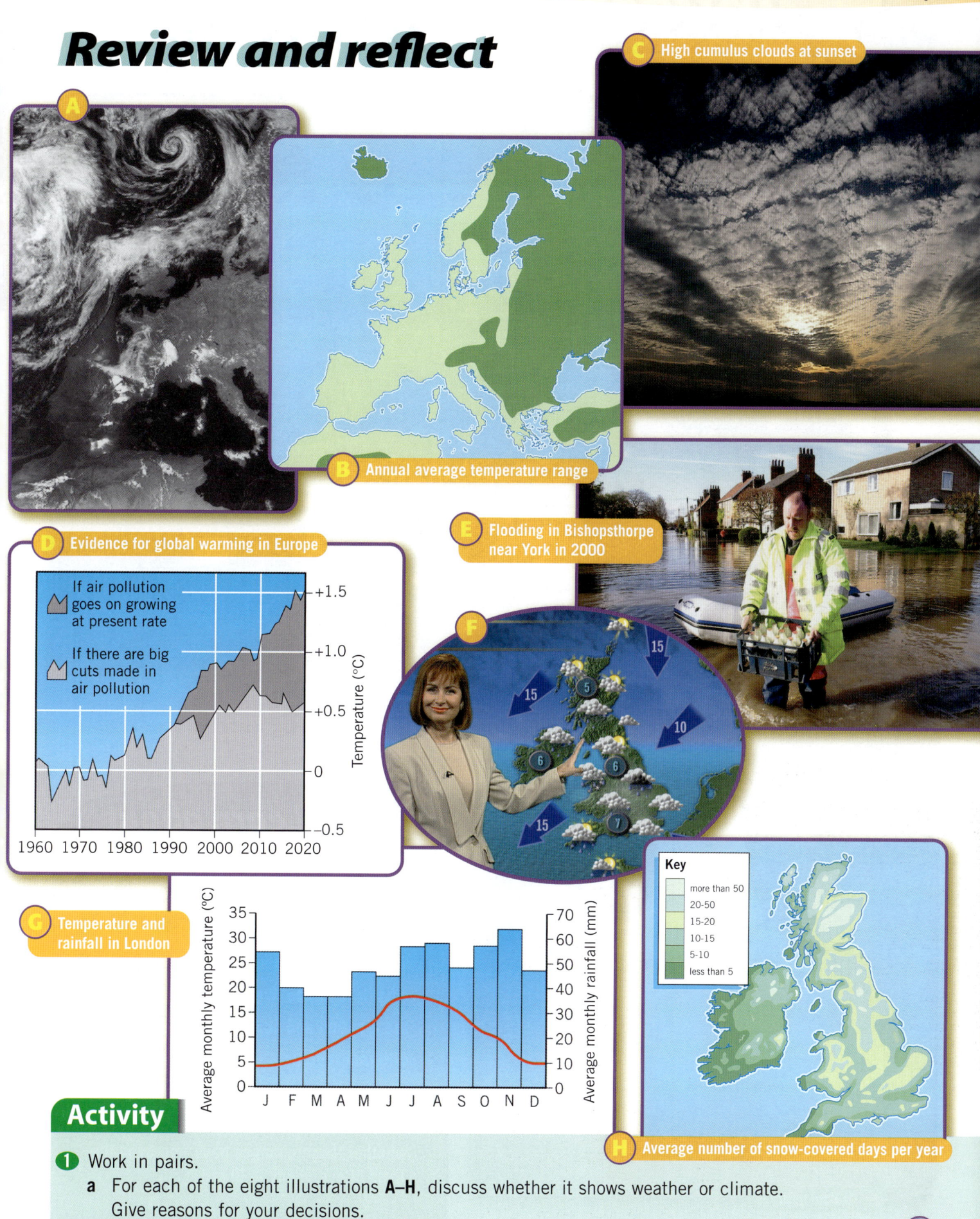

1. Work in pairs.
   a. For each of the eight illustrations **A–H**, discuss whether it shows weather or climate. Give reasons for your decisions.
   b. Name the type of source shown in each case, e.g. *Source A is a satellite image of Europe.*

5 Investigating Brazil

A São Paulo, Brazil

B A dam in Brazil

Learn about

This unit is about Brazil. You will develop your investigation skills so that you can then research other countries. You will investigate:

- what Brazil is like
- what it is like to live in Brazil
- the location and scale of the country
- different regions
- whether Brazil is economically developed
- what changes are occurring in the country
- whether these changes have improved the lives of everybody in Brazil.

What do you know about Brazil?

Brazil is a wonderful country – it has everything to offer!

Fact file 1

Brazil is big.	Brazil is the 5th largest country in the world. It has an area of 8.5 million km^2.
Brazil is rich.	It has the 9th largest economy in the world.
Brazil has many resources.	Brazil has more forest than any other country.
Brazil has a large population.	The population is 163 million, the largest in South America.

C Ipanema beach, Rio

What goes on in these high-rise buildings? Look closely at the photograph to find out whether they are office blocks or flats.

What is the temperature? Use the climate maps in an atlas to find the temperatures experienced in Brazil.

D

Activities

1 a What do you think of when you think of 'Brazil'? Write down the first ten words or images that come to mind.

b Compare your list with a partner's. Do you have similar ideas?

2 Now look at photos **A–C** on these pages. Write down two things that each photo tells you about Brazil.

3 a Look at each photo again and think of one good geographical question for each one. Write it down.

b Compare these questions with a partner and decide on the four best ones.

c You could either make a list of the questions, or label them on a sketch of the photograph, like **D**.

help!

- This activity is about how to carry out an investigation, so don't worry about the answers to your questions.
- Remember that nearly all geographical questions will include at least one of the words: *What? Where? Why? How? Who?*

5 Geography Matters

Other images of Brazil

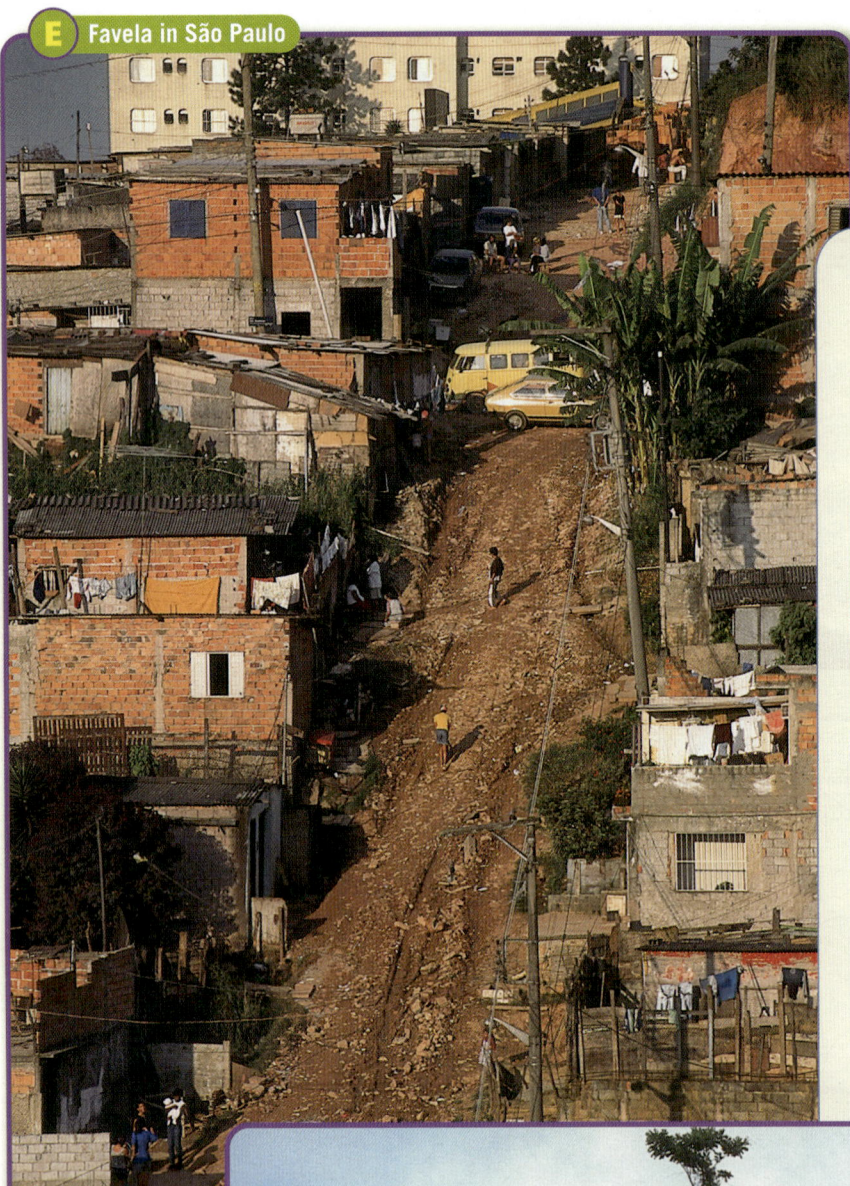

E Favela in São Paulo

Brazil fact file 2

Brazil is an amazing country, but it is also a country of contrasts. Some parts of the country are completely different from other places. Brazil has many problems.

There are many poor people in Brazil.	One third of homes lack either clean water or sanitation.
Brazil has some of the worst inequality in the world.	Just 1 per cent of Brazilians own 50 per cent of the land in Brazil.
Working conditions are poor.	Most people work long hours in bad conditions for low wages.
Many children are poor.	7 million children have to work instead of going to school.

F Sandy river banks being eroded following deforestation in Para State, Amazonia

Investigating Brazil

G Satellite image of South America

Key

- Andes Mountains
- Tropical rainforest
- Desert and semi-desert
- Grassland and savannah

help!

Try to think about
- Stresses on the natural environment
- Stresses on people.

Activities

1 a In pairs, look at the photos on page 66. Make a list of the problems that you can find.

b Write one geography question for each photograph.

2 a Make a copy of the assessment grid below.

ugly	1	2	3	4	5	6	7	beautiful
polluted	1	2	3	4	5	6	7	clean
noisy	1	2	3	4	5	6	7	quiet
crowded	1	2	3	4	5	6	7	spacious
unfriendly	1	2	3	4	5	6	7	friendly
unhappy	1	2	3	4	5	6	7	happy

b Look back at all the text and photos on pages 64–67 and decide what you now think of Brazil. Circle one number for each row. Why is this quite difficult to do?

c Use your answers to write a paragraph to summarise what you now know about Brazil.

5 Geography Matters

Location, location, location

When geographers investigate a place, they often look first at its **location**. Location is usually described by linking the position of that place to the positions of other places. This is called the **situation** of the place. The starting point for your detailed investigation of Brazil is to ask the enquiry question:

Where is Brazil located?

All the maps on this page show Brazil.

- Map **A** shows Brazil in its global situation.
- Map **B** shows Brazil in its continental situation.
- Map **C** shows São Paulo as a city within a region of Brazil.

The location of any place can be built up within a precise geographical **hierarchy**, like the one in diagram **D**.

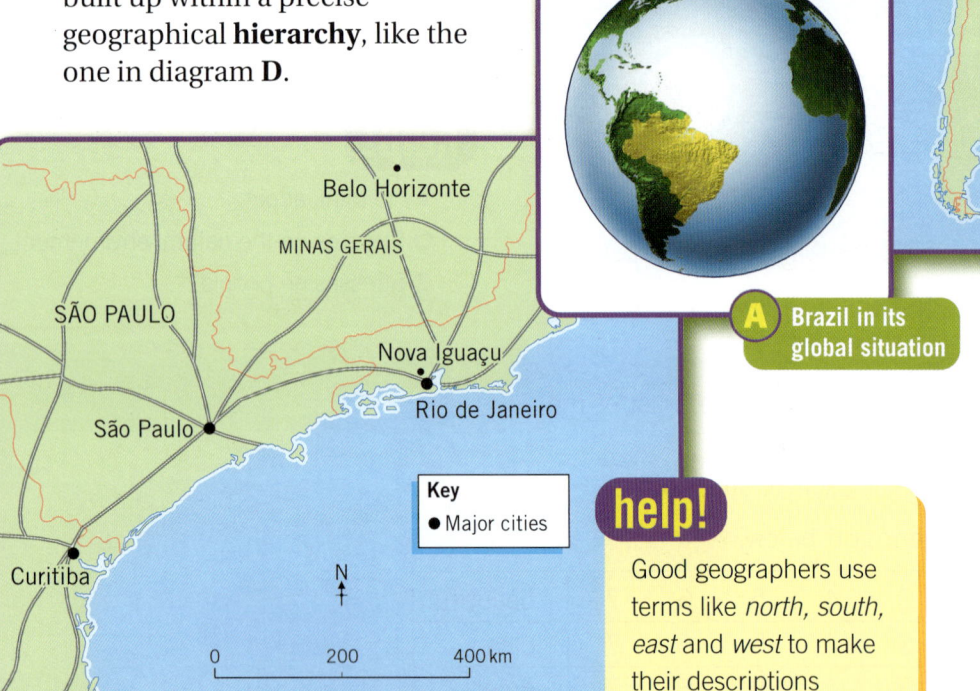

B The situation of Brazil within the continent of South America

A Brazil in its global situation

C The situation of São Paulo in its region

D Building up a geographical hierarchy

help!

Good geographers use terms like *north, south, east* and *west* to make their descriptions precise. Using latitude and longitude also helps to locate places exactly.

Activities

1. Use maps **A** and **B** to describe where Brazil is located in the world. Write three sentences and use as many of these words as you can.

   South America   Tropic   Equator
   degrees   Hemisphere   Ocean

2. Look at map **B**. Draw a sketch map to show the situation of Brazil within the continent of South America.

3. Use your atlas to describe an air journey from the UK to Brasilia, the capital of Brazil.

   - Name the countries and oceans you fly over. Give your direction and the distances you cover as well.
   - The aircraft needs refuelling at an international airport every 2500 km. There are a number of ways you could do it – safe journey!

Investigating Brazil

How big is Brazil?

If you look at maps **A** and **B**, you will not only see the situation of Brazil but also get a clear idea of the size or **scale** of the country. This gives a second aspect to the investigation, so you can ask a second enquiry question:

How big is Brazil?

The answer is more useful when the size is given in relation to the size of other countries.

Brazil is a very large country – it is the fifth largest in the world. You can see in table **C** how it compares with some other countries in South America.

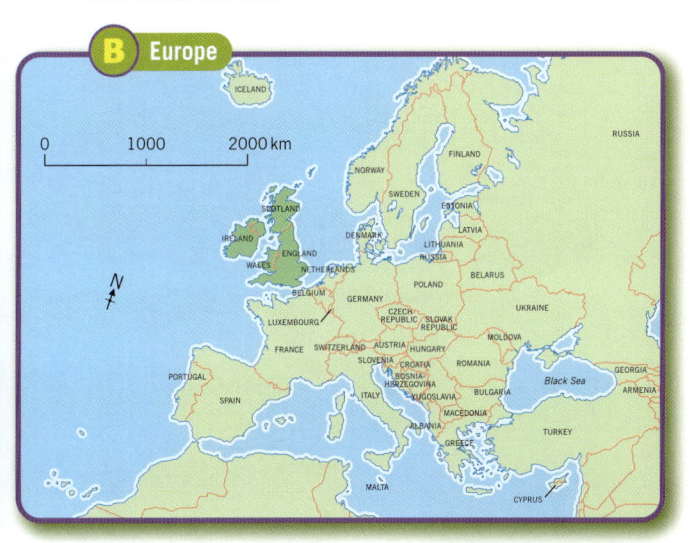

A South America

B Europe

help!
Use the scale line on your map. Measure the distances using a ruler or by marking the edge of a piece of paper.

C The areas of some countries in South America (thousands of square kilometres)

Country	Area
Argentina	2767
Bolivia	1099
Brazil	8512
Chile	757
Ecuador	272
Paraguay	407
Surinam	164
Uruguay	176
Venezuela	912

Activities

1 a Make a copy of the table below.

Country	Distance north to south	Distance east to west
Brazil	km	km
UK	km	km

b On a map of Brazil, measure the distance from north to south across the country. Then measure from east to west. Write your answers in your table.

c Now do the same for the UK and complete the table.

d Look at your table. Work out approximately how many times the UK could fit into Brazil.

e Look at map **B**. How does Brazil compare with Europe in size?

2 Table **C** does not show all the countries in South America.

a Estimate the size of the missing countries: French Guiana, Guyana, Colombia and Peru.

b Now list all the countries in South America in order of size. Start with the largest.

5 Geography Matters

What is Brazil like? What are the main differences within the country?

Case Study

Planning a trip to Brazil

Activities

A group of geography students and teachers want to go to Brazil on an educational holiday. You must plan their three-week trip. Use the information on the following six pages to make some decisions about:

1. which regions to travel to
2. which places to visit
3. when to go.

ICT idea There is also some interesting travel information about Brazil on the Internet. Try the two travel company websites at:

www.heinemann.co.uk/hotlinks (insert code 1631P)

When you have made these decisions, you must present your ideas to the rest of the class. You must explain your ideas. The most educational tour will win the contract.

Brazil is the size of Europe. The north of Brazil is very different from the south, just as Greece is different from Finland! People on this study tour want to see as much as they can. The tour is called: 'Amazing Brazil – land of contrasts', so make sure that you make it a trip of a lifetime. Include the following:

- a route map showing where they will go and how long they will stay in each place
- information about each place that they will visit
- the reasons for visiting each place
- advice about what to do and precautions to take.

There are four main regions in Brazil. Each one is bigger than the UK. Start by comparing the climate, population and physical geography of the four regions. This will help you to decide when to go on the trip.

A The regions of Brazil

B Population density

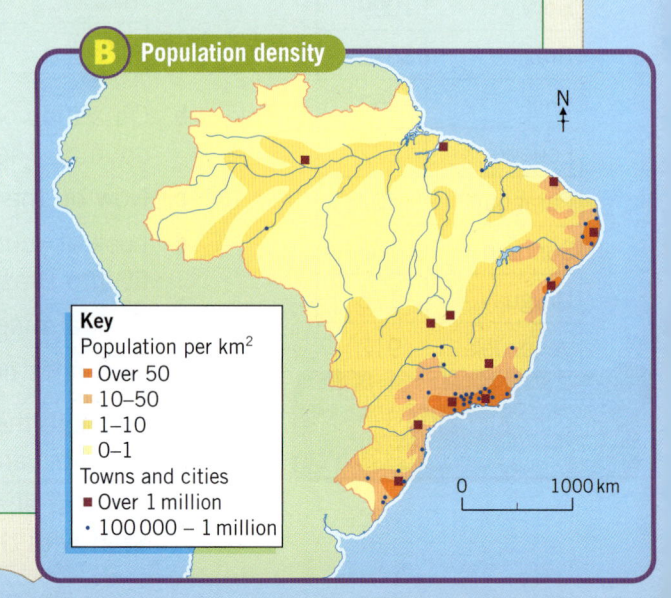

Key
Population per km²
- Over 50
- 10–50
- 1–10
- 0–1

Towns and cities
- Over 1 million
- 100 000 – 1 million

Activities

Investigating Brazil

1. Look at maps, **A**, **B**, **C** and **D**. Copy and complete this table of information, using the statements below.

	Cities and population density	Rainfall	Physical geography
South-East Region			
North-East Region			
Centre-West Region		Quite dry and hot most of the year because it is inland from the coast.	
North Region	Very low population density.		

Very wet and hot all year round.

Most Brazilians live in this region. The biggest

Dense rainforest in the Amazon Basin covers much of this region.

An area of grassland and swamps. Mostly a

Very hot and dry for much of the year.

Very low population density.

Very low population density, although the capital city is here.

Low population density, except along the coast.

Some inland areas are like desert, with scrub vegetation.

Quite dry and hot most of the year because it is inland from the coast.

The most hilly region of Brazil. Many tropical forests are now cleared.

The coolest region, although it is hot in the summer months between November and February.

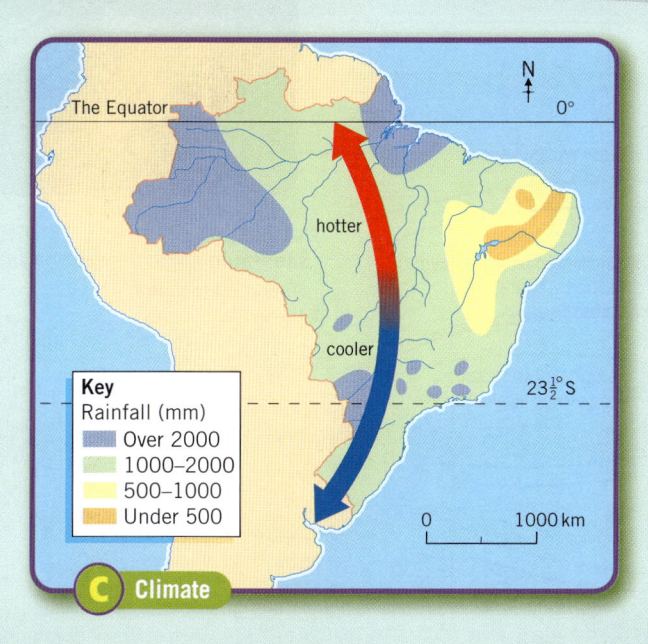

C Climate

Key
Rainfall (mm)
- Over 2000
- 1000–2000
- 500–1000
- Under 500

D Physical geography

Key
- Lowland swamp
- Lowland
- Hills and low plateaus
- Plateaus and mountains

2. What time of year seems to be the best time to travel to Brazil? Explain your answer.
3. Give three types of vegetation that would be interesting to see.

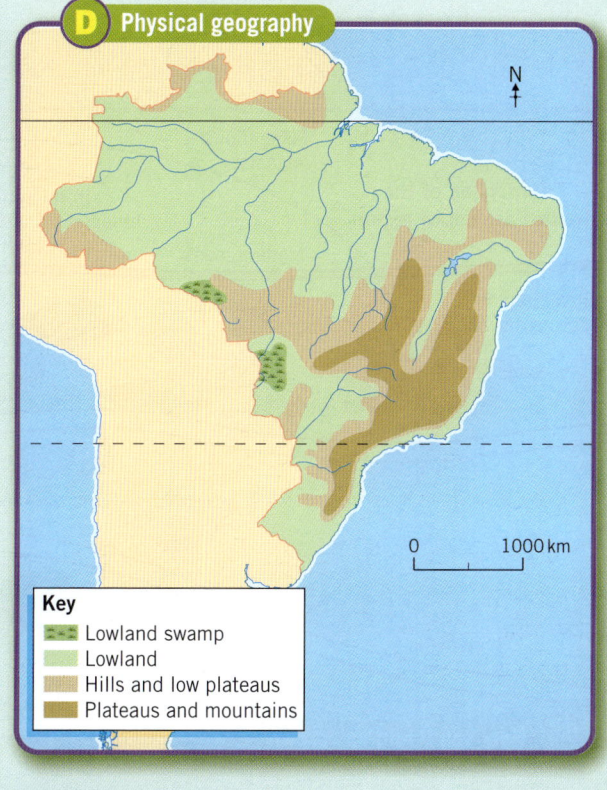

5 Geography Matters

What is the South-East Region like?

This region is divided into two: the South and the South-East. The photograph and diagram on this page will help to give some idea of what this region is like.

The South-East is an important farming region. It produces most of Brazil's food, and is famous for its huge coffee estates. The South-East has the three biggest cities in Brazil:

- São Paulo grew as the centre for the coffee industry in the 1800s and is now Brazil's business centre. It is the biggest city in South America, with modern buildings, headquarters of international firms and many large factories. Ford, Mercedes and VW all have big car factories here.
- Rio de Janeiro was the capital of Brazil until 1960. This carnival city is still the country's biggest tourist centre, with world-famous beaches such as Copacabana.
- Belo Horizonte is the third largest city of the region, and centre for the steel industry.

Activity

1. Make a large copy of the table below. Use it to make notes on each of the four regions. In the end, you will have to decide which places to include, and which to leave out.

Region	Important sights to see	Interesting geographical tours to arrange	Leisure time activities to include
South-East	The city of Rio – when is the carnival?	Tour around a coffee estate	A day on the beach at Copacabana
North-East			
Centre-West			
North			

E Growing sugar cane is highly mechanized

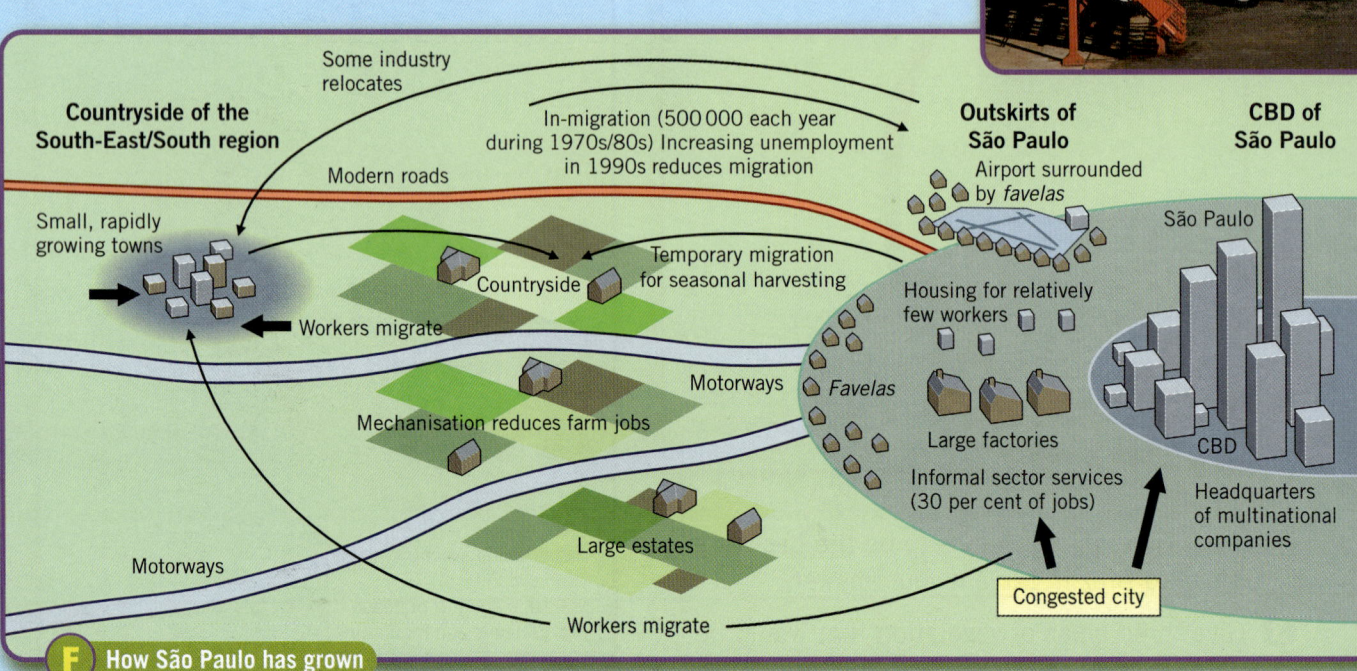

F How São Paulo has grown

Investigating Brazil

What is the Centre-West Region like?

Early settlers in Brazil did not travel this far. This region is so far inland that it rains less than on the coast, and it is very hot in summer, when most of the rain falls. The Centre-West is famous for its vast grasslands and swamps, many of which are rich in wildlife. The Brazilian government is keen to develop farming in this region, to provide useful food crops to sell abroad as exports.

G Cattle ranching in the Centre-West Region

Traditional life in the Centre-West Region
- Poor soils only allowed **extensive ranching** of cattle: fewer than one cow per hectare.
- The few mineral resources were quickly mined.
- Towns were few and far between. They were local market and services centres.

Changes to life in the Centre-West Region
- In 1960 a new capital city, Brasilia, was built.
- People migrated here as farming became more **mechanised**.
- Growing soya beans changed the farming landscape greatly during the late twentieth century.

H Brasilia

5 Geography Matters

What is the North-East Region like?

The tropical climate of the North-East is ideal for growing sugar cane, and millions of people settled here over the last few centuries to work in the plantations. Unfortunately it is also the **drought** region of Brazil. Water shortages in the 1970s forced thousands of people to migrate to the big cities on the coast.

One scheme to solve the water shortage is the Sobradinho Dam on the São Francisco River. Making a reservoir provides a steady supply of water all through the year.

The coast has hundreds of miles of unspoiled beaches.

I The dam at Sobradinho

Brazil invests in alcohol
Sugar cane can be processed to make ethanol (pure alcohol), which may be used as an alternative to petrol. The Brazilian government started a programme in the 1970s to increase ethanol production in the north-east. The aim was to help poor farmers in this underdeveloped area, as well as reducing the need to import oil. This idea may seem good, but sugar cane is grown on large farms, so valuable land is taken away from growing food.

Fact file

The North-East Region of Brazil

- The poorest area of South America.
- Many people in rural areas lack the most basic needs.
- Cities are growing as thousands migrate in search of work.

J Farming in the north-east of Brazil

Disaster, famine, disease and drought ravage the land!

Starving mobs ransacked market stalls in a small town in the State of Pernambuco yesterday. A thousand people queued to fill their tins with drinking water. There have been lootings by hungry peasant farmers all over Ceará State. 90 per cent of all crops have been destroyed by severe drought, which has followed three years of below average rainfall.

Many people in the area farm very small plots and are unable to save money. Large-scale projects don't seem to make much difference to the plight of the poor.

The Brazilian government declared a state of emergency in the area last night.

K Newsflash from the North-East Region of Brazil, 24 January 1992

Investigating Brazil

What is it like in the North Region?

An unending 'sea' of jungle full of exotic creatures

A landscape laden with moisture

Daily downpours of rain

Massive system that helps stabilise the global climate

Tall trees, both evergreen and broad-leaved

Contains 1 in 30 of the world's butterflies

Home to 2000 species of fish

One in five of the world's bird species live in one-fiftieth of the Earth's land surface

Hot and wet throughout the year, rotting even people's clothes

Full of stinging and biting creatures

Crawling with huge spiders, many with deadly bites

Home to tribal people who are threatened by 'western ways'

L Amazonia – the final frontier?

M How a rainforest works: an unending 'sea' of jungle full of exotic creatures

In the north of Brazil the climate is **equatorial**, with no dry season. The Amazon River flows through this region from west to east. Large boats can sail a long way up the Amazon, so it is an important transport route.

The Amazon rainforest is the last large area of undeveloped tropical rainforest in the world. For centuries people have farmed or gathered natural products like Brazil nuts, cocoa and natural rubber from the rainforest. These activities were **sustainable** because they did no long-term damage to the forest environment. More recent developments have often been larger in scale and have had a much greater impact.

ICT idea Find out more on www.heinemann.co.uk/hotlinks

5 Geography Matters

What is a developed country?

The students threw a party when they got home from their trip to Brazil. Several of them started talking about what a developed country was. It was a lively party and the discussion became quite heated …

A developed country is simply a rich country! The rich countries of the world, places like the UK or the USA, are very developed.
Asma

Surely there is more to development than just money – hasn't happiness got something to do with being a developed person? A developed country is simply a country made up of mainly happy people.
Amy

Development is easy to measure. In developed countries, people on average have a high income. In poor, developing countries people on average have a low income.
Heidi

I'd say a developed country is one where there is a good education system, a good medical system and a fair government.
Kerrie

Things like inequality must count in development. I don't feel that Britain is a very developed country. Since the 1980s the gap between the rich and the poor has been getting greater.
Su-yin

I think that the tribal people of the Amazon are among the most developed people in the world. They have lots of leisure time, and their lifestyle is **sustainable**.
Joe

People are happy when they have money to do what they want – this means that they've probably got a good job which pays well. People in developed countries have got good jobs. Certainly most of them aren't sweating in the fields trying to farm on poor soils with little machinery to help.
Carl

How can a country get developed if it is in debt? No country can be developed if it **imports** more than it **exports**.
Brett

Developed countries have met the basic needs of all their people, like having enough food, access to water and proper housing.
Jasbir

Investigating Brazil

Activities

1 Some people think that development is about money. Other people think that other factors are more important. Copy and complete the table below, putting each person in the correct column.

Development is about money	Development is about other factors
Amy	Asma

2 Read the views of the nine people on page 76.

   a Choose the person that you agree with most and give a reason for your decision.

   b Repeat the activity for the person you disagree with most.

3 Jasbir gave some examples of basic human needs. What other human needs can you think of?

4 Use a full page to produce a brainstorm diagram showing all the factors that could be used to define development. Use all the views of the people involved in the discussion as well as some of your own ideas.

help!

Set out your ideas as a development compass rose:

Natural factors:
to do with the environment

Who decides:
to do with government and politics

Economic factors:
to do with money and jobs

Social factors:
to do with people

Tide~

5 Now it is time to come to a conclusion:

   What is a developed country?

Imagine you were at the party. Write down what you would have said after hearing all nine views. Try to end up with the best definition of what you think 'a developed country' is.

6 a Add your definition of 'a developed country' to your geography word bank.

   b Look back through pages 64–75 and add any other key words you need to remember.

5 Geography Matters

How developed is Brazil?

Would you like to live in Brazil? It probably depends on how Brazil compares with the UK. Geographers use indicators to see how well developed a country is. Some indicators measure a country's economy and others measure people's standard of living. Map **A** shows the global pattern of **economic development** using Gross National Product (GNP) as an indicator. Table **B** shows six other indicators for six South American countries and the UK.

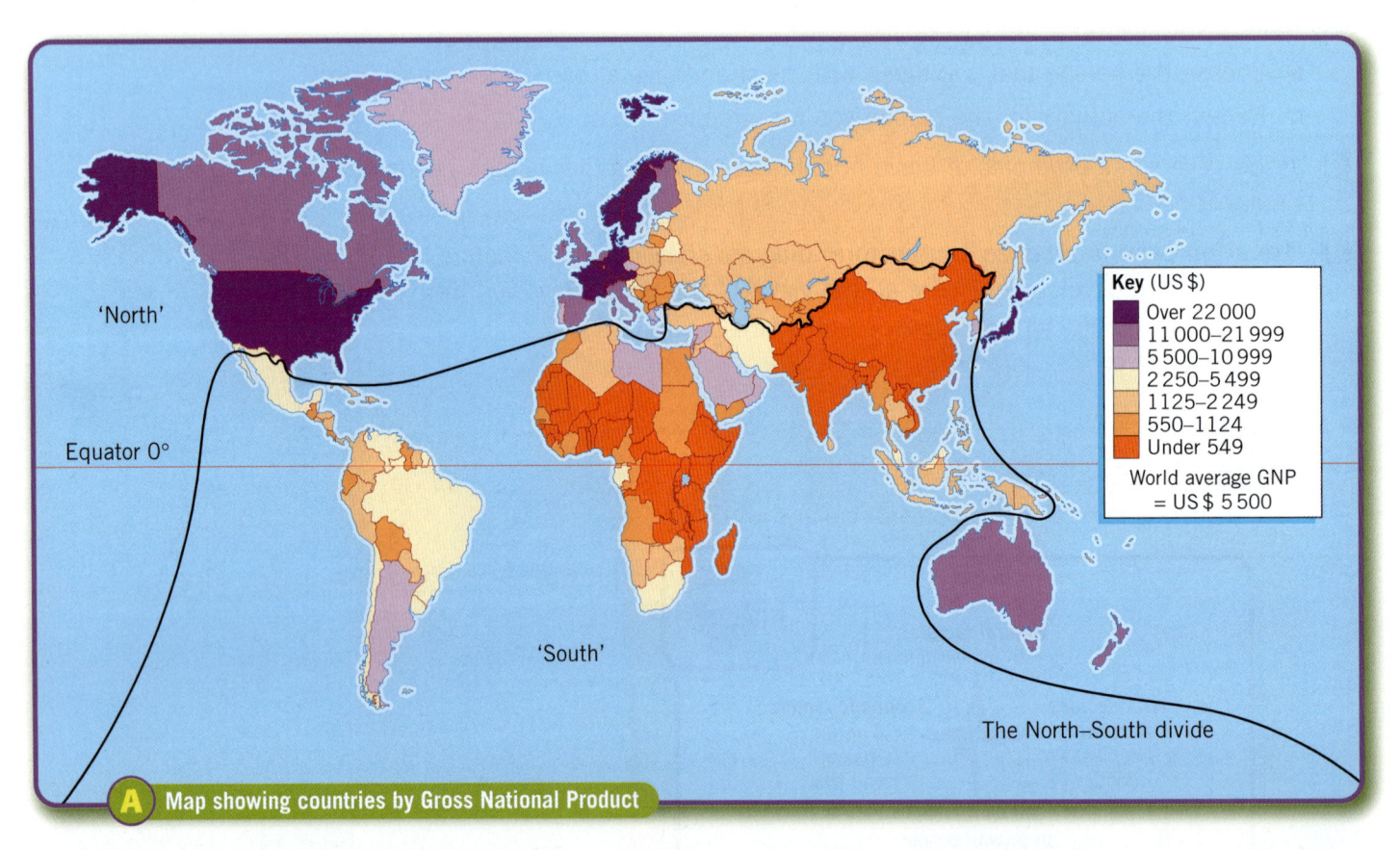

Key (US $)
- Over 22 000
- 11 000–21 999
- 5 500–10 999
- 2 250–5 499
- 1 125–2 249
- 550–1 124
- Under 549

World average GNP = US $ 5 500

A Map showing countries by Gross National Product

Country	GNP (US $)	Safe water (%)	Adult literacy (%)	Life expectancy (years)	IMR (per thousand)	Population growth (%)	Energy consumption (kg oil equivalent)
Argentina	11 728	65	97	73	19	1.4	1 730
Bolivia	2 205	55	87	62	60	2.2	548
Brazil	6 460	72	85	67	33	1.7	1 051
Chile	8 507	85	95	75	10	1.6	1 574
Guyana	760	83	98	64	57	0.8	426
Venezuela	5 706	79	94	73	21	2.4	2 526
UK	20 314	100	99	77	6	0.3	3 863

Data taken from 1980–1998

B Development indicators

Investigating Brazil

Getting Technical

- **Gross National Product (GNP)** – the money a country produces, divided by the total population. GNP is measured in US dollars.
- **Safe water** – percentage of people who have access to clean water.
- **Adult literacy rate** – percentage of adults who can read and write.
- **Life expectancy** – the average number of years people can expect to live.
- **Infant mortality rate (IMR)** – the number of babies who die before their first birthday, out of every thousand born.
- **Population growth** – how fast the population is growing, in percentage each year.
- **Energy consumption** – the average energy each person in a country uses.

Activities

1 Look at Table **B** and the information in 'Getting Technical'. Try to work out what each indicator tells you about a country. Match each indicator with the correct statement. For example **1 = E**

1 GNP per person	A if this is high, then people are obviously very poor because many babies die young
2 safe water	B this tells us if parents have lots of children. This is common in poor countries.
3 adult literacy	C this shows whether people are well fed, healthy and have a good standard of living
4 life expectancy	D this shows whether the country has lots of factories and a good power supply to homes
5 infant mortality rate	E this shows whether the country has lots of successful businesses
6 population growth	F this shows whether the country has a good education system
7 energy consumption	G if this is unsafe, then people will die from diseases

2 Now use the development data to see how the seven countries compare.

   a Copy the table below.

GNP	Indicator:	Indicator:	Indicator:	Total scores
1 UK	1	1	1	1
2	2	2	2	2
3	3	3	3	3
4	4	4	4	4
5	5	5	5	5
6	6	6	6	6
7 Guyana	7	7	7	7

   b Start with column 1. Use the GNP data to rank the countries in order, with the most developed country first.

   c Choose three other indicators that you think show a country's development. Use the data to rank the seven countries in columns 2, 3 and 4.

5 Geography Matters

How successful has development been in Brazil?

The government in Brazil has tried to develop the country, so that it is richer and people live better lives. Some of the developments in Amazonas are shown on the next few pages. Are they good or bad, or is it not this simple?

Transport developments

European settlers first colonised the coastal areas of Brazil. It has taken many years to develop the Centre-West and North regions. The Amazon rainforests could not be developed until a huge network of roads was built in the 1970s. This network was called the Trans-Amazonian Highway, and is thousands of kilometres long. It is very expensive to build and repair these routes.

Once the roads were built, farmers could clear land and grow crops. Goods could be transported into settlements in the area. Raw materials and other products could be transported out.

A The Trans-Amazonian Highway cuts through the rainforest in Amazonia

Activities

1. Before roads were built, how do you think people travelled into the rainforest?
2. Why are roads so important for the development of settlements, mining and farming in the rainforest?

Investigating Brazil

B Main roads in Brazil

Cattle ranching

Cattle ranching has become one of the main reasons why the rainforest has been destroyed in Amazonas. The ranches are usually very large and many are owned by large, powerful companies. Trees are cut down to make room for cattle pasture. There is a great demand for beef in the 'hamburger' culture of the USA, Japan and Europe, and Brazil exports much of the beef it produces.

Cattle ranching does provide jobs, but one cowboy can manage over 3000 cattle.

Unfortunately grass does not grow well in Amazonas, and weeds spread quickly. After a few years, ranchers have to move on to another area of forest, and then sell their poor land. As more roads are built, the cattle ranches extend further into the rainforest, and more minerals are discovered. Land prices are now rising.

C During and after the destruction of the rainforest

Activities

❸ Give one reason why the Brazilian government wants cattle ranches in the Amazon.
Cattle ranches are good for Brazil because …

❹ Give one reason why the government might not want cattle ranches.
On the other hand, cattle ranches cause problems because …

5 Geography Matters

Developments in Rondônia

Many poor people in Brazil have no land to farm. So in the 1980s the government encouraged thousands of people to move into the Rondônia rainforests by giving away free land. They first had to build a proper road to Pôrto Velho (BR364). Unfortunately much of the land which used to support lush tropical rainforest became useless for farming after a few years. Many new settlers abandoned their land and headed further on into the jungle to see if they had better luck with the next piece of land they cleared.

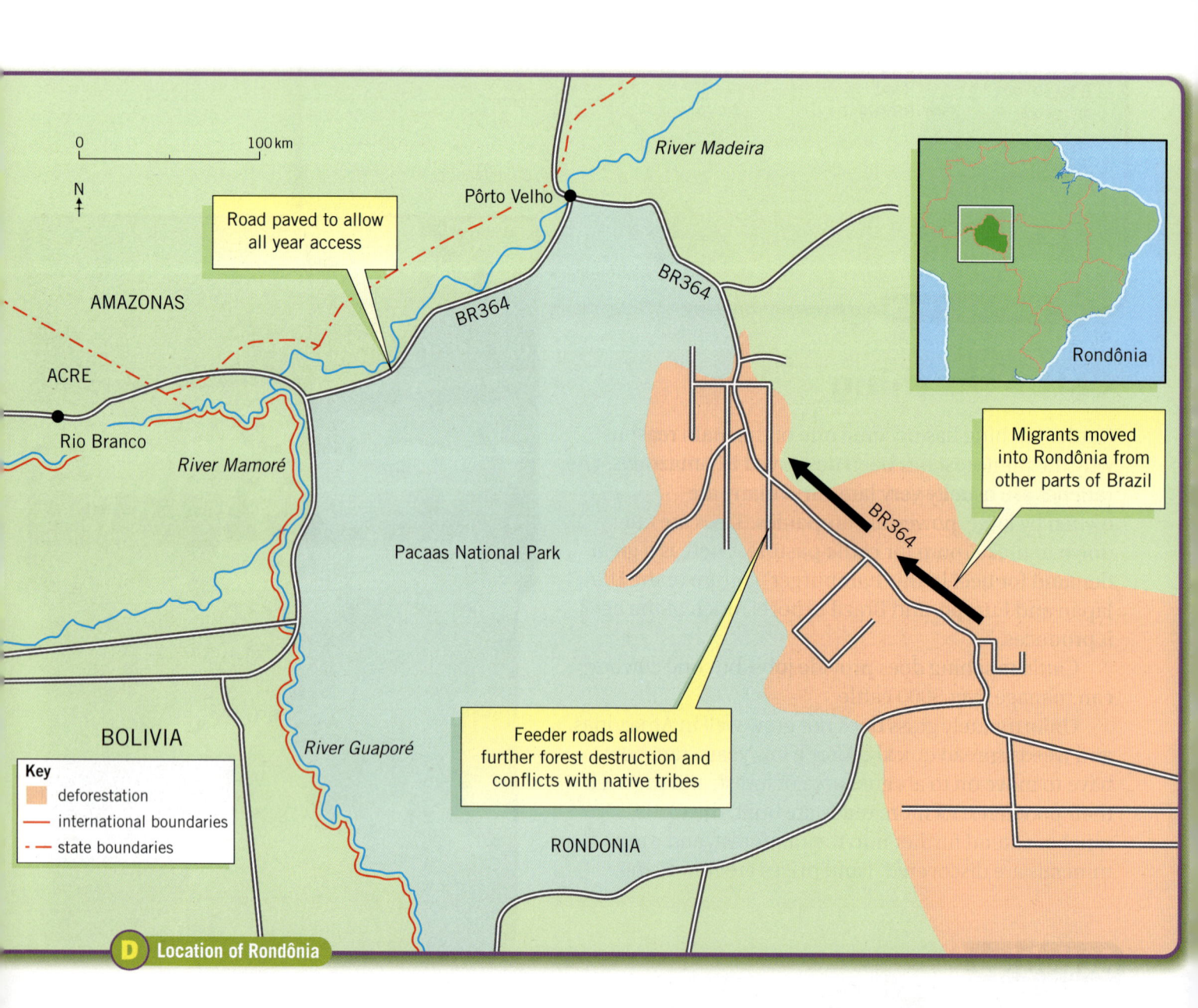

D Location of Rondônia

Map labels:
- Road paved to allow all year access
- Migrants moved into Rondônia from other parts of Brazil
- Feeder roads allowed further forest destruction and conflicts with native tribes

Places: Pôrto Velho, River Madeira, BR364, AMAZONAS, ACRE, Rio Branco, River Mamoré, Pacaas National Park, BOLIVIA, River Guaporé, RONDONIA, Rondônia

Key:
- deforestation
- international boundaries
- state boundaries

Investigating Brazil

E Rainforest destruction in Rondônia

Key

- Dense vegetation
- Marsh
- Deforested areas

5 Geography Matters

Mining in the Amazon jungle

The Amazon has great mineral wealth. One of the largest mining projects is in the Carajás mountains. There are huge iron deposits here that will last for many years. The ore is very pure and the mine has been carefully developed. A 900 km railway line takes the ore to the coast at São Luis from where it is exported.

The project uses power **generated** by the nearby Tucurui **Hydro power plant**. Building this meant that another 2000 square kilometres of forest was destroyed. Nearby forest is also under pressure for making charcoal, which is needed to produce the iron.

The company that developed the area has now agreed to protect 12 000 square kilometres of land and the native people who live there. In exchange, it wants to mine a further 4120 square kilometres.

Many environmentalists ask if twenty years' supply of iron ore is worth the ecological damage.

F Development at Carajás

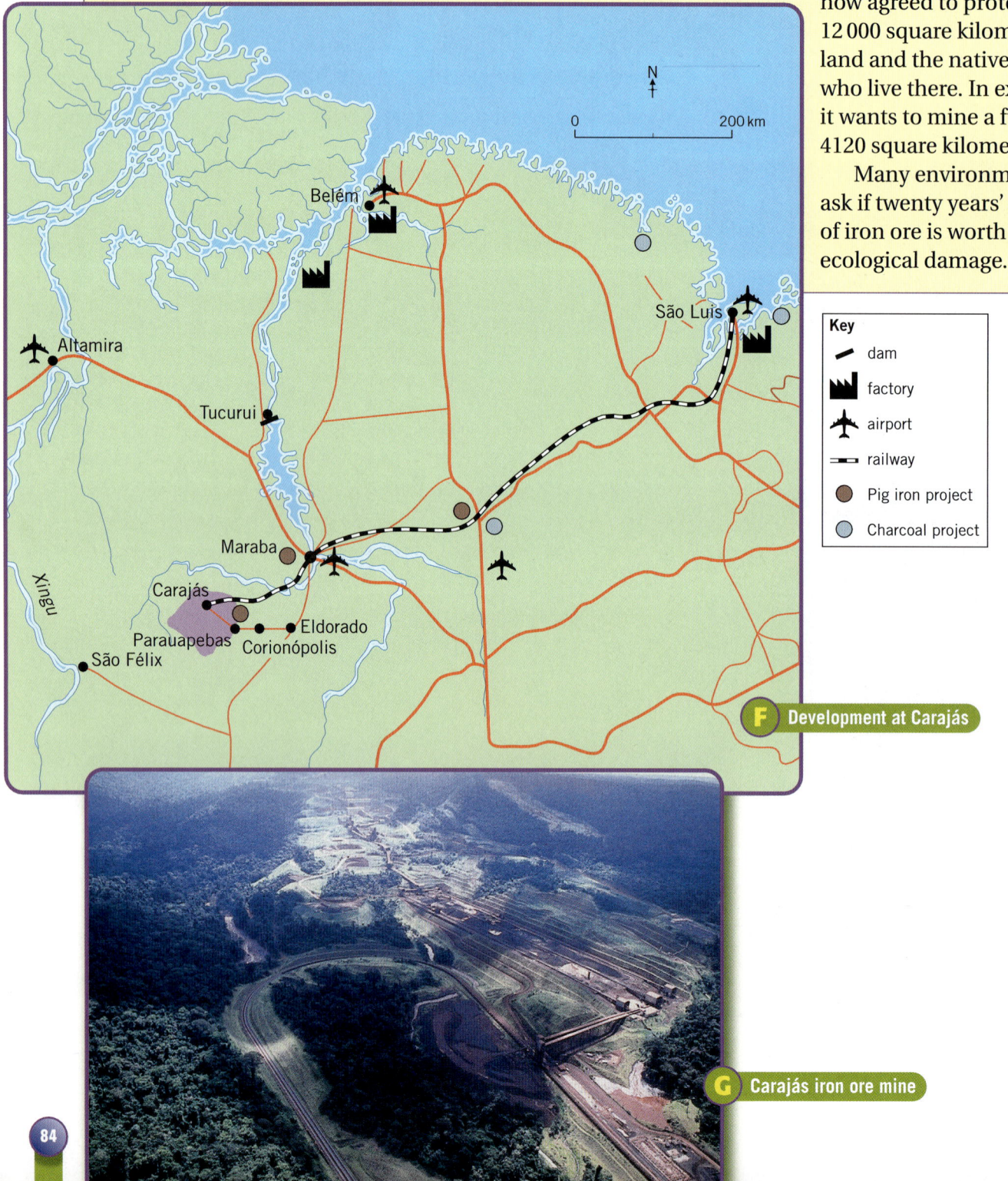

G Carajás iron ore mine

How is Brazil changing?
What are the impacts of these changes?

help!
Don't re-read every single sentence! Try to skim read and look out for dates quoted in the text.

Activities

1 Draw a timeline to record the important events in Brazil's attempts to develop the country since 1960. You will need to look back over earlier pages of this unit. Set your timeline out like this. Remember to allow lots of space – if things start to get cluttered, use a key.

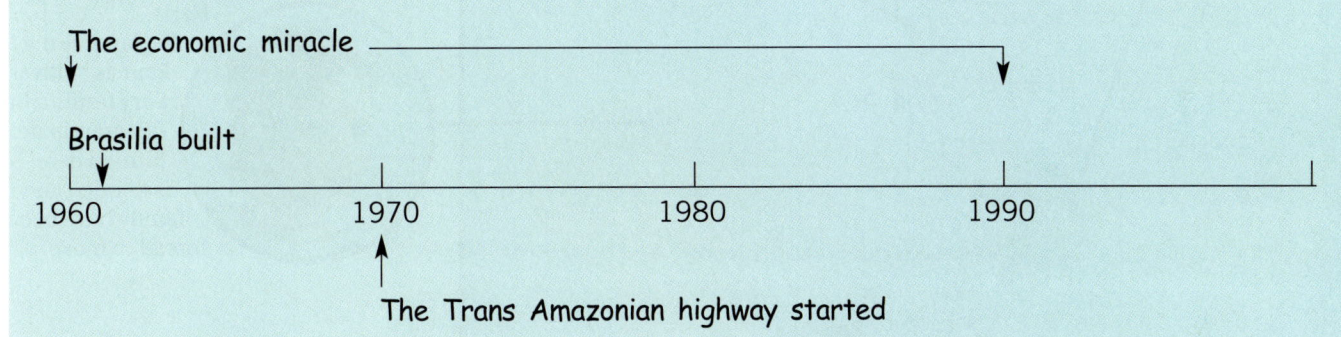

```
The economic miracle ─────────────────────────────────┐
         ↓                                            ↓
Brasilia built
     ↓
├─────────────┼─────────────┼─────────────┼─────────────┤
1960         1970          1980          1990
              ↑
    The Trans Amazonian highway started
```

2 Choose a colour for each of the regions you studied earlier in the unit and make a key. For each change that you have marked on your diagram, shade neatly behind the writing to show which part of Brazil was affected.

3 Write a short paragraph to describe what your timeline diagram shows about the developments that have occurred in Brazil since 1960.

4 Choose three of the changes that you have marked on your diagram. Try to assess how successful each of the developments has been. Set your work out like this.

Development: Sobradinho Reservoir	Region: NE Brazil
Brief description of development:	
Good things about the change:	
Bad things about the change:	
Verdict:	

5 Work out a league table for the developments that you looked at in activity **4**. Put the most successful development first. Write a short summary to describe any pattern that your league table shows.

5 Geography Matters

Review and reflect

Looking at the lives of six Brazilians

Renato
I was brought up on a coffee estate, but the boss thinks that machines are better than workers now! I took my family to Rondônia to make a living in the rainforest on our own piece of land. My son has a small café in town, I help him when my health allows. I've never really got used to the climate.

Yano
Every day it is harder for us to survive. More and more people want to destroy the forest and the land. We can trade forest products. Now there is so much pressure to change that our old way of life will soon be a memory.

Maria
The land by the São Francisco River was very fertile when my grandparents farmed here. Now it is flooded and my family have been forced to move.

Somália
I live with my family in Rio de Janeiro. We built a shack in a favela on the edge of the city. Life is hard, but I hope that my six daughters will have a future here.

B.A.
Everyone in this Pepsi factory knows me. This is a great job, and I am lucky to have it because the company gives me loads of benefits, like holidays and health care.

Luiz Boaz
I live and work in São Paulo. I have a smart city centre apartment, and my children go to a good school. My company exports beef, so I spend time abroad. Brazil is a land of opportunity.

A

Investigating Brazil

To do these activities well, you will need to look back at the information in this unit.

Activities

1 a Sort yourselves into groups of six people. Read the statements on the opposite page. Choose one character each.

b For each character that you represent, write a full description of the kind of life they lead.

> **help!**
>
> Start off by using what the character has said on page 86. Then think about the topics which have run through this unit:
> - the **location** of where they live within Brazil
> - the **natural** environment there, e.g. climate, vegetation and relief
> - the **economy** of the area, e.g. the sort of jobs people do
> - the **social** geography of the area, e.g. family life, population density, birth and death rate, life expectancy
> - the **changes** that are occurring in the area.

2 What will each character think about the big projects in Brazil, like the Carajás mine, cattle ranching, the São Francisco dam and the big factories? Copy the table below. Work out a conflict matrix for each of the characters. Each person must say what they think.

Somália	Renato	B.A.	Luiz	Maria	Yano
Somália					
	Renato			✓	
		B.A.			
			Luiz		
				Maria	
					Yano

- If you think the two characters would share many of the same interests and agree with each other about how Brazil was being developed, mark with a tick (✓). One has been done for you.
- If you think they would disagree, mark with a cross (✗).
- If you think they would have no strong feeling mark with a wavy line (〜).
- Put two ticks (✓✓) or two crosses (✗✗) if the agreement or disagreement is very great.

3 Give reasons for the decisions you have made in activity **2**. Focus in particular on the character or characters you represent.

4 Extension

Work out a new conflict matrix for how you think things might change over the next ten years. Remember to give reasons for your decisions.

6 Limestone landscapes of England

A Stalactites in a limestone cave

B Limestone quarry

C Limestone scar

D This cathedral is built of limestone

Learn about

Limestone is a unique rock that creates a very special landscape. In the north of England the Yorkshire Dales National Park is a famous area of limestone. Here people come to enjoy the landscape, but there are also problems. In this unit you will learn about:

- different rocks in upland areas in England
- what makes limestone so special
- the special features of limestone areas
- the problems of limestone areas.

E In a dark, dark cave there's a shaft of light

the
stalactites
are
shining
bright

F Going for Gold in a limestone landscape – Terry, Tom, Andrew and Daniel on their Duke of Edinburgh expedition

G Limestone pavement

H Karst landscape

I Natural limestone arch

Activities

With a partner, look at all the photos on these two pages. They all show **limestone** rock.

1 a Where do you think these photos were taken? For each one, decide whether it:
- Is definitely in England.
- Could be in England.
- Is definitely not in England.

b Do other people agree with you?

2 a What use is limestone? Make a list of five different ways that people use limestone in the photos.

b What else do the photos tell you? Write down two other things that the photos tell you about limestone rock.

3 Choose the photograph that you like best. Explain to your partner why you like it.

4 Extension

Figure **E** is a 'shape poem' inspired by the **stalactites** and **stalagmites** shown in **cave** picture **A**. Write a shape poem about your chosen photograph – remember, it need not rhyme. You might prefer to describe the things that you see as a story instead.

6 Geography Matters

England rocks!

England has a huge variety of landscapes. There are some areas of flat land (**lowland** areas) and also some hills and mountains (**upland** areas).

Look carefully at map **A**, which is a relief map of England and Wales. The map is shaded using a series of colours to show the highest and lowest land. This is called **layer shading**. The highest land on map **A** is shaded in brown and the lowest land in green.

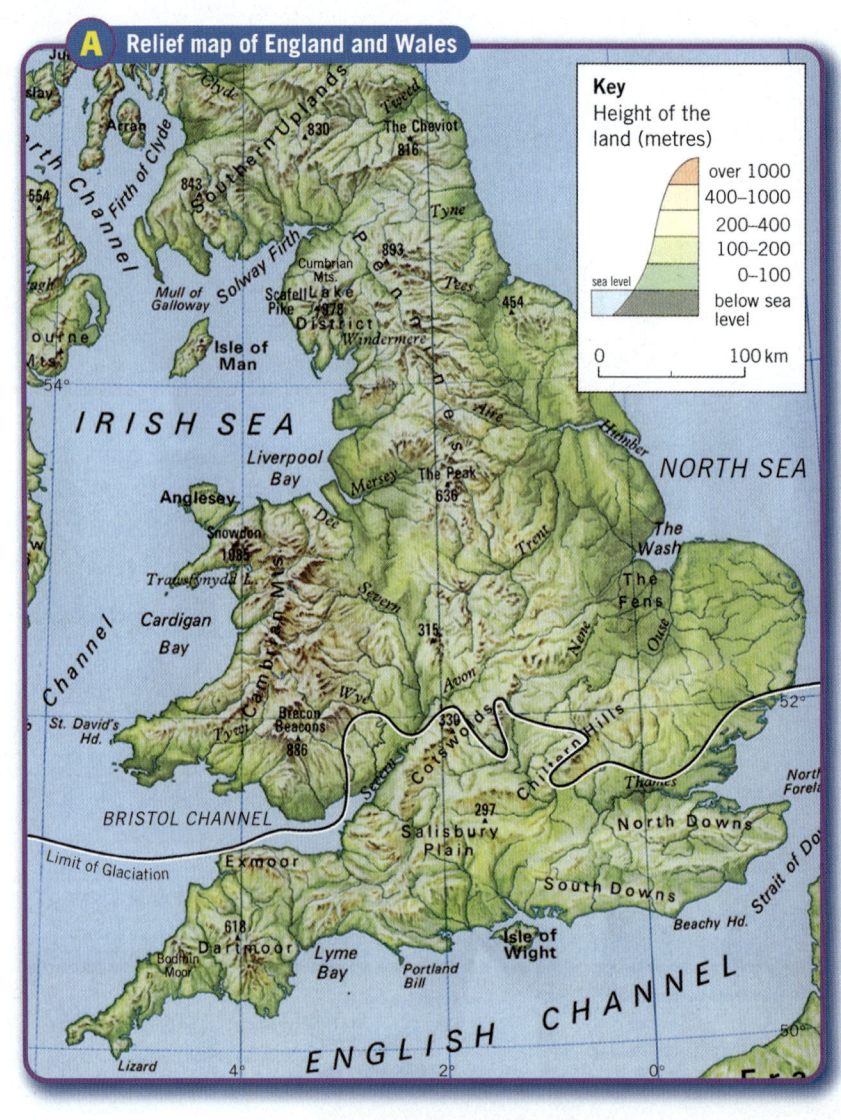

A Relief map of England and Wales

Key Height of the land (metres)
- over 1000
- 400–1000
- 200–400
- 100–200
- 0–100
- below sea level

sea level

0 — 100 km

Activities

1 Look at relief map **A**. Find the place where you live. Use the key to work out how high it is in metres above sea level.

2 a Look at the statements below. Write down the ones that are true.
- There is no land above 300 metres in England.
- The highest peak in England is 619 metres above sea level.
- All low-lying land, below 100 metres, is in the east.
- The highest mountain in England is called Scafell Pike.
- Most of the upland areas are in the north of England.

b Rewrite the other statements by changing just one word (or number), so these are also correct.

3 Extension

Write a paragraph to describe England's relief. Use your sentences from question **2**, and try to add the names of places from the atlas, such as:

the Lake District   the Fens
the Pennines   Dartmoor

Limestone landscapes of England

Rock types

Map **C** shows the main rock types in England. Our land surface is made up of lots of different types of rock. Some rocks are hard and others are quite easily eroded. Some rocks are very old, while others were formed more recently. All the different rocks can be classified into three types:

- Sedimentary
- Igneous
- Metamorphic.

Limestone is a **sedimentary rock**. The hardest limestone rock in England is called Carboniferous limestone. It was formed between 600 and 225 million years ago, during the Carboniferous period. The different time periods are shown on the geological timescale **B**.

Getting Technical

Sedimentary rocks are made of bits of rock (sediments) which were laid down in layers, usually under water. Over a very long time the sediments are squeezed (compressed) into new rocks (0–600 million years).

Igneous rocks were formed when molten rock (**magma**) from deep inside the Earth interior cooled down to form rocks (290–600 million years).

Metamorphic rocks are sedimentary or igneous rocks which have been changed by heat or pressure (over 500 million years).

Activities

4. Compare relief map **A** with map **C** showing the rock types of England.
   a. Name two rocks that make mountains or hills.
   b. Name two rocks that make lowland areas.

5. a. Make a copy of the geological timescale **B**.
   b. Label sedimentary, **igneous** and **metamorphic** rocks against the correct period on the scale: 'Getting Technical' will tell you how old these rock types are. Use different colours for your labels.
   c. Label Carboniferous limestone on your scale.

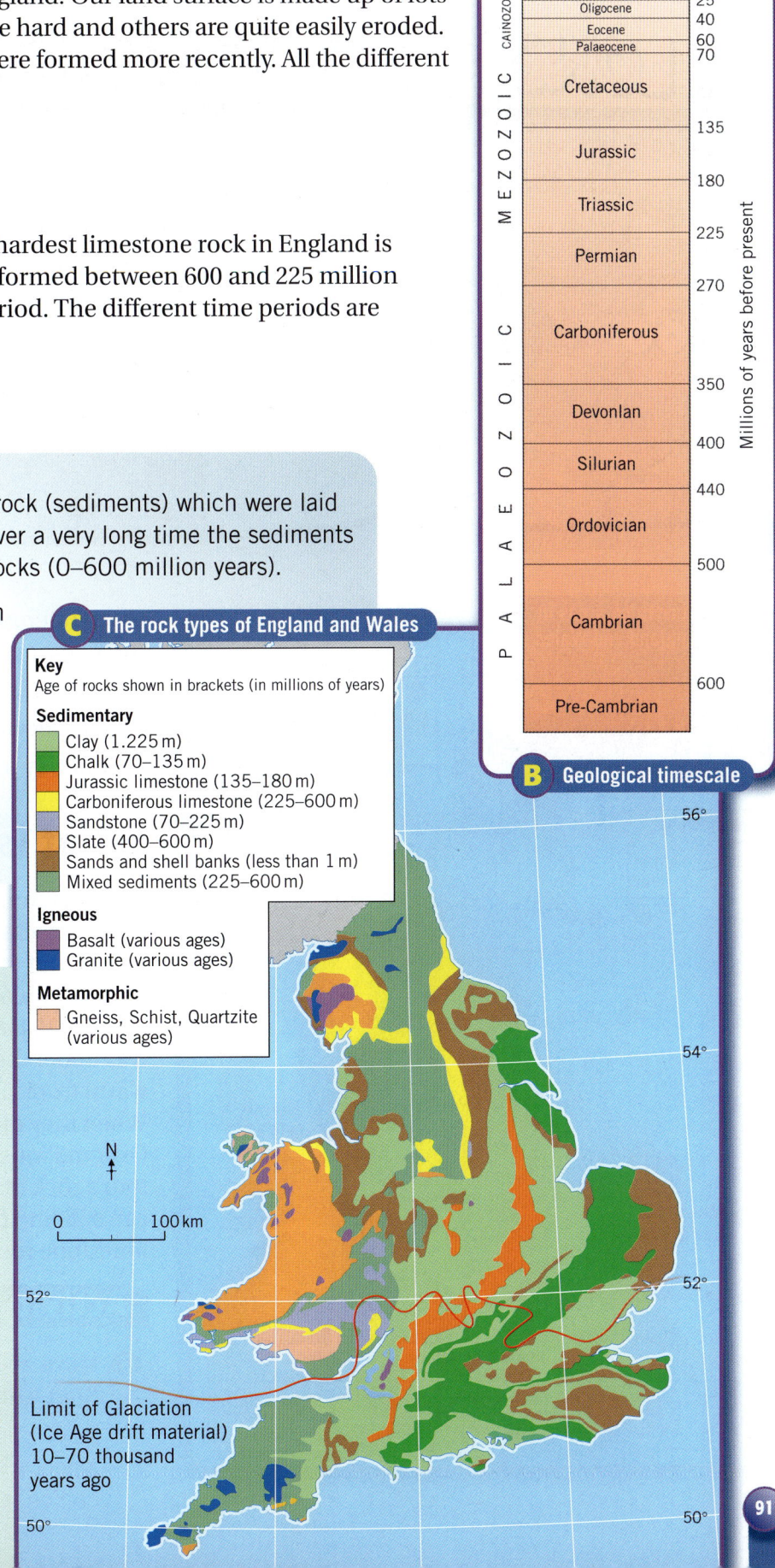

C The rock types of England and Wales

Key
Age of rocks shown in brackets (in millions of years)

Sedimentary
- Clay (1.225 m)
- Chalk (70–135 m)
- Jurassic limestone (135–180 m)
- Carboniferous limestone (225–600 m)
- Sandstone (70–225 m)
- Slate (400–600 m)
- Sands and shell banks (less than 1 m)
- Mixed sediments (225–600 m)

Igneous
- Basalt (various ages)
- Granite (various ages)

Metamorphic
- Gneiss, Schist, Quartzite (various ages)

Limit of Glaciation (Ice Age drift material) 10–70 thousand years ago

B Geological timescale

Era	Period	Millions of years before present
CAINOZOIC	Pleistocene	
	Pliocene	1.0
	Miocene	11
	Oligocene	25
	Eocene	40
	Palaeocene	60
		70
MEZOZOIC	Cretaceous	
		135
	Jurassic	
		180
	Triassic	
		225
	Permian	
		270
PALAEOZOIC	Carboniferous	
		350
	Devonian	
		400
	Silurian	
		440
	Ordovician	
		500
	Cambrian	
		600
	Pre-Cambrian	

6 Geography Matters

Why is limestone so special?

A LONG, LONG TIME AGO....

...EVEN BEFORE THE DINOSAURS

England was covered by a shallow tropical sea – a bit like where the Great Barrier Reef is forming today.

As the small animals and corals that lived in the sea died, their shells and skeletons fell to the bottom.

A thick layer built up over millions of years. As it squashed and hardened, it eventually turned into limestone.

A

B Limestone areas in England and Wales

Key:
- National parks
- Carboniferous limestone
- Jurassic limestone
- Chalk

Northumberland NP
North York Moors NP
Lake District NP
Yorkshire Dales NP
Peak District NP
Snowdonia NP
Norfolk Broads NP
Brecon Beacons NP
Pembrokeshire Coast NP
Exmoor NP
Dartmoor NP

Carboniferous limestone: hard, grey, full of fossils, e.g. coral

Jurassic limestone: soft, yellowish, many fossils

Chalk: soft, white, full of remains of many microscopic sea organisms

0 — 100 km

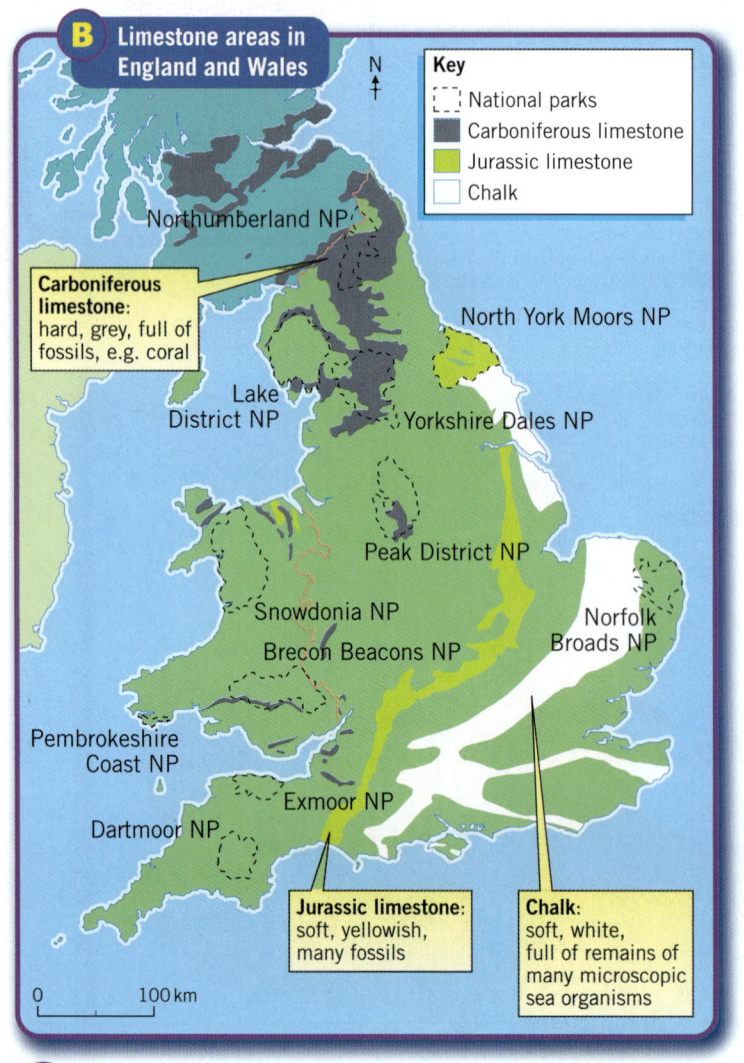

Carboniferous limestone is special for three reasons:
- what it is made from
- its special structure
- the way it is worn away.

What is it made from?

Carboniferous limestone is one of our oldest and hardest rocks. This is quite surprising when you know what it is made from – sea animals!

Cartoon **A** shows how limestone is formed. Around 350 million years ago northern England was under the ocean near the Equator. These warm tropical seas were rich in sea creatures. When they died, their shells sank to the sea bed. Over millions of years the shells were squashed into a rock made from **calcium carbonate**. You can still find fossils in limestone rock. Different limestone rocks are shown on map **B**.

Activity

6 Make a word bank about rocks and limestone. Start with these words.

relief   upland   lowland   sedimentary rock
igneous rock   metamorphic rock
carboniferous limestone

Limestone landscapes of England

What is its special structure?

Carboniferous limestone formed in layers under the sea. As the sediments dried out, the rock cracked into huge blocks, like bricks in a wall. The cracks are called **joints** and are shown in diagram **C**. Now that the limestone is above sea level, the joints let water seep through the rock.

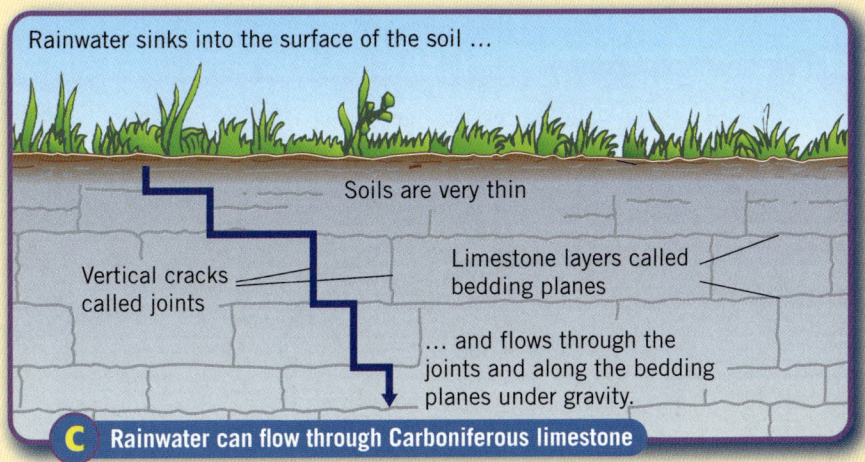

Rainwater sinks into the surface of the soil …

Soils are very thin

Vertical cracks called joints

Limestone layers called bedding planes

… and flows through the joints and along the bedding planes under gravity.

C Rainwater can flow through Carboniferous limestone

D The cracks in this rock are called joints

E This limestone statue has been weathered by rainwater

How is it worn away?

Like other rocks, Carboniferous limestone can be eroded by rivers, glaciers and wind, but it is a very tough rock. Its only weakness is from rainwater. Rainwater is a weak acid, and this attacks limestone, which is made of calcium carbonate. The acidic water dissolves the alkaline rock. This is called **chemical weathering**.

$$CaCO_3 + H_2O + CO_2 = Ca(HCO_3)_2$$
calcium carbonate + water + carbon dioxide = calcium bicarbonate (soluble)

F The chemical reaction between rainwater and limestone

Activities

1. Look at photo **E**.
   a. What do you think the statue looked like when it was new? Do a 'before' and 'after' sketch of the statue.
   b. Label your sketch to explain what has happened to the statue. Use these words: calcium carbonate, acid, rainwater, chemical, weathering.

2. Limestone is an amazing rock. Draw a poster that would be suitable for junior school children. Give it the title 'Amazing Limestone'. Try to show something interesting about limestone. Explain things simply, using pictures and words. You could use an ICT package to present your information. **ICT**

6 Geography Matters

What are typical limestone features?

Limestone is a rock that produces unique scenery because of its special structure and properties – it is permeable and is dissolved by rainwater. These two properties lead to the creation of landforms like **swallow holes**, **limestone pavements**, **caves** and **caverns**, and **limestone scars**.

You can see typical limestone features in diagram **A** and read about them in the boxes on pages 94–96.

Getting Technical

- **Permeable** rock allows water to pass through it. Water cannot pass through **impermeable** rock.

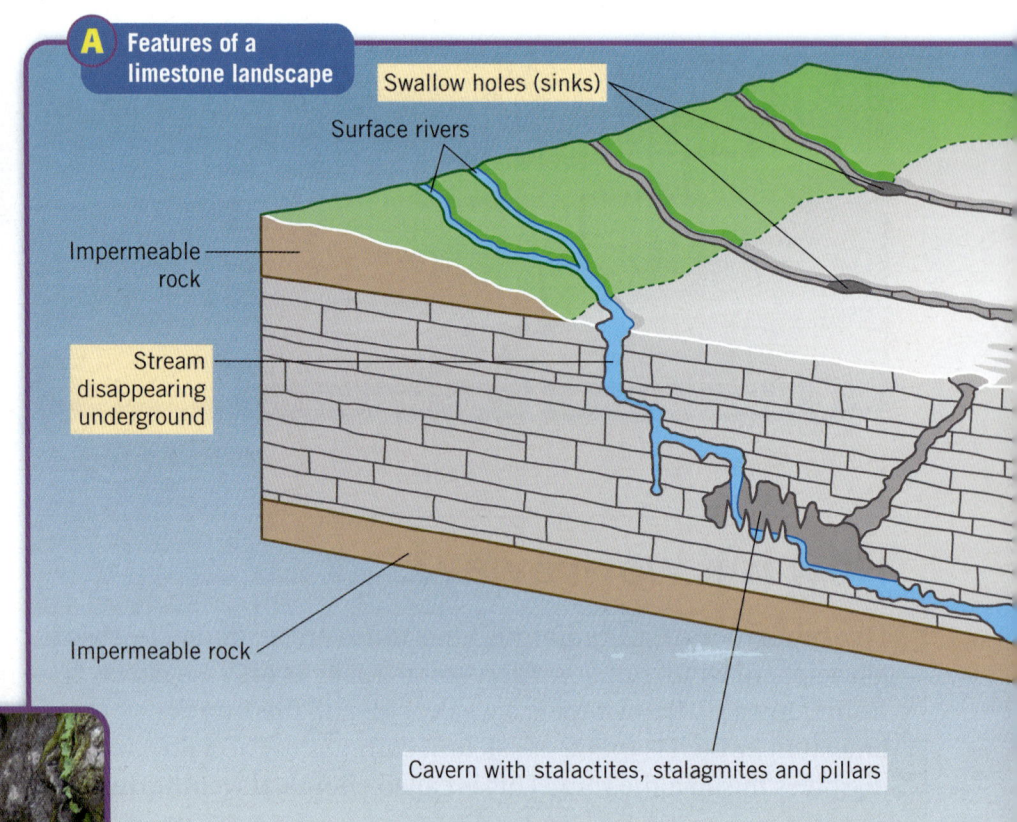

A Features of a limestone landscape

- Swallow holes (sinks)
- Surface rivers
- Impermeable rock
- Stream disappearing underground
- Impermeable rock
- Cavern with stalactites, stalagmites and pillars

Sinks and swallow holes

Some rivers simply disappear underground when water seeps into cracks in the limestone – this is called a **sink**. A big sink is called a **swallow hole**.

Photograph **B** shows Gaping Gill in Yorkshire. It is one of the most famous swallow holes in England. Here the Fell Beck river falls 110 metres into a cavern the size of a cathedral!

B The swallow hole at Gaping Gill

Limestone landscapes of England

Springs and resurgences

Photo **C** shows where the underground river eventually comes out again at the surface. This is called a **resurgence** or **spring**. Some spring water is bottled and sold.

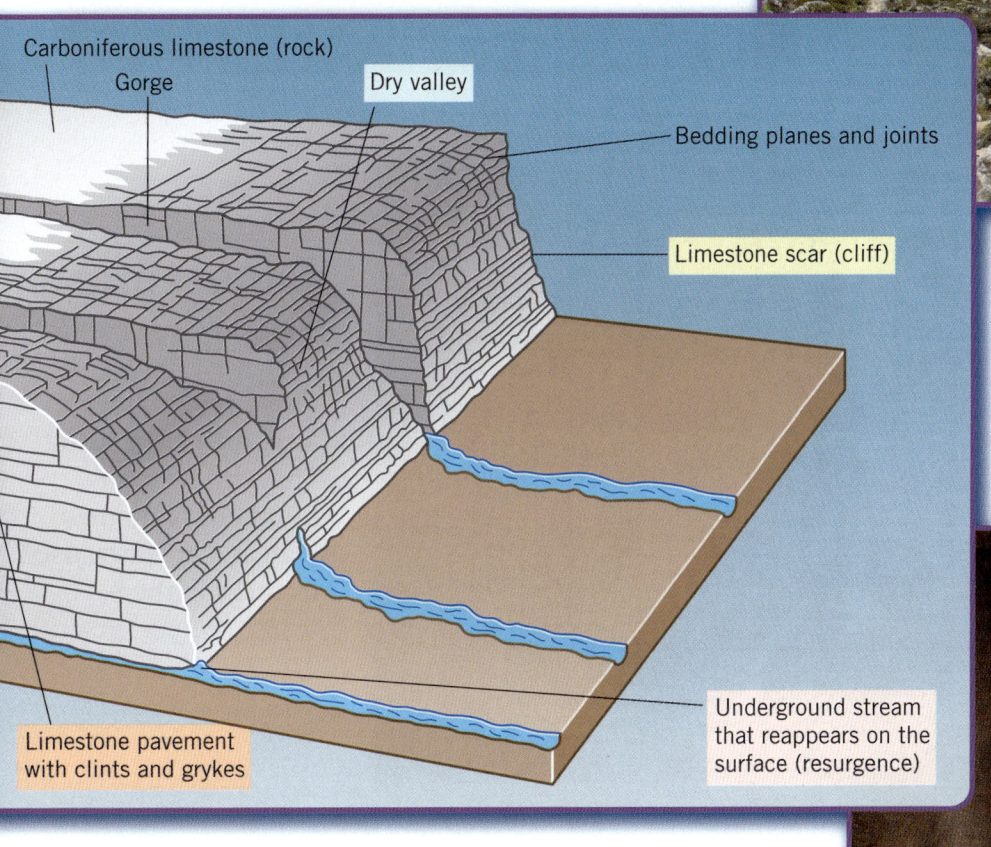

C The resurgence at Malham Cove

D This cavern at Gaping Gill is the largest underground chamber in England

Labels on diagram:
- Carboniferous limestone (rock)
- Gorge
- Dry valley
- Bedding planes and joints
- Limestone scar (cliff)
- Underground stream that reappears on the surface (resurgence)
- Limestone pavement with clints and grykes

Caves and caverns

Over millions of years, rainwater seeps through the joints in limestone and slowly dissolves the rock. As the joint gets bigger it becomes a **cave** and then a big **cavern**. The calcium carbonate from limestone is dissolved in the water. Sometimes it gets deposited again when water drips from the roof of a cave. This slow process makes **stalactites** that hang from the roof, like icicles. **Stalagmites** stick up from the cave floor, and sometimes make big **pillars** of new rock.

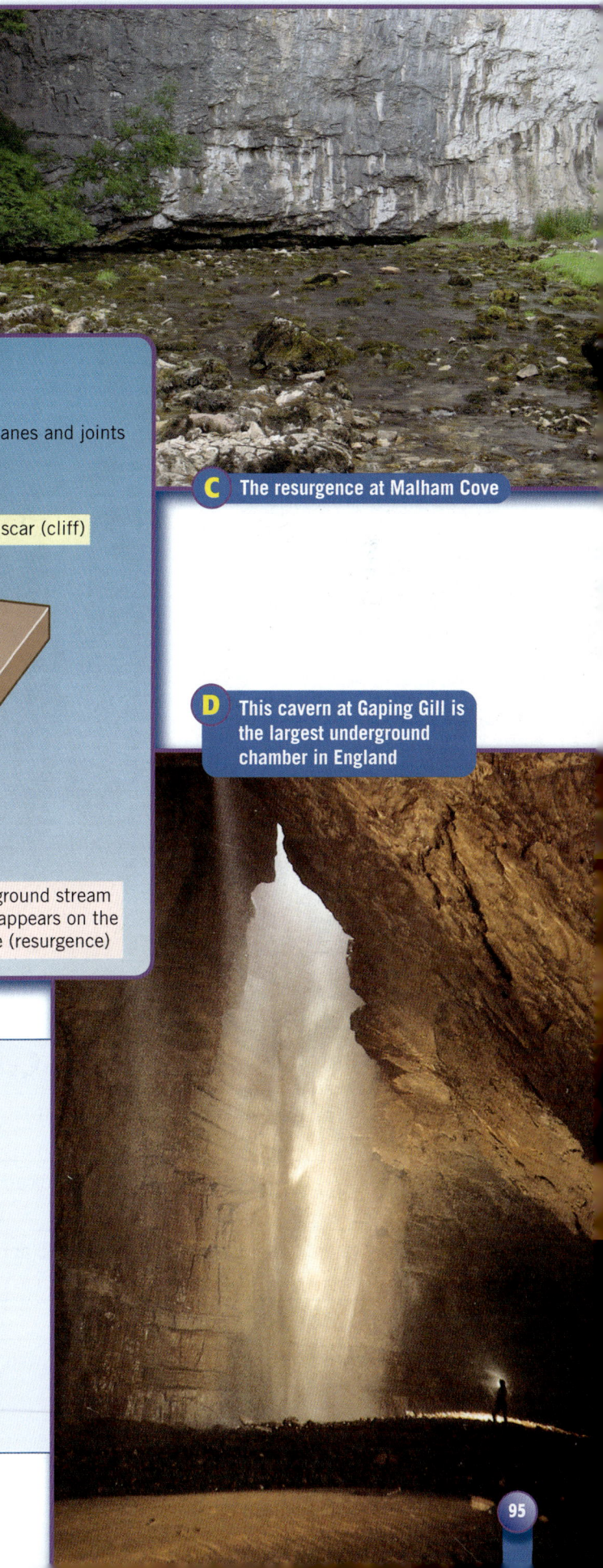

6 Geography Matters

Dry valleys

These formed during the Ice Age when the ground was frozen. Today these valleys have no rivers. The water has sunk into the ground. These features are called **dry valleys**.

E Watlowes Valley in Yorkshire is a dry valley

Limestone pavements

Limestone pavements have flat blocks of rock called **clints** with gaps between them, which have been enlarged by weathering, called **grykes**.

F A limestone pavement in Yorkshire

G Gordale Scar in the Yorkshire Dales

Limestone scars

These vertical rock faces are called **scars**. They can be many hundreds of metres high and are often used by rock climbers.

Activities

1 a Make a copy of the table below and match the words with their correct definitions.
   b Add these words to your word bank.

sink	where an underground river comes back to the surface
cave	where a river suddenly disappears underground
dry valley	when water has enlarged an underground joint
swallow hole	a valley with no river!
spring	a flat piece of limestone with surface cracks, called grykes
cavern	a steep limestone cliff
scar	a big hole where a river disappears
limestone pavement	a big cave

2 Extension

In groups, choose one of the features in question **1** and make a fact card about it. You could present your work as part of a display, using sketches as well as writing.

help!

Your fact card should include:
- *What* is the name of the landform?
- *Where* is it found in a limestone area?
- *How* is it formed?
- *Why* is it only found in a limestone area?
- *Name* some examples. You could use other textbooks, the Internet or an encyclopaedia.

Limestone landscapes of England

What is the limestone like in the Yorkshire Dales?

Case Study

The Yorkshire Dales National Park is a special area of limestone. Although only 19 000 people live in the Yorkshire Dales, more than one million people visit the National Park every year. Visitors come to view the spectacular scenery. Many people go hiking in the hills. The area is famous for its pretty villages, hills, valleys and farms with their old stone walls.

A National Parks in northern England

B

- Pen-y-Ghent
- Whernside
- The Settle viaduct in Ribblesdale
- Malham village

The Yorkshire Dales National Park is a popular area to visit for day trips, short breaks or longer holidays. Postcard **B** shows some of the most attractive areas and two of the region's three highest peaks: Pen-y-Ghent (694 m) and Great Whernside (704 m). From these hills you get marvellous views of the surrounding limestone areas.

Activities

1 What is so special about the Yorkshire Dales?

a Look at the photos on these two pages and make a copy of the survey below:

noisy	1	2	3	4	5	6	7	quiet
crowded	1	2	3	4	5	6	7	uncrowded
boring	1	2	3	4	5	6	7	exciting
ugly buildings	1	2	3	4	5	6	7	beautiful buildings
completely spoilt	1	2	3	4	5	6	7	completely unspoilt
dull landscape	1	2	3	4	5	6	7	interesting landscape
monotonous	1	2	3	4	5	6	7	different and varied

b Now give your opinion about the Yorkshire Dales. Circle your score for each set of words

c Use these words to write two sentences to describe the Yorkshire Dales.

2 Sketch a large copy of one of the photos in **B**. Use the sketch to make a wordshape drawing of the photo.

6 Geography Matters

Rocks and rain in Yorkshire

The area around Ingleborough in Yorkshire is famous for its limestone landscape. The area around Ingleborough Hill is shown on these pages.

The brown contour lines on maps **C** and **F** show the height of the hills. When the contours are close together, it shows that the slopes are steep.

If you look at the maps, you can see small streams flowing down from the top of Ingleborough Hill. One stream, Fell Beck, flows from A to B on the cross-section diagram **D**. It is also shown on map **F**. When Fell Beck reaches the limestone rock it disappears from the map! The water falls down Gaping Gill and flows underground until it comes out again at Beck Head.

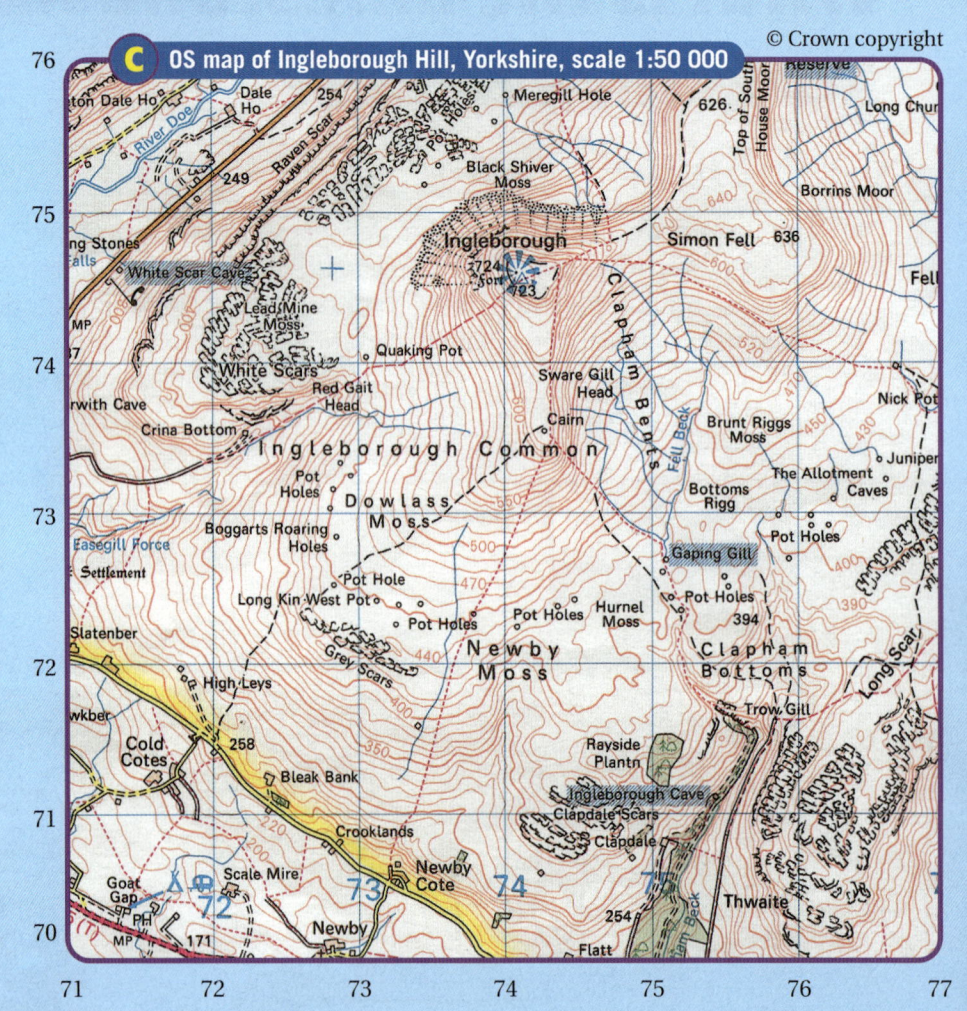

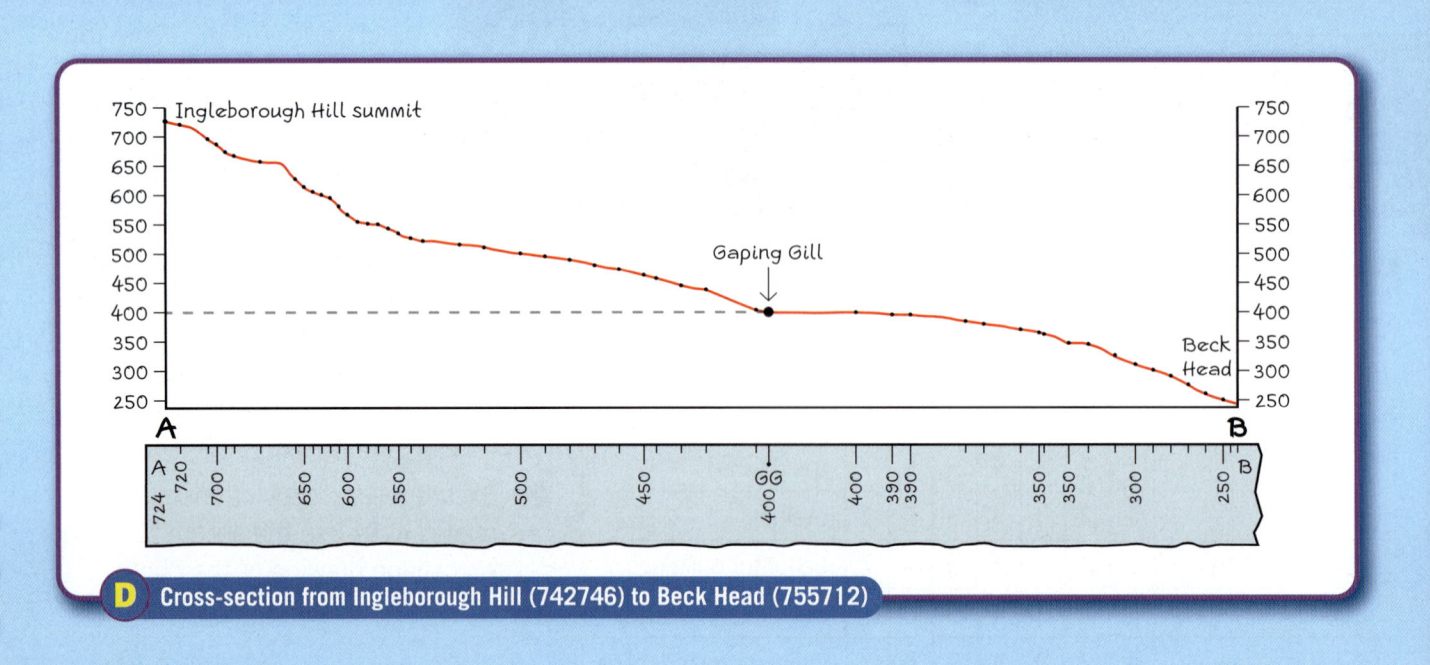

C OS map of Ingleborough Hill, Yorkshire, scale 1:50 000

© Crown copyright

D Cross-section from Ingleborough Hill (742746) to Beck Head (755712)

Getting Technical

- Contour lines join places of the same height at 10 metre intervals.

  The closer together the contour lines are, the steeper the land.

- Hills are shown as contour rings.

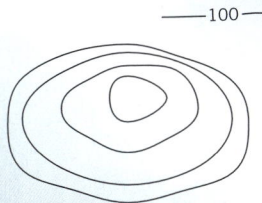

Limestone landscapes of England

E Ingleborough Hill

F OS map of Ingleborough Hill, scale 1:25 000

© Crown copyright

Activities

1. Which map, **C** or **F**, is better for hikers to use? Give one reason for your answer.

2. **a** Draw your own copy of the cross-section from A to B on map **F**. If you need help, look back at the How to … box on page 9.

   b Add these labels to your cross-section: Ingleborough Hill, spring, impermeable rock, Gaping Gill, limestone rock.

   c Add the river, Fell Beck, to your cross-section using a blue line. Remember to make it go underground at the right place.

3. Have you ever been in a cave? Imagine that it is a hot summer day. You go down Gaping Gill and into the cavern below. Describe what it is like in the cave. Include these details:

   - What do you do? *'As I climbed down the rope ladder, the bright sunshine …'*
   - What can you see? *'At first …'*
   - What does it feel like?
   - Can you hear anything?
   - What does it smell like?

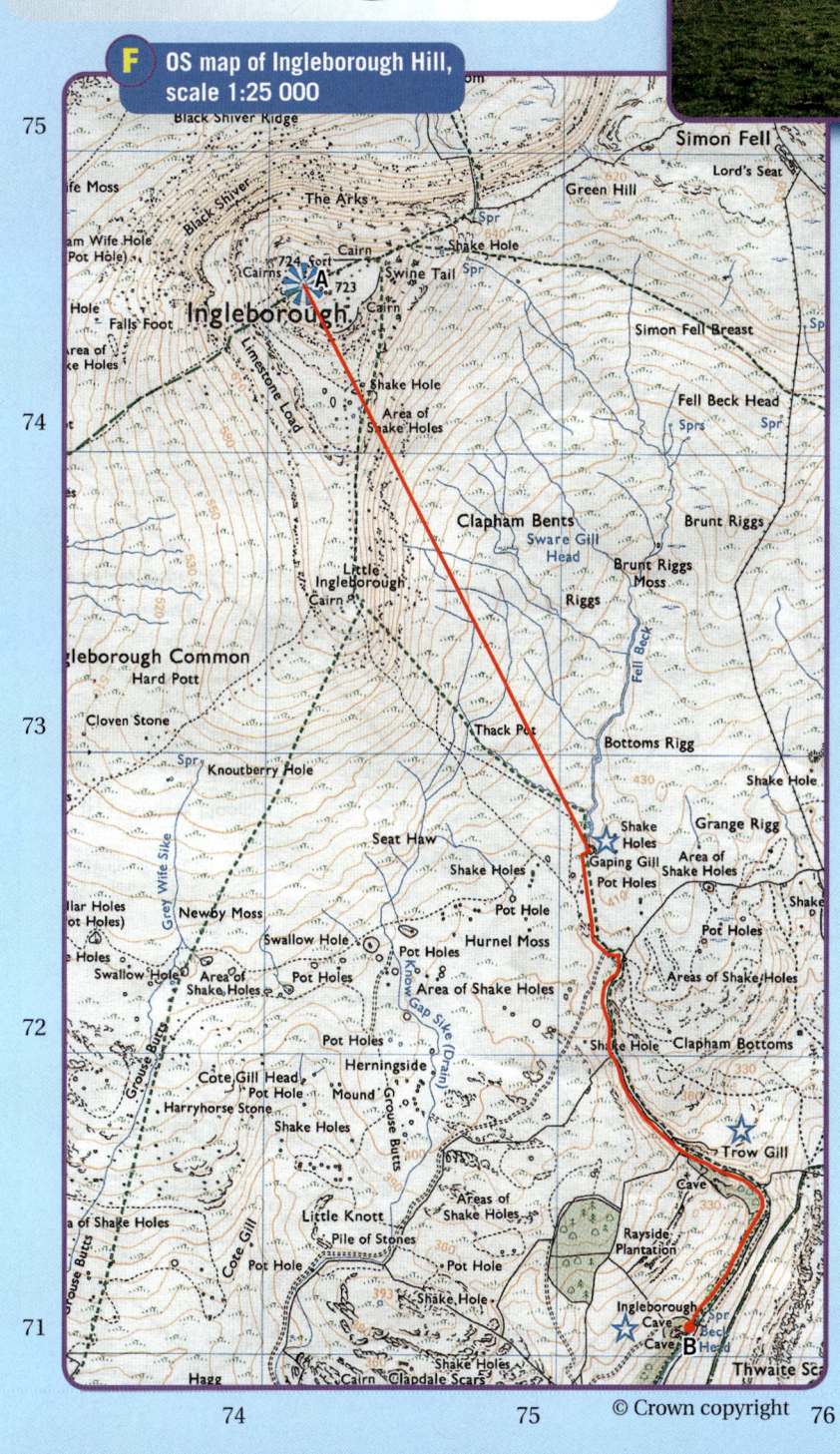

6 Geography Matters

A walk in the Dales

The Yorkshire Dales are very popular with walkers. A group of five students chose the area for their Duke of Edinburgh Gold Award expedition. They hiked 75 km in four days. One section of their walk is shown on Route Card **H**. It goes past some interesting limestone features, including a disappearing river!

Their route can be followed on map **I**. It is a 1:25 000 map so 4 cm = 1 km. It gives lots of detail. Two checkpoints are shown: the parking area (893658) and the campsite (899633).

G Duke of Edinburgh Award students

AWARD GROUP: Gina, Claire, Helen, Steven, James Cockshut Hill Technology College Gold D of E						DAY 3	DATE 31st August
Place with Grid Reference	Direction or bearing as required	Distance (km)	Time estimated	Time for meals, stops, etc.	Time for leg	ROUTE INFORMATION	
START Home Farm GR 885 674 TO Footpath and road junction CHECKPOINT G GR 893 658	SE	2.7	52 min	5 min	57 min	Turn right out of Home Farm onto a track. Follow it until forest boundary. Path joins with Pennine Way and enters forest. Keep Malham Tarn to the right and follow it round, keeping to footpath closest to the river (i.e. turn right at footpath and track junctions). Carry straight on, taking the footpath directly ahead coming off the Pennine Way. Follow the path, at crossroads turn right and head towards the car park. Path joins with the road.	
TO Campsite CHECKPOINT H GR 899 633	S	3.8	1 hr 04 min	10 min	1 hr 14 min	Here turn right onto road and cross the river before taking left path. At the junction take the right footpath (not the Pennine Way). At fork turn left. Pass Dean Scar. Take left path onto Pennine Way. Walk past Ing Scar Crag and down onto Malham Cove (steep descent), turn right at path junction and cross footbridge coming off the Pennine Way taking left path at fork. Follow path to campsite.	

H Route card for the students' expedition

Limestone landscapes of England

© Crown copyright

1 OS map of Malham area, scale 1:25 000

Activities

Can you help the expedition group to complete their report?

1 Look at the route card and follow their instructions on the map.

 a How far did the students walk between the two checkpoints?

 b What was the general direction of the route?

2 Read the list of limestone features below. Write them down in the order that the group would see them on their walk.

- Water Sinks (where Malham Beck river disappears)
- Watlowes dry valley
- Malham Tarn (lake formed on slate rock)
- Malham Cove (a limestone scar)
- Shake Holes (holes where water can disappear)
- Resurgence at the foot of Malham Cove (where the river comes out as a spring)
- Scars (e.g. Ing Scar and Raven Scar)

3 Find each feature and give it a grid reference. Decide whether to use a four-figure reference or a six-figure grid reference for each feature – some features will cover whole grid squares while others are just in one spot.

Why do limestone areas face problems?

Limestone is a tough rock and is very useful for buildings. You have already seen photos of some of its different uses. Some people want to develop huge quarries to dig up the limestone. It is a good building stone and is also used in industry. The huge boulders can even be used to protect the coast from the sea.

Another problem is that more than 8 million visitors visit the National Park every year. This can damage the area. The limestone environment provides an important habitat for particular plants and animals. Some rare plants, such as the rock rose, grow in the Yorkshire Dales. Diagram **L** shows how the scenery is under threat.

It is the job of the National Park Authority to protect the Yorkshire Dales. Diagram **J** shows that this is not an easy matter, because they must also help local people to find jobs and earn money.

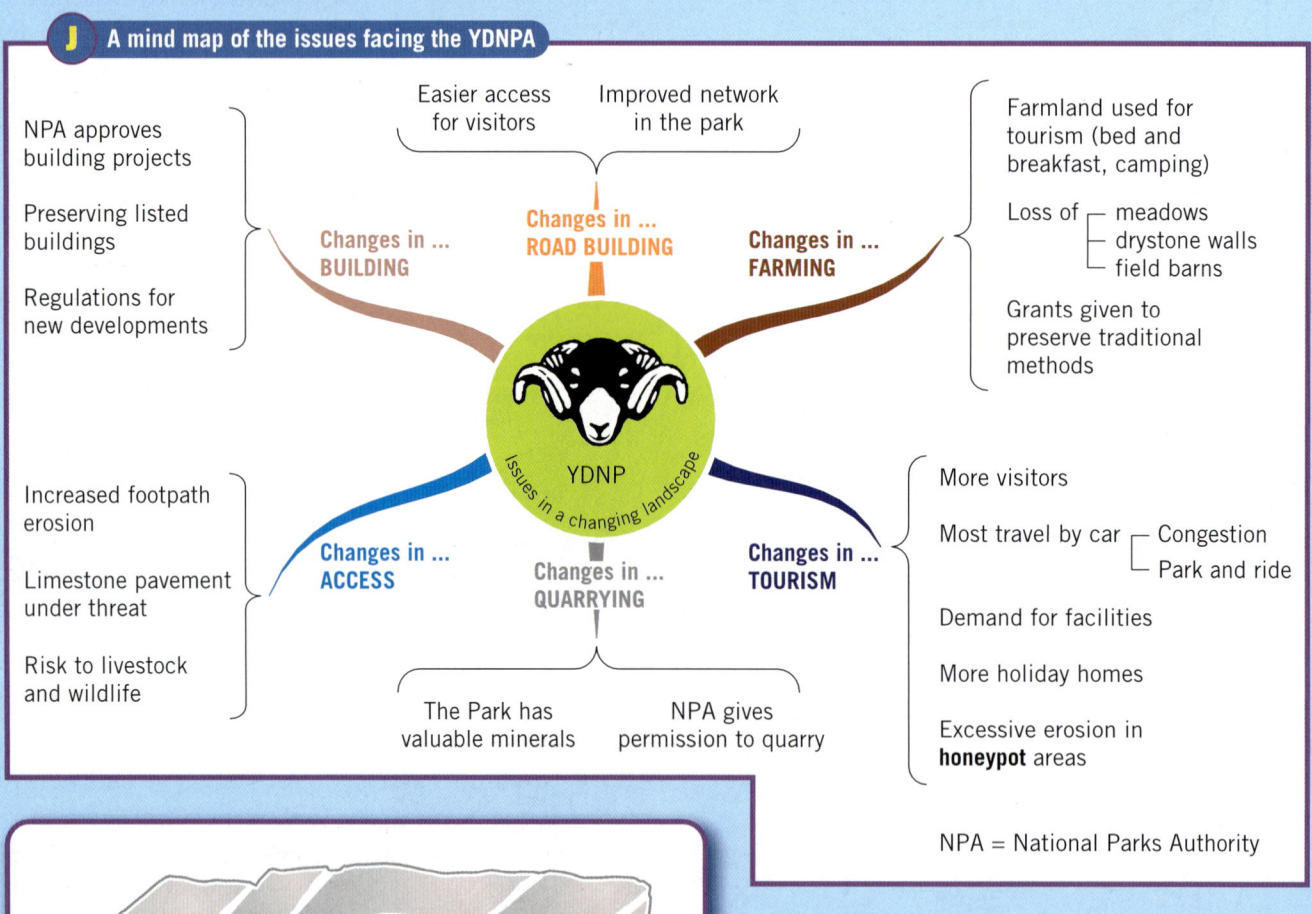

J A mind map of the issues facing the YDNPA

Changes in ... BUILDING
- NPA approves building projects
- Preserving listed buildings
- Regulations for new developments

Changes in ... ROAD BUILDING
- Easier access for visitors
- Improved network in the park

Changes in ... FARMING
- Farmland used for tourism (bed and breakfast, camping)
- Loss of meadows, drystone walls, field barns
- Grants given to preserve traditional methods

Changes in ... ACCESS
- Increased footpath erosion
- Limestone pavement under threat
- Risk to livestock and wildlife

Changes in ... QUARRYING
- The Park has valuable minerals
- NPA gives permission to quarry

Changes in ... TOURISM
- More visitors
- Most travel by car — Congestion, Park and ride
- Demand for facilities
- More holiday homes
- Excessive erosion in **honeypot** areas

YDNP — issues in a changing landscape

NPA = National Parks Authority

The most important resource in the Yorkshire Dales National Park is the limestone scenery. Limestone areas are important **habitats**. Many species of plants and animals can only be found in this alkaline environment. Examples are lime-loving plants like the birds eye primrose and rock rose. But because limestone has many uses, the scenery is under threat (**K**).

K Limestone is a very useful material

Uses: Cement, Concrete, Rockery stone, Road building, Fertiliser, Glass-making, Buildings, e.g. St Paul's Cathedral, Steel-making

Limestone landscapes of England

Should the Malham quarry be developed?

A British cement company wants to open a big quarry near Malham. It has applied for planning permission for the development. The quarry will be located in grid square 8864 on map **I** (page 101). Details of the proposal are shown in diagram **L**.

Different people have different opinions on developments such as this. The National Park Authority must decide whether to give planning permission for the new quarry.

L Plans for a new quarry near Malham

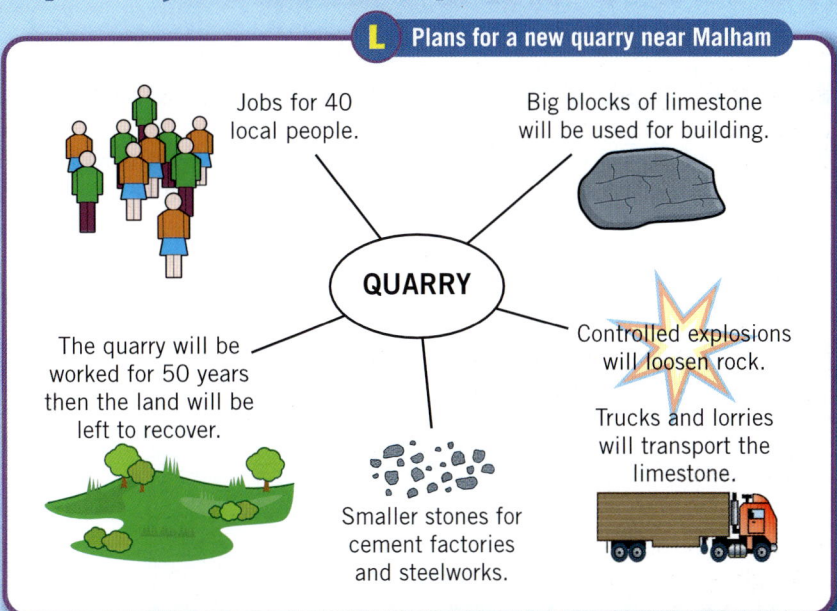

- Jobs for 40 local people.
- Big blocks of limestone will be used for building.
- Controlled explosions will loosen rock.
- Trucks and lorries will transport the limestone.
- Smaller stones for cement factories and steelworks.
- The quarry will be worked for 50 years then the land will be left to recover.

Activities

1 Read the different viewpoints below.

'This is a very special area. We only found out about it when we did our expedition here last summer.'
Student

'Malham is a small unspoilt village. We need to think of future generations.'
Local resident

'It is very difficult to find full-time jobs in the National Park. Tourism employs people in the summer, but farming has had a terrible time recently.'
Farmer

'We have come on holiday to the Malham area for many years. We love the landscape and know a lot about the different plants and animals that can be found here.'
Tourist visitor

'Limestone is a valuable resource. This is not the most important area of scenery.'
Cement company spokesperson

'We must try to do the best for everyone. Any developments should not harm the local environment.'
Environmental campaigner

a In pairs, choose one of the six roles and decide what opinion the person will have about the quarry development. Prepare a few sentences to put forward your point of view. You might need to do some research, so that you know what you are talking about.

b The Park Authority must decide what to do. They hold a meeting so that everyone can voice their opinion. The debate will allow people to ask questions and to give their opinions. Make notes on what people say. In the end, the National Park Authority must decide what to do.

2 **Extension**

Write a report on the class debate. Try to summarise what different people said. Explain what the final decision was, and whether you agree with it.

6 Geography Matters

Review and reflect

What do you know about limestone?

In this unit you have looked at limestone in England. Limestone is a unique rock that forms an interesting landscape. The Yorkshire Dales have many special limestone features. Some **economic activities** such as quarrying and tourism can damage the landscape. The area needs careful management.

A Karst region of Croatia

B Limestone in Hvar, Croatia

Limestone landscapes of England

Activities

1. Make a large copy of the cross-section diagram below.

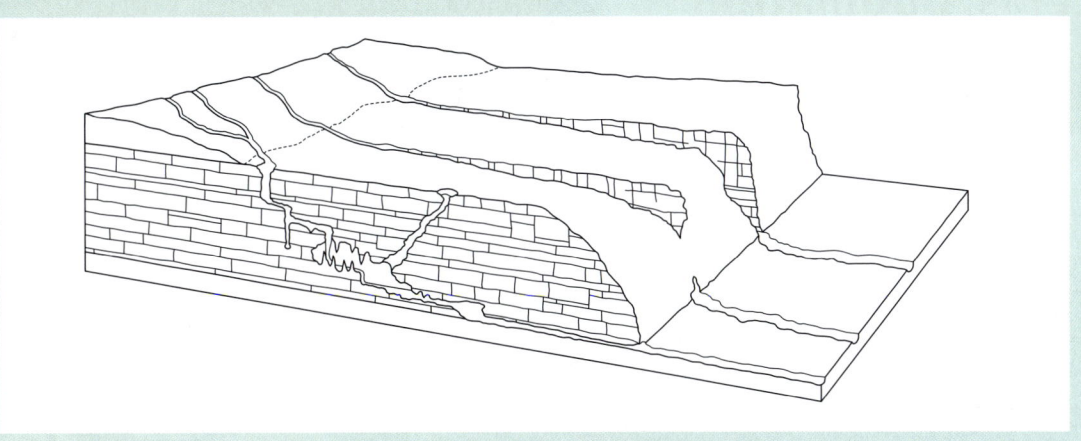

   Add each of these labels in the correct place on your diagram:

cavern	stalactite	limestone pavement	joints
swallow hole	stalagmite	clints	scar
impermeable rock	pillar	grykes	spring

2. As a final review of what you have learned, try this 'odd one out' activity with a partner.

   a Take each set of words A–F in turn and work out which word is the odd one out. Explain why, and what the other three have in common.

Set A:	1	10	13	20
Set B:	6	4	17	22
Set C:	2	3	9	12
Set D:	7	14	18	21
Set E:	11	15	16	23
Set F:	5	8	19	24

1 Limestone	9 Clints	17 Pillar
2 Grykes	10 Granite	18 Swallow hole
3 Scar	11 Malham	19 Fossils
4 Stalactite	12 Pavement	20 Clay
5 Joints	13 Sandstone	21 Gaping Gill
6 Dry valley	14 Spring	22 Stalagmite
7 Sink	15 Ingleborough	23 Dartmoor
8 Calcium carbonate	16 Yorkshire Dales	24 Impermeable

   b Try to use these words to do three more 'odd one out' sets of your own. Try them on your partner.

7 Can the Earth cope?

Ecosystems, population and resources

A Smoke emissions in New Orleans, USA

B The problem of waste: Stockton-on-Tees, UK

C Deforestation in Johor State, Malaysia

D Rock slide following an earthquake, India

E Confiscated ivory being burned in Kenya

Learn about

Can the world cope with its growing population? This unit will help you investigate ecosystems, population and resources, and how they are linked together. You will explore:

- what ecosystems are and where they are found
- how vegetation is related to climate, soil and human activity
- how population and resources are linked
- how a resource can best be managed
- what the future is for global resources.

F Protecting the Earth

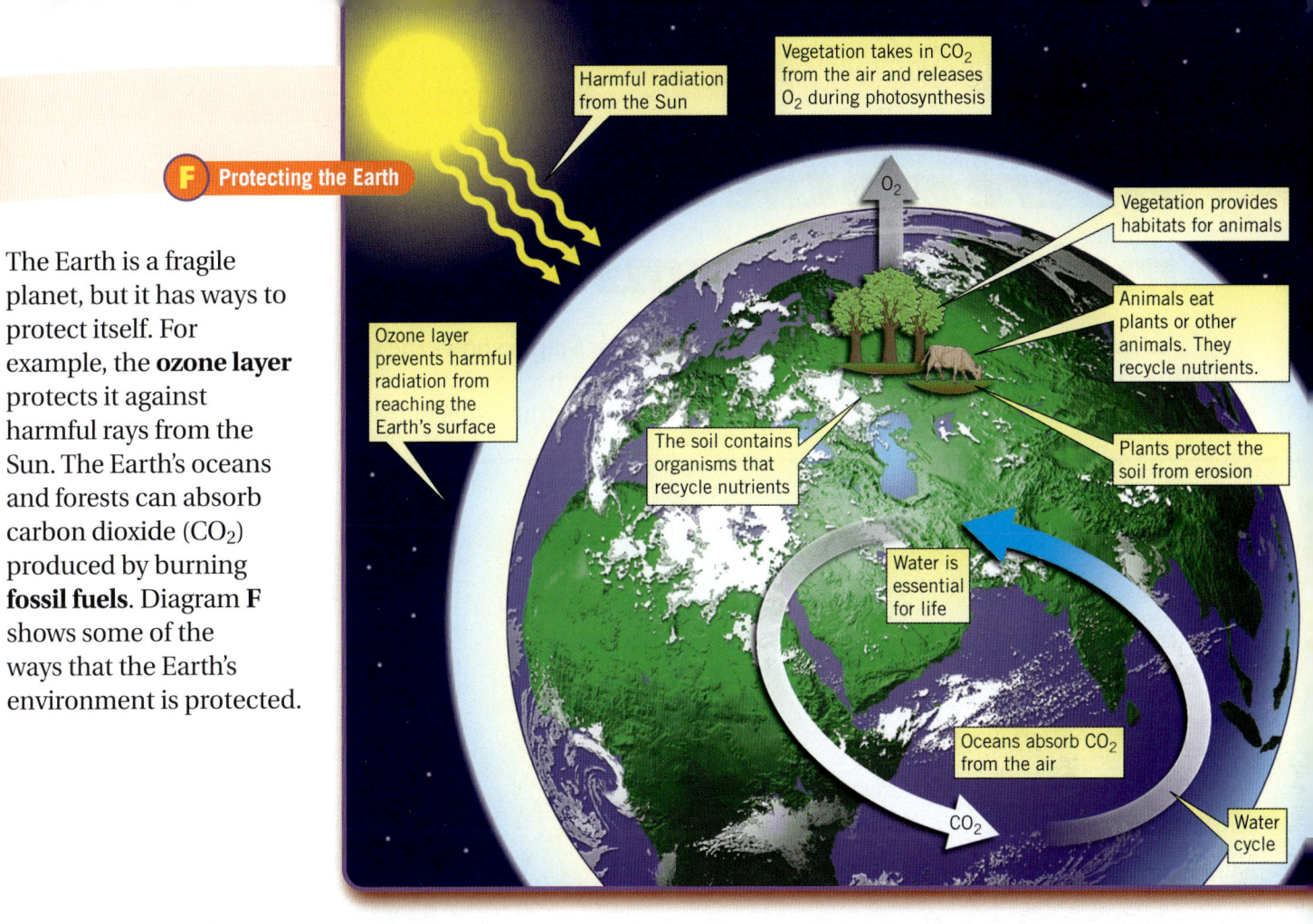

The Earth is a fragile planet, but it has ways to protect itself. For example, the **ozone layer** protects it against harmful rays from the Sun. The Earth's oceans and forests can absorb carbon dioxide (CO_2) produced by burning **fossil fuels**. Diagram **F** shows some of the ways that the Earth's environment is protected.

Diagram F labels:
- Harmful radiation from the Sun
- Vegetation takes in CO_2 from the air and releases O_2 during photosynthesis
- Ozone layer prevents harmful radiation from reaching the Earth's surface
- Vegetation provides habitats for animals
- Animals eat plants or other animals. They recycle nutrients.
- The soil contains organisms that recycle nutrients
- Plants protect the soil from erosion
- Water is essential for life
- Oceans absorb CO_2 from the air
- Water cycle

But can the Earth cope with the increasing pressure of human beings? People need food, clothing, shelter and a huge range of other goods. As the world's population continues to grow, the extra people use up more and more of the Earth's resources.

Activities

1 In a small group, discuss ways that the Earth can protect itself. Make a copy of the table and look at diagram **F**. See if you can add ideas of your own to the table.

Problem	How the Earth's environment is protected
Animals need somewhere to live	vegetation provides habitats for animals
Too much CO_2 in the air	
Harmful radiation from the Sun	
Soil erosion	
The environment needs nutrients	

2 Look at all the photographs. Work out how people are damaging the environment in each picture. Copy and complete this table.

	Photograph	Country	Continent	What is happening to the environment?
Air pollution				
Soil erosion				
Water pollution				
Landscape damage				
Animals endangered				

7 Geography Matters

Where are the Earth's major ecosystems?

The Earth is made up of many different **ecosystems**. Map **A** shows the world distribution of three types of ecosystems: tropical rainforest ecosystems, hot desert ecosystems and coral reef ecosystems. A **biome** is an ecosystem that covers a huge area of the world.

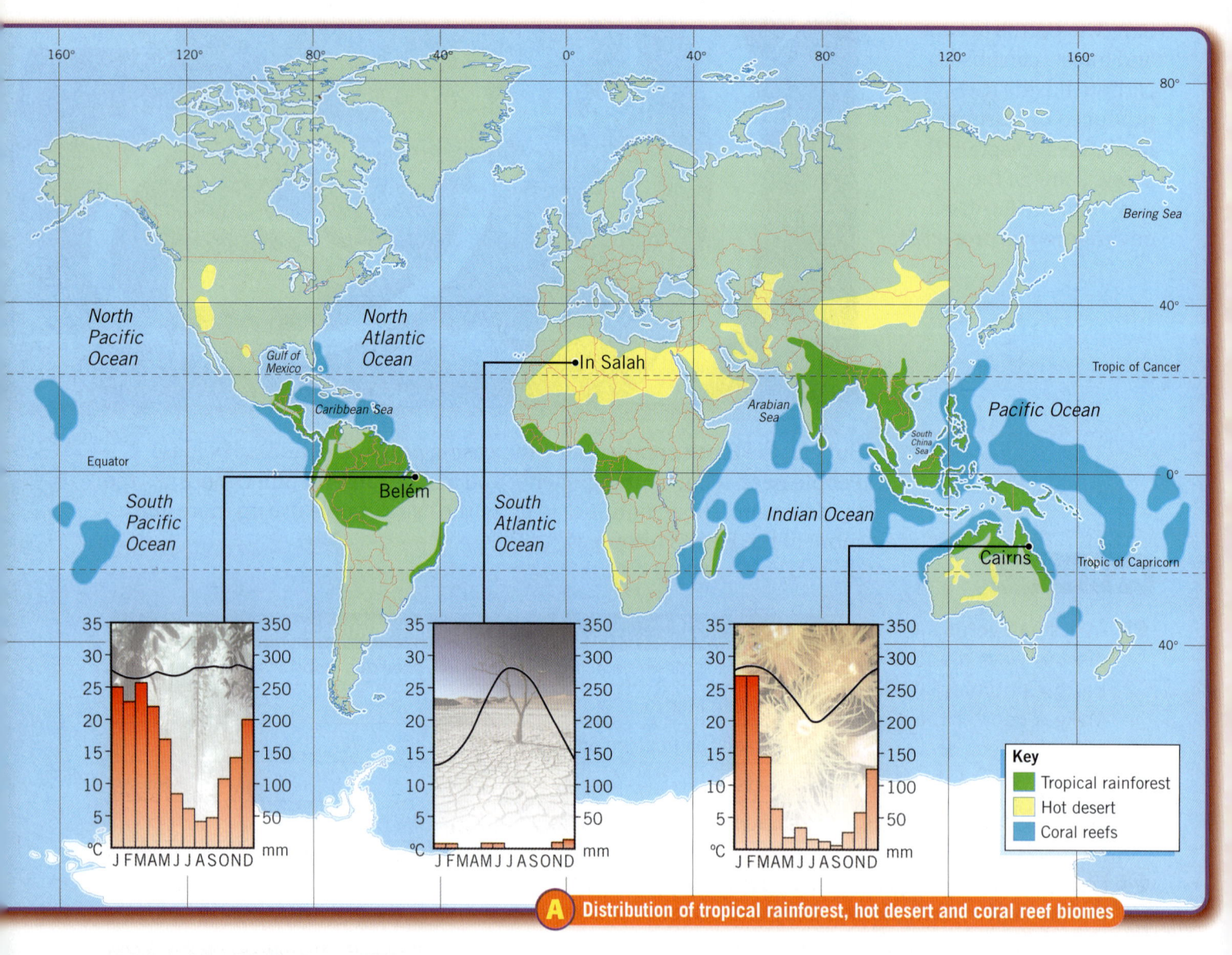

A Distribution of tropical rainforest, hot desert and coral reef biomes

Key:
- Tropical rainforest
- Hot desert
- Coral reefs

Getting Technical

- An **ecosystem** is a community of plants and animals living in an environment. It can be small, like a pond, or huge, like a rainforest. The **flora** (plants), **fauna** (animals), climate and soil of an ecosystem all depend on each other.
- A **biome** is a global scale ecosystem where similar plants grow in different parts of the world.
- A **community** is a group of plants and animals living closely together.

Can the Earth cope?

How does vegetation adapt to its environment?

Plants must **adapt** to their environment or they will die. Diagram **B** shows how the saguaro cactus has adapted to survive in desert conditions.

B Saguaro cactus, Arizona desert

C Mahogany tree in the Amazon rainforest

Desert conditions:
- very little rainfall every year
- heavy rainstorms bring lots of water in short bursts
- hot conditions evaporate water
- wind takes moisture from leaves

Equatorial conditions:
- heavy rain all year
- hot all year
- lots of plants: shortage of sunlight
- thin, poor soil

Activities

1 The saguaro cactus is found in the Arizona desert, in North America.

a Make a large copy of the cactus in diagram **B**.

b The four labels show the ways that the cactus has adapted to its environment.
For each one, explain how it helps the cactus survive in desert conditions.
- The cactus has no leaves because …
- In order to photosynthesize it has a …
- Its roots are … so that …
- Its trunk is …

c Look at map **A**. Name three other places were the desert biome is found.

d Use the graph in **A** to describe the desert climate at different times of the year.

e Some desert plants are different. They are small and have very deep roots. Give two reasons for this.

2 a Make a large copy of the rainforest tree in diagram **C**.

b Find four differences between the tree and the cactus. Give reasons why the mahogany tree has adapted in this way.
- The tree has big leaves so that …
- Another difference is that it … This is because …

c Is there anything similar? Can you suggest why?

7 Geography Matters

How are ecosystems linked to human activity?

An ecosystem is a **community** of plants and animals in one place. Diagram **A** helps you to understand what an ecosystem is and how the four parts of an ecosystem are closely interconnected.

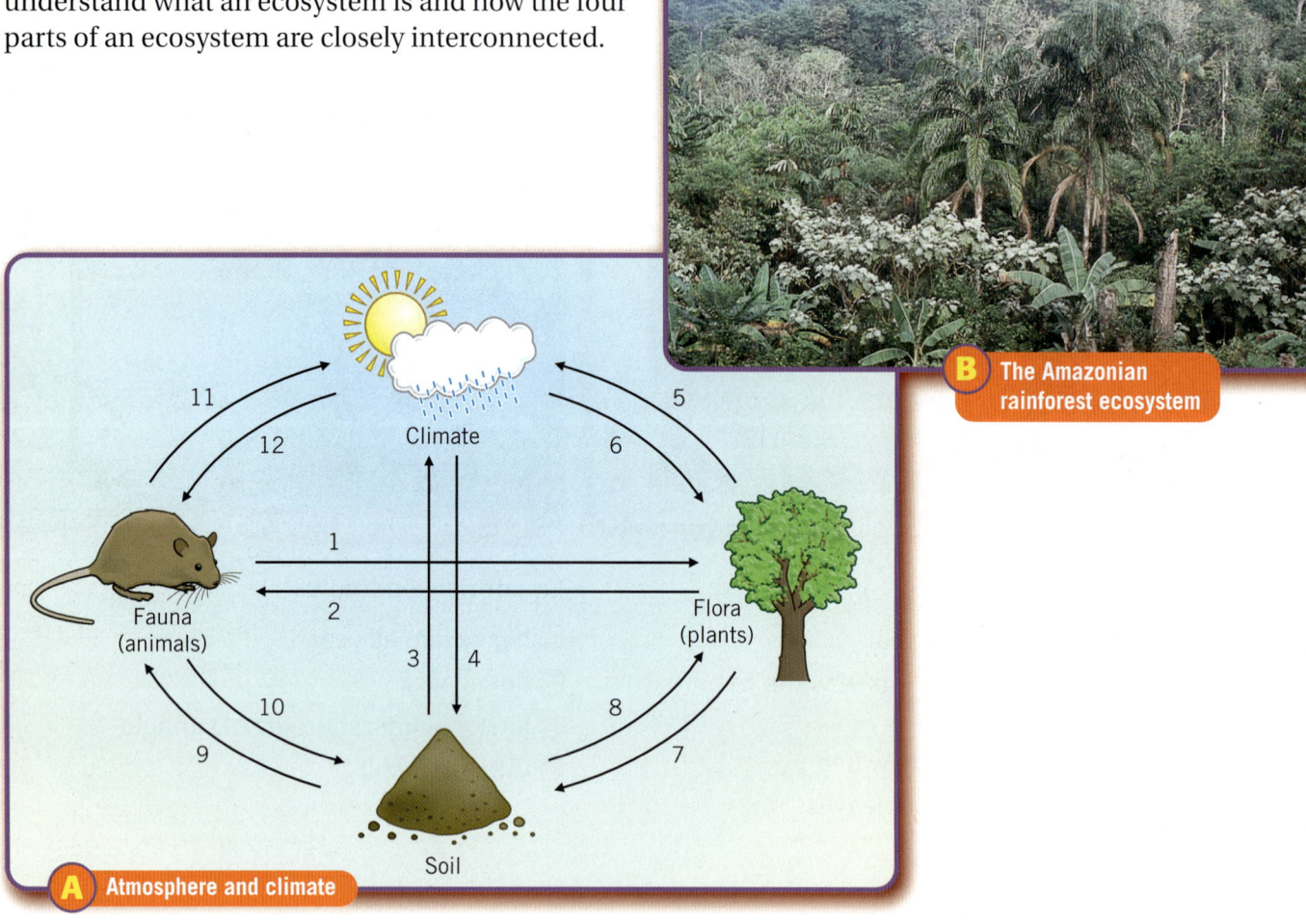

B The Amazonian rainforest ecosystem

A Atmosphere and climate

Human activity has an **impact** on ecosystems. People use natural environments for food, shelter and to extract mineral resources like coal and oil. Some resources are not **renewable** – they will run out. So people have to manage the Earth's resources in a **sustainable** way.

Getting Technical

- **Renewable resource:** a resource which can be used again and again, for example trees, which can be replanted, or wind, which can be used to make electricity.
- **Non-renewable resource:** a resource like minerals or oil, that cannot grow again once it has been used up.
- **Sustainable development:** To be sustainable, we must use renewable resources and then let them grow again. We must also try to recycle non-renewable resources.

Can the Earth cope?

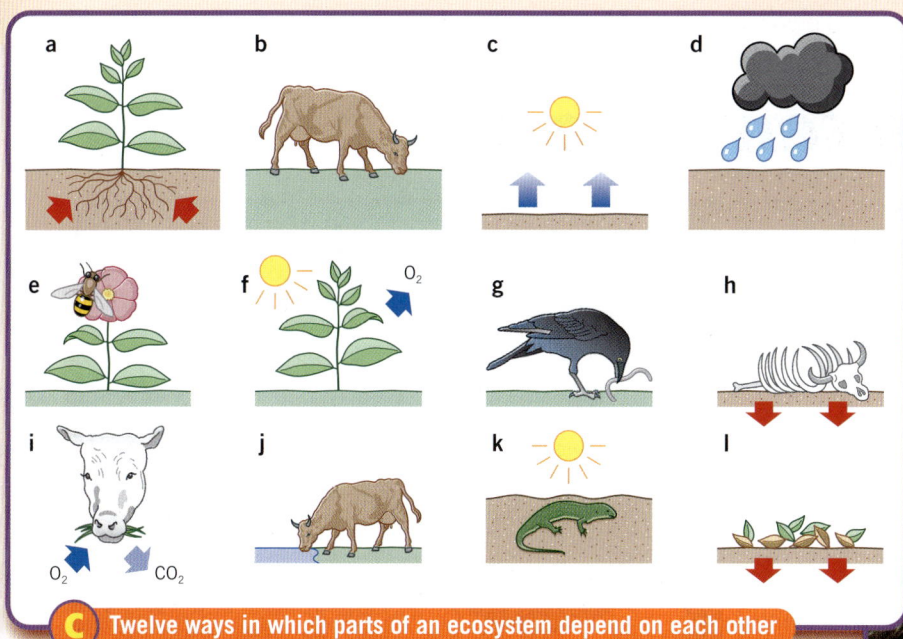

C Twelve ways in which parts of an ecosystem depend on each other

D Human impacts on an ecosystem in Amazonia

Activities

1 a Study diagram **A**. On a sketch of a tropical rainforest, label the four main parts of the ecosystem.

b Add arrows copied from diagram **A** to show how the different parts of the ecosystem are linked.

2 Look at diagram **A** and the sketches in **C**.

a Copy and complete the table below by matching each sketch in **C** with the correct arrow in **A**. Some sketches match two numbers.

Description of the link	Sketch	Arrow
An insect pollinates the flower	e	2
Water evaporates from the soil		
Leaves rot		
Rain falls onto the ground		
Animals breathe out carbon dioxide		
Animals eat plants		
The Sun gives energy to plants		
Plants take up nutrients		
Dead animals decompose		
Plants give out oxygen		
Soil is food for worms		
Reptiles need warmth to survive	k	12

3 Photograph **D** shows the effects of human activity on an ecosystem.

a Work in pairs at first for this activity. First discuss which ecosystem is shown in **D**. Talk about how human activity has changed it. It may help you to write notes on rough paper.

b Use diagram **A** to discuss how changes will affect the fauna, flora, soil and climate in this ecosystem.

For example:

> By cutting down the trees, people have removed protection from the soil. This allows rain to wash the soil away ...

c Write a paragraph to describe and explain the impact people have had on this ecosystem. Include the following information:
- name and location of ecosystem
- the change brought about by human activity
- the effects on fauna (animals)
- the effects on flora (plants)
- the effects on soil
- the effects on climate.

help!

Remember that:
- good descriptions include details or examples
- good explanations say why things change – they use linking words like *why*, *because*, and *so*.

7 Geography Matters

How do ecosystems work?

All living things need energy. Animals such as humans get their energy by eating plants or other animals. Plants can make their own energy from sunlight using their green leaves. This process is called **photosynthesis** (see **A**). Photosynthesis happens faster where there is plenty of sunlight, warmth and water. So plants can grow faster in some parts of the world than in others, and will grow slowly at some times of the year.

Without plants there would be no **food chain** because there would be no energy for other animals to eat. Diagram **B** shows how energy flows through the food chain in an ecosystem.

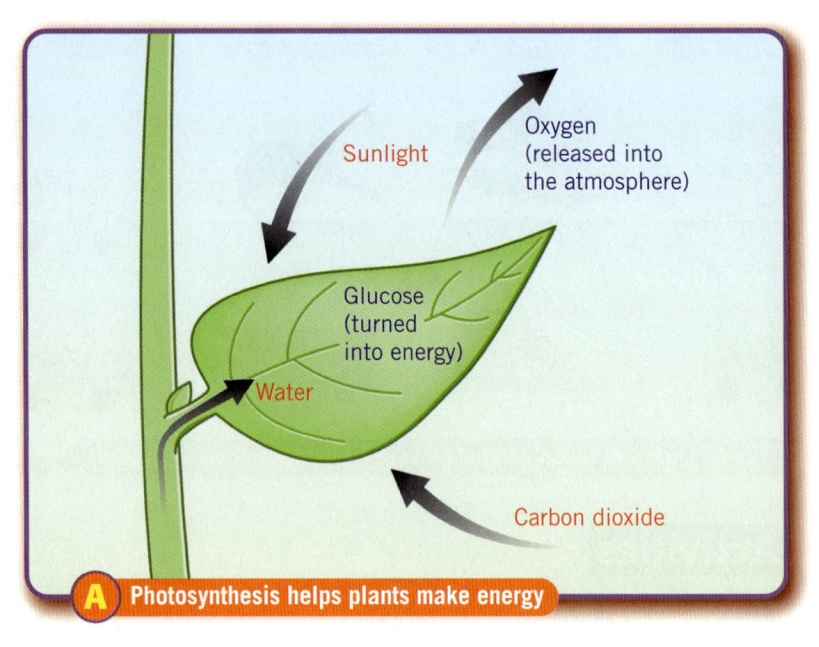

A Photosynthesis helps plants make energy

How nutrients are recycled

Plants and animals need **nutrients** as well as energy. Plants take nutrients like nitrates from the soil through their roots. Nutrients are passed through the food chain and eventually end up back in the soil. Diagram **C** shows how bacteria and fungi help to recycle nutrients back into the soil.

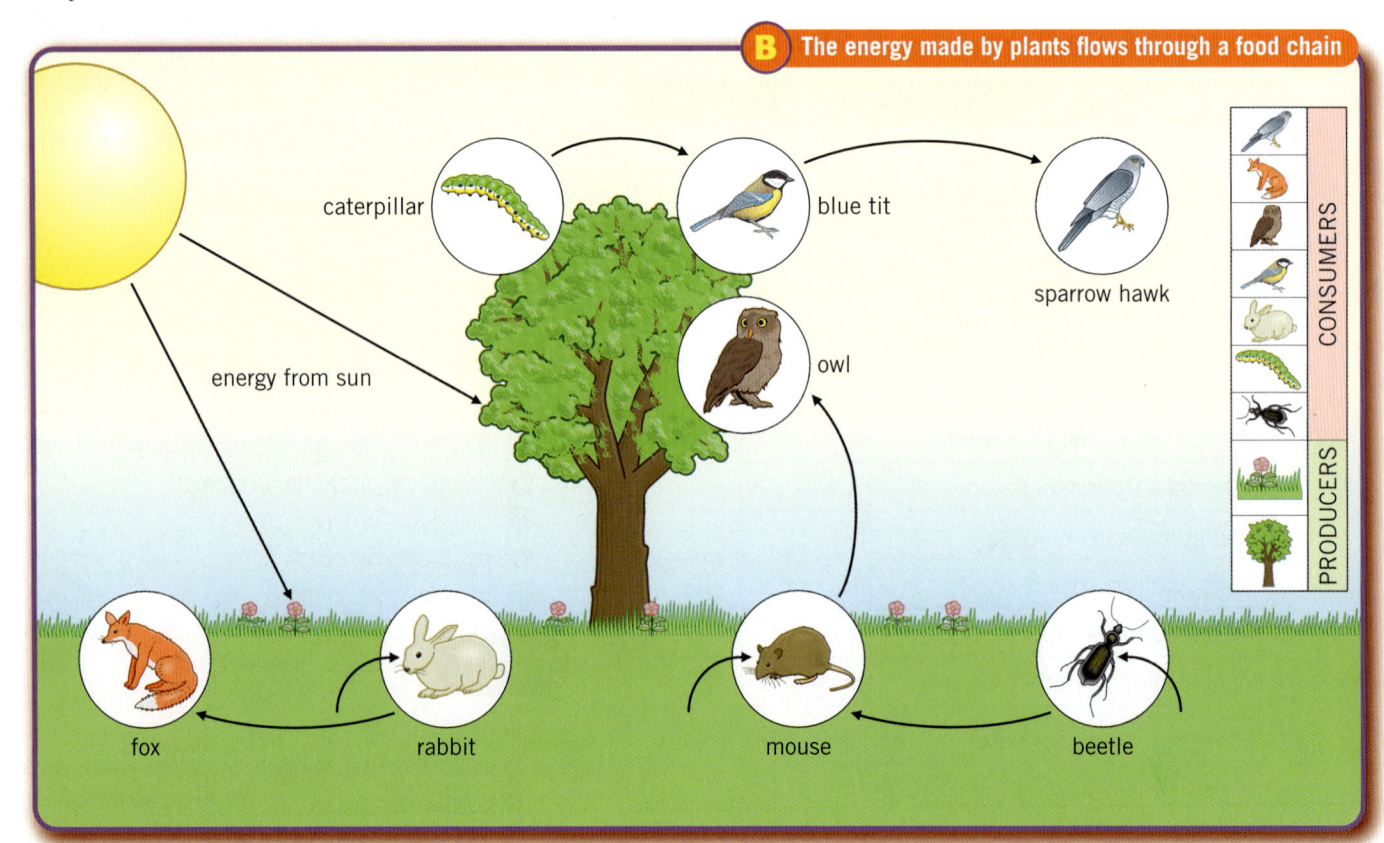

B The energy made by plants flows through a food chain

Can the Earth cope?

C Nutrients are recycled through plants and animals

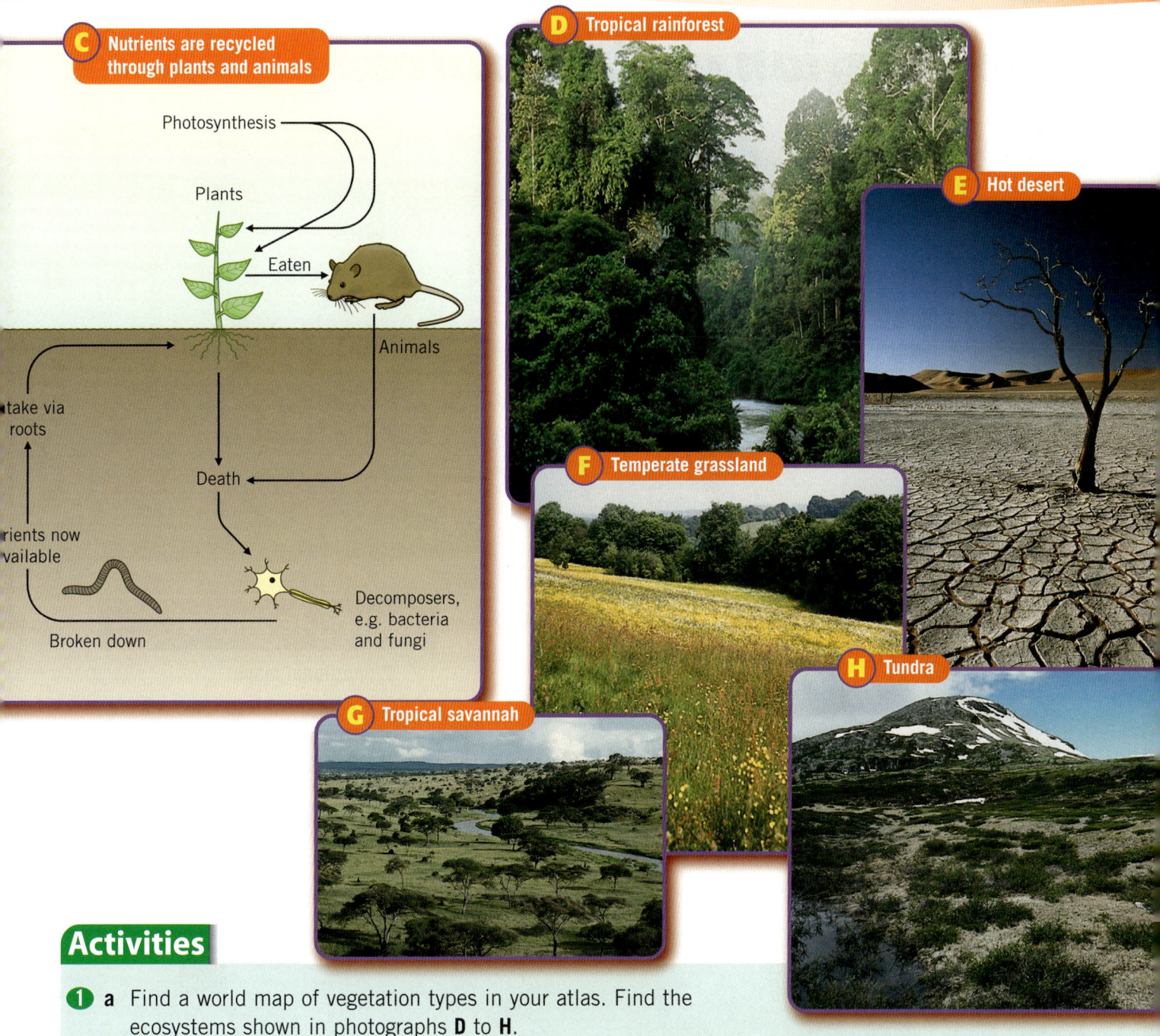

Photosynthesis
Plants
Eaten
Animals
take via roots
Death
rients now available
Broken down
Decomposers, e.g. bacteria and fungi

D Tropical rainforest

E Hot desert

F Temperate grassland

G Tropical savannah

H Tundra

Activities

1. **a** Find a world map of vegetation types in your atlas. Find the ecosystems shown in photographs **D** to **H**.
   b Make a list of the ecosystems. You could set your work out in a table like the one here.
   c Study the photographs and find out about their climates. Decide which ecosystems will have plants that grow fast (a high rate of photosynthesis).
   d Now decide which ecosystems will have plants that grow more slowly or are smaller. Explain your choices.

Ecosystem	Climate	Photosynthesis	Reasons
Tropical rainforest	Hot and wet most of the year	High	High temperatures and rainfall

2. Look at diagram **C**, and ecosystems **D** to **H**. In which one do:
   - Nutrients pass through slowly? Give a reason for your choice.
   - Nutrients pass through quickly? Give a reason for your choice.

3. Check that you understand the definitions of the key words in **bold**, then add them to your geography word bank.

7 Geography Matters

Population and resources

We all need resources to survive, but the Earth's resources are not shared out evenly between people in different parts of the world. For example, the richest 20 per cent of the world's population use 80 per cent of the resources.

One reason is that some parts of the world have more natural resources than others.

Another is that rich countries can buy the resources they need. For example, Japan has few natural resources of its own, but is rich enough to buy resources from poorer countries.

The USA uses more of the Earth's resources than any other country. Unlike Japan, it has many resources of its own.

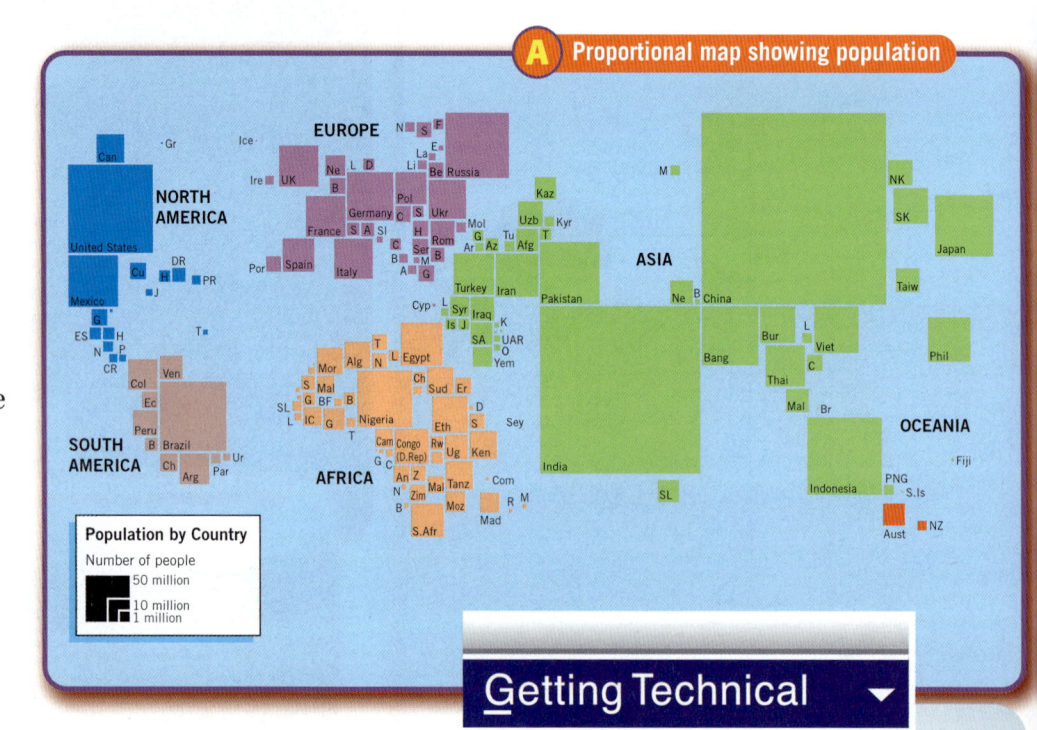

A Proportional map showing population

Getting Technical

Proportional maps

A **proportional map** uses a value, such as GNP, to map the world, rather than land area. So Switzerland, which looks small on a traditional map, looks big because it has a high GNP.

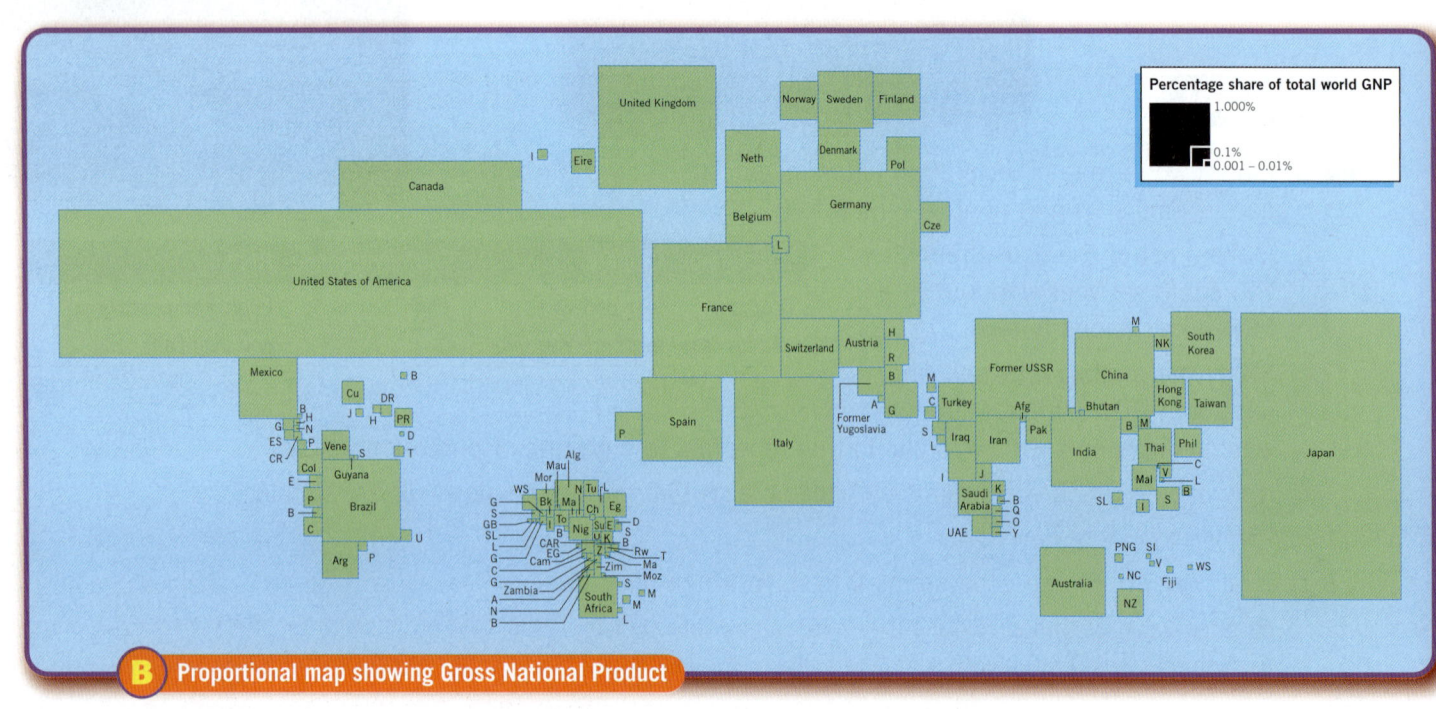

B Proportional map showing Gross National Product

Can the Earth cope?

C Natural resources: minerals

Key
- ▽ Gold
- ⌂ Silver
- ◇ Diamonds
- ● Iron
- ■ Nickel
- ⌐ Chrome
- ▲ Manganese
- ☐ Cobalt
- ▽ Tungsten
- ☐ Copper
- ▲ Lead
- ● Aluminium
- ▽ Tin
- ◆ Zinc
- ⌐ Mercury

Equator

help!

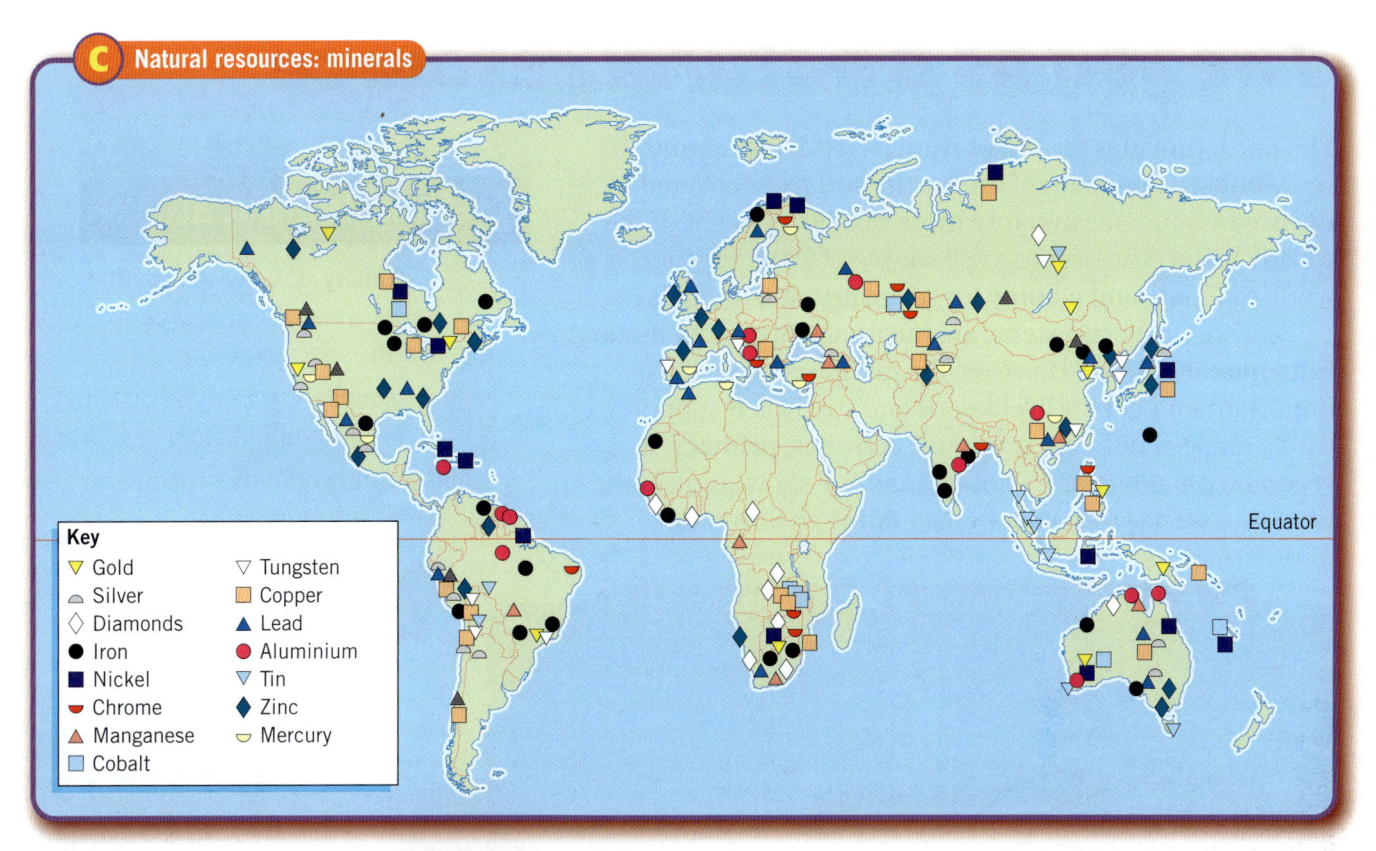

Natural resources include:
- minerals
- wool and cotton
- wood
- rubber
- oil (used to make plastics)
- clay

Activities

1 In pairs, choose ten objects in your classroom. List the natural resources that were used to make them. Discuss which resources are **renewable** and which are **non-renewable**. Colour code your list into these two groups.

2 Look at maps **A** and **B**. Now match the heads to the correct tails:

a wealthy region of the world with a high population	Australia
a poor region of the world with a high population	USA
a poor region of the world with a low population	Tanzania
a wealthy part of the world with a low population.	India

3 Work in pairs or groups of three and use maps **A**, **B** and **C**.

  a Each choose an important resource from map **C** and explain why it is useful. Then answer these questions.
  - Which continents or countries is it mainly found in?
  - Which parts of the world lack the resource?
  - Is the resource found in parts of the world where many people live?
  - Is the resource found in parts of the world which have a high, medium or low GNP?

  b Compare your results with those of your partner. What are the main similarities and differences between the resources?

4 Add the key words in **bold** on these two pages to your word bank.

115

7 Geography Matters

The sea as a natural resource

The Earth provides resources from its land, the air and the sea. Almost 71 per cent of the Earth's surface is covered by the oceans, and oceans store more than 97 per cent of the world's water. The oceans are a source of water for the world's climate and a home for sea plants and animals.

Marine (sea) ecosystems are fragile and are under threat from human activity. However, the marine ecosystem is important for people's livelihoods and survival. It supports a whole range of different economic activities: **primary**, **secondary** and **tertiary**. Photographs **A–F** show some of the ways that we use resources in the marine environment.

Getting Technical

- A **primary** activity is one that takes a natural resource from the Earth.
- A **secondary** activity is one that makes a product from resources.
- A **tertiary** activity provides a service to people.

A People enjoying the seaside at South Bay, Scarborough, UK

B Fishing trawler, Bering Sea

C Japanese whaling in the Southern Ocean

D An oil rig in the North Sea

116

E Diving off the coast of Kenya

F Fish grading in Orkney, Scotland

Can the Earth cope?

Activities

1 a With a partner, study photographs **A** to **F**, then discuss the different ways they show people using the sea as a resource.

b Copy the table below. For each photograph, describe at least one way in which the sea is being used.

c Decide whether each activity is primary, secondary or tertiary, then add an explanation to your table. One example has been done for you.

hint

Be careful – there may not be a simple answer for some of these photographs. It all depends on the reason you give.

Photograph	Location	How the sea is used as a resource	Primary, secondary or tertiary activity
F	Scotland	The photo shows the sea is being used as a source of food for people.	This is a secondary activity because the fish will be made into products like fish cakes.

2 a Work in pairs. Choose three of the photographs you have investigated. Work out ways in which the activities they show may have an impact on the marine ecosystem. Share your ideas with another pair.

b Using the photographs to help you, list the ways you or your families use the sea as a resource. Are there any links between your use of the resources and impacts on the environment?

3 Below are examples of resource chains. Copy and complete the table. Use the photographs to help complete the two resource chains that start in the marine environment. You may be able to think of some more.

Resource	Primary activity	Secondary activity	Tertiary activity	Consumer
fish	fishing boat	fish finger factory	shop	people eating fish
		oil refinery		

117

7 Geography Matters

Threats to marine ecosystems

Over time, seas and oceans have become polluted as a result of human activities. Waste is dumped straight into the sea, flows into seas from rivers, or falls from the atmosphere. Table **A** shows the main sources of marine pollution.

Source		Pollutants	Percentage of total
Atmosphere		Particles blown by the wind, and gases from industry and vehicles	33%
Run-off and discharges from the land		Sewage and waste from farms and industry	44%
Ships		Oil spills and leaks, and cargo spills	12%
Dumping at sea		Waste from dredging, sewage sludge, and ships' rubbish	10%
Offshore oil and gas production		Waste from oil and gas drilling	1%

A Sources of marine pollution

People often think that oil spills are the most serious form of marine pollution. When an oil spill happens, it can be a disaster for the marine environment. However, everyday pollution is more of a problem, and is difficult to stop.

The oil industry

Oil is one of the Earth's most valuable resources. **Crude oil** was formed millions of years ago and it is a **non-renewable** resource. It is found in some rocks beneath the land and the sea.

Once it has been extracted from the rocks, we transport oil across the sea by pipelines and huge tankers. Map **C** shows the world's major oilfields and the main transport routes. Transporting oil can be a risky business. Diagram **B** shows how oil can affect the marine ecosystem.

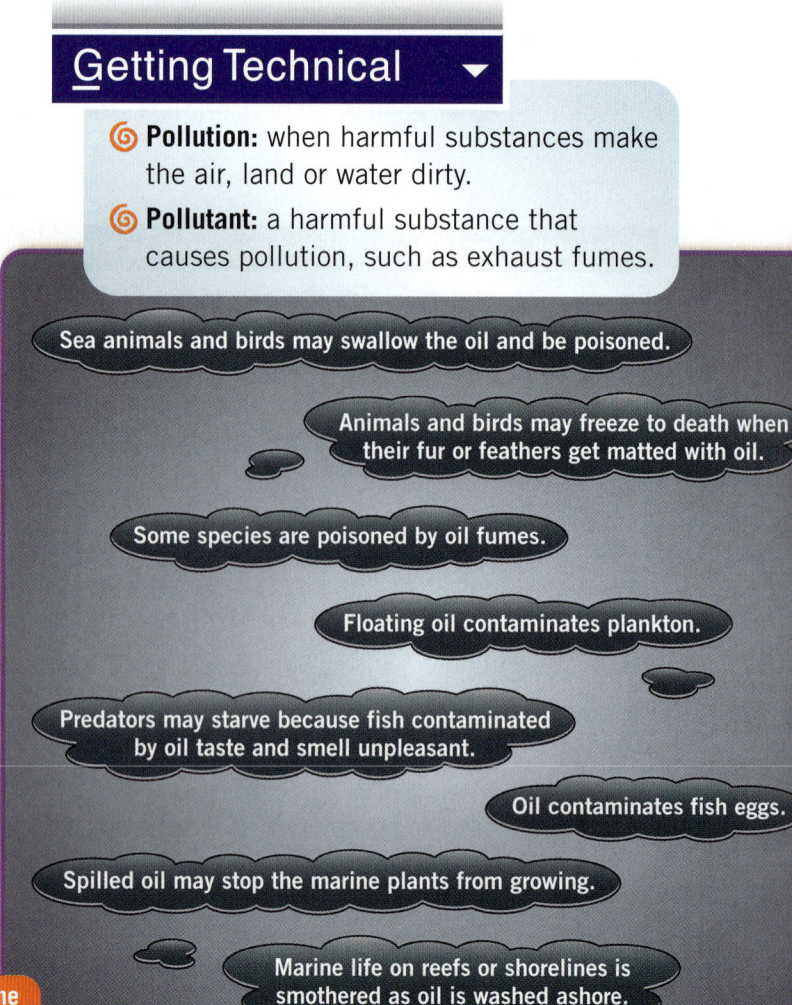

Getting Technical

- **Pollution:** when harmful substances make the air, land or water dirty.
- **Pollutant:** a harmful substance that causes pollution, such as exhaust fumes.

- Sea animals and birds may swallow the oil and be poisoned.
- Animals and birds may freeze to death when their fur or feathers get matted with oil.
- Some species are poisoned by oil fumes.
- Floating oil contaminates plankton.
- Predators may starve because fish contaminated by oil taste and smell unpleasant.
- Oil contaminates fish eggs.
- Spilled oil may stop the marine plants from growing.
- Marine life on reefs or shorelines is smothered as oil is washed ashore.

B Effects of oil on the marine ecosystem

Can the Earth cope?

Key
- Oilfields on land
- Offshore oilfields
- Most polluted seas
- Transport of oil by tanker

C Oil production and transport both use seas and oceans

Activities

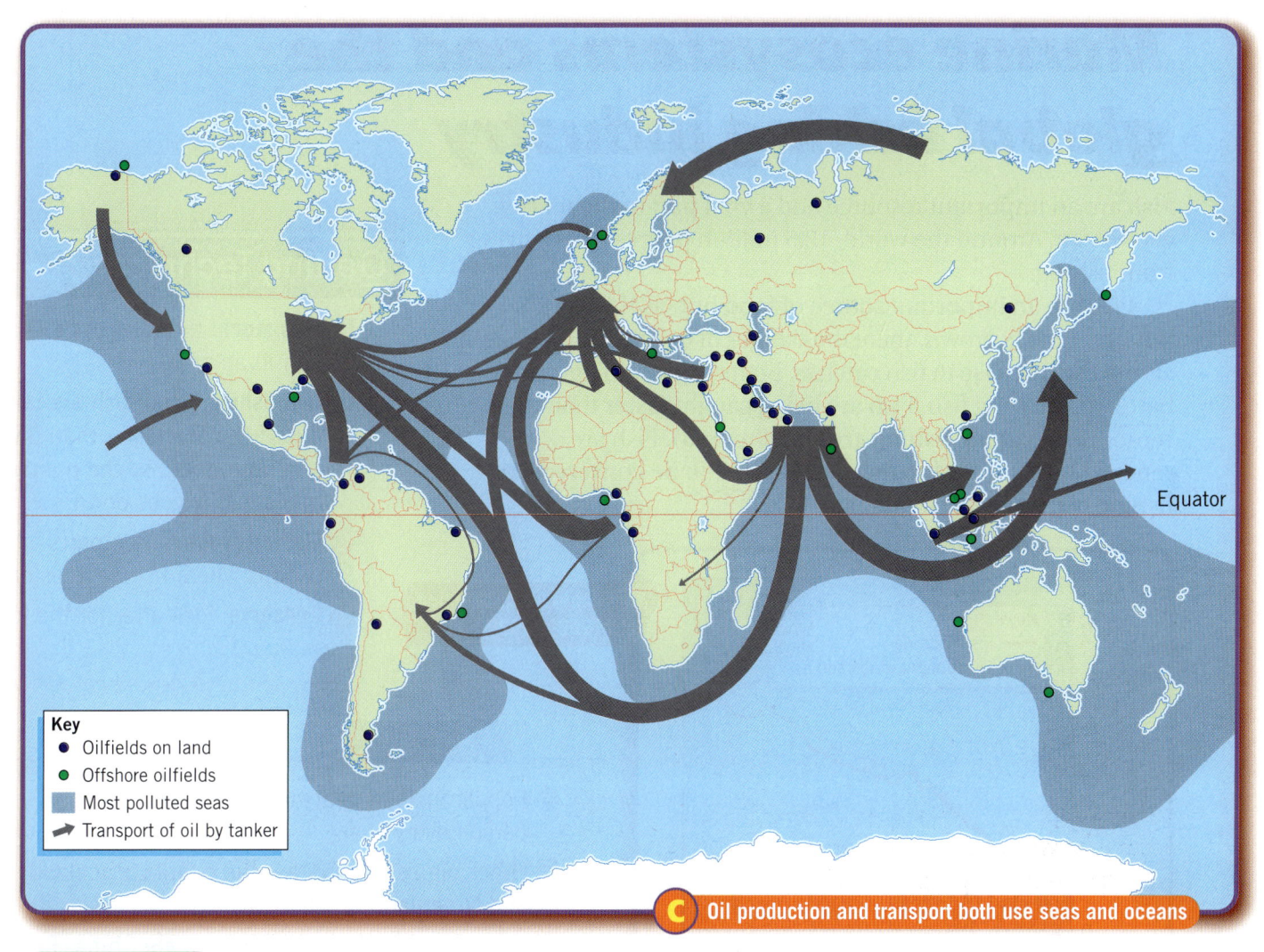

1. Draw a pie chart to show the data in table **A**. Add a title and a key. The 'How to...' box on page 133 will help you.

2. Look at map **C** and use an atlas to answer these questions.

   a Put these places in the correct column in the table below:
   - Europe
   - The Middle East
   - West Africa
   - Japan
   - USA

Big producers of oil	Big consumers of oil

   b Name two places where oilfields are in the sea.

   c Name two seas or oceans that are most at risk from oil spills.

3. Study diagram **B**, which shows the impact of oil on a marine ecosystem.

   a Choose the impact that you think would affect the marine ecosystem most quickly. Explain your choice.

   b Which of the impacts do you think would take the longest to affect the marine ecosystem?

4. Map **C** also shows the most polluted seas in the world. Use table **A** and your answers to question 2.

   a Explain why pollution is worse in some places than others.

   b Is it worse if the middle or the edge of the oceans are polluted? Explain your answer carefully.

7 Geography Matters

Marine ecosystems and the global fishing industry

Fish are an important resource and a vital part of the marine ecosystem. Around the world, 12.5 million people earn a living from fishing.

Fish are an important source of food but, as the world's population has grown, there is a danger of **overfishing**. Graph **A** shows the increase in fish catches. Boats are now bigger and better at catching fish. Fish are being caught faster than they can reproduce in many **fishing grounds** (map **B**). Fish are a renewable resource, but **fish stocks** need to be conserved, or fishing will not be sustainable.

Getting Technical

- **Fish stock:** the total number of fish in an area
- **Overfishing:** when fish are taken out of the sea faster than they can reproduce, so the number of fish steadily goes down
- **Fishing grounds:** the parts of the oceans where fishing goes on
- **Conserve:** look after for the future.

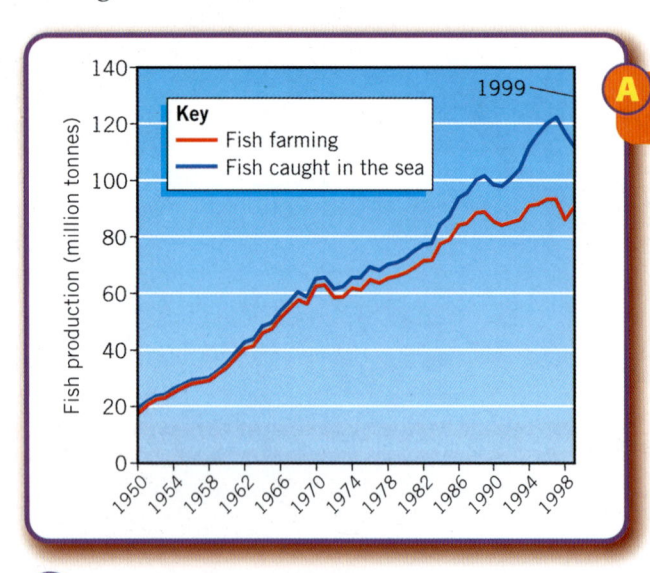

A World fish production, 1950–1999

Fact file

- People in Japan eat the most fish: 72 kg per person every year.
- Other big fish-eaters are the people of Iceland and Greenland.
- The four biggest fishing nations are China, Peru, Chile and Japan. They take 42 per cent of the world's fishing catch.

B The world's fishing grounds

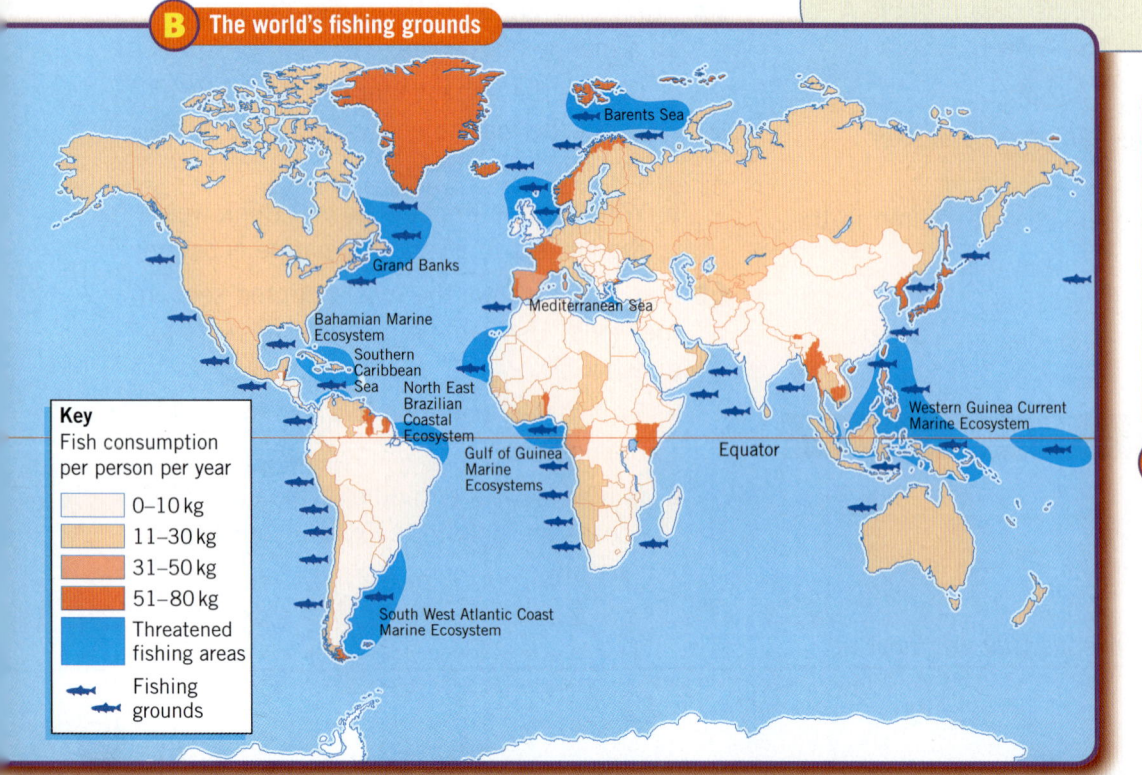

Key — Fish consumption per person per year
- 0–10 kg
- 11–30 kg
- 31–50 kg
- 51–80 kg
- Threatened fishing areas
- Fishing grounds

Ocean	Fish catch in million tonnes
North Atlantic	21
South Atlantic	4
Indian	8
Western Pacific	34.3
Eastern Pacific	18.9

C The world fish catch, 1997

Can the Earth cope?

Traditional types of fishing, like **D**, often fish quite close to land. They provide many jobs for local people. The boats or nets are too small to catch too many fish, so overfishing is not a problem.

Huge modern factory ships, like the one in **E**, use electronic equipment to find fish. They can travel to distant seas and use massive nets to catch fish. The fish catch can be processed and frozen on board. The boats are expensive, so they must catch a lot of fish.

Fish farms, like **F**, are set up to breed fish. They are specially fed so they grow fast. When they are big enough, they are easy to catch. Waste from fish farms is a problem because it pollutes the surrounding water.

D Traditional fishing in Kerala, India

E Processing fish aboard a trawler in the Bering Sea

F Salmon farm in Dover, Tasmania

Activities

1 a Use the figures in table **C** and an outline map of the world. Draw a bar graph to show the weight of fish caught in each ocean.

  b Shade your map to show the endangered fishing grounds.

  c Label the information in the fact file onto your map.

2 a Compare the three types of fishing on this page. Complete the table below. Try to use the following words in your answer.
- expensive/cheap
- sustainable/unsustainable
- polluted/clean
- easy/difficult

	Advantages	Disadvantages
Traditional fishing boats		
Large factory ships		
Fish farming		

  b On balance, which type of fishing is best for:
- the environment
- the people who catch the fish?

3 Using your work from activities **1** and **2**, write a short summary to explain what you have learned about the problem of overfishing. Use this framework to help you:

Although fish is a renewable resource, overfishing is a serious problem. Overfishing is when fish stocks ...

It is a problem now because fishing boats ...

The threatened fishing grounds are in places such as ... This is because ...

There are several ways to make fishing sustainable in future such as ...

121

7 Geography Matters

Case Study
Overfishing in the North Sea

The North Sea is suffering from overfishing. The World Wide Fund for Nature (WWF) say that in some places cod is an **endangered species**.

This is because most of the big fish have been caught, so fishermen now catch smaller and younger fish. Eighty per cent of the cod they catch are too young to breed so there will be even fewer cod in future.

A The North Sea

The European Union
Most countries around the North Sea are in the European Union (EU). The EU has a difficult job; it has to:

- be fair to the fishermen from each country
- make sure that fishing is sustainable
- keep people supplied with fish.

There are so few mackerel it is not worth fishermen leaving port. Herring are now recovering after numbers went so low in 1995 that fishing for them was banned. Cod, haddock, plaice and prawns are heading the same way. However, this does not have to be the case. During the First and Second World Wars no fishing took place in the North Sea. For five years after the wars finished, all fish species saw healthy recoveries. This could happen again!

B The views of Amy Chang, North Sea environmentalist

Even before the fishing ban, we were struggling to make ends meet. I understand the need for conservation, but I need to catch 170 tonnes of cod a year to make a profit. Three years ago I invested £250 000 in my trawler, but our catches have gone down for the past two years. I now travel further in search of fishing grounds where I am allowed to fish, towards the coast of Holland. This will increase my costs and I'll have to be out at sea longer. This ban is too harsh and the government should compensate us.

C Sam Douglas, fisherman from the Port of Grimsby

Can the Earth cope?

Saving the cod

Ban on North Sea cod fishing – 24 January 2001

THE EUROPEAN COMMISSION announces that 100 000 square kilometres of the North Sea, almost 20 per cent of its entire area, will be out of bounds to boats fishing for cod, haddock, and whiting. This is a desperate attempt to ensure that there will be cod left in the North Sea next year.

The UK will be worst affected by the ban since it has the longest coastline bordering the North Sea. Britain also has a long tradition of cod fishing – British people eat one-third of the world's cod catch.

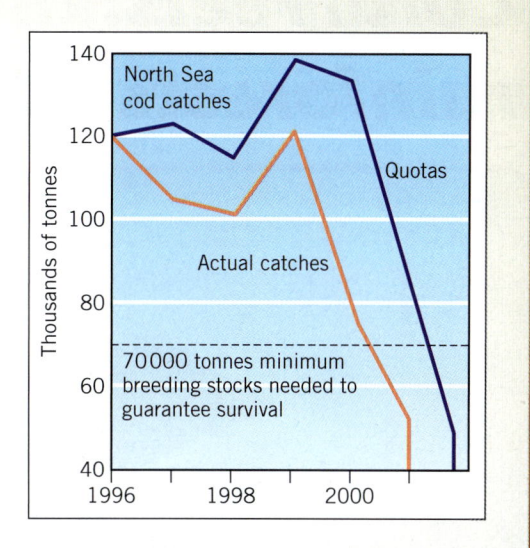

D

Graph showing North Sea cod catches (Thousands of tonnes) from 1996 to 2000, with lines for Quotas and Actual catches, and a dashed line at 70 000 tonnes minimum breeding stocks needed to guarantee survival.

Conservation choices

Most people think conserving fish is a good idea, but it means making difficult decisions. These affect everybody who catches, processes or eats fish. The decisions also affect the future of the whole marine ecosystem. Ideas for conservation include:

- banning fishing from some areas of the North Sea
- a **quota** (limit) on the amount of fish that people can catch
- paying fishermen to scrap older boats
- limiting the number of days that fishermen can go fishing.

Activities

1 List the countries that border the North Sea which might want to fish there.

2 Look at figure **D**.
   a Describe what the graph tells you about changes in North Sea cod catches.
   b When was the last time fishermen matched the quota set by the EU? What does this tell you about cod numbers in the North Sea?

3 a Work in pairs. Make a list of the ideas for conservation in the North Sea, then explain how they would work. Make notes in a table like the one below.

Conservation ideas	How they would work	Ranking	Ranking
Banning fishing from some areas	This would help conserve fish because ...		

   b Decide which you think would be the best idea from the point of view of fishermen. Use a blue pen and rank this idea 1, then the next best 2, and so on.
   c Decide which you think would be the best idea from the point of view of the environmentalist. Use a green pen, and rank this idea 1, then the next best 2, and so on.
   d Make a short presentation to explain *your* point of view. Include any ideas of your own.

7 Geography Matters

Coral reefs: the 'tropical rainforests' of the sea

A Aerial view of Kuata Island, south west of Fiji

B Stone coral

Coral reefs are one of the most important ecosystems in the world. They are home to huge numbers of different fauna and flora. Although coral reefs cover less than 1 per cent of the Earth's surface, over 25 per cent of all ocean fish live there.

What is a coral reef?

A coral reef is made up of millions of coral polyps. These are tiny animals that contain plants called algae. The algae use photosynthesis to convert sunlight into energy. The algae are very colourful and make beautiful reefs.

Over thousands of years the coral polyps build up to make massive reefs of calcium carbonate like the Great Barrier Reef in Australia.

Getting Technical

Biodiversity: the number of different species of plants and animals in an ecosystem. Human activity has reduced the world's biodiversity, with some species of plants and animals becoming extinct.

E Conditions that encourage coral growth

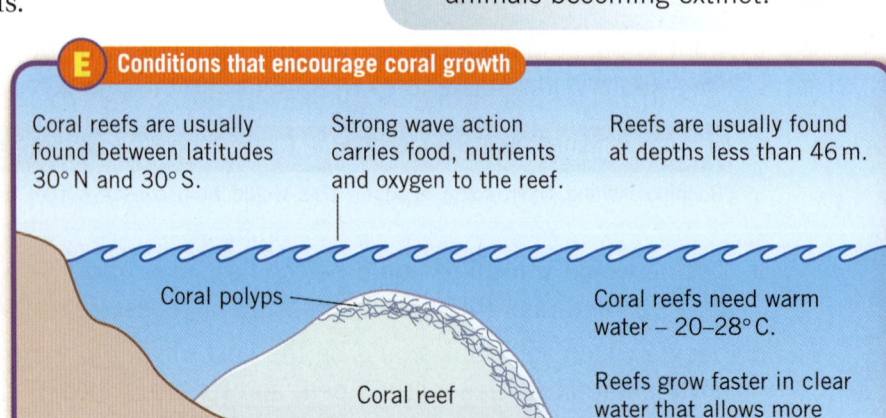

Coral reefs are usually found between latitudes 30° N and 30° S.

Strong wave action carries food, nutrients and oxygen to the reef.

Reefs are usually found at depths less than 46 m.

Coral polyps

Coral reef

Coral reefs need warm water – 20–28° C.

Reefs grow faster in clear water that allows more sunlight to penetrate.

Can the Earth cope?

C Coral reefs are rich in plant and animal life

D The world's coral reefs

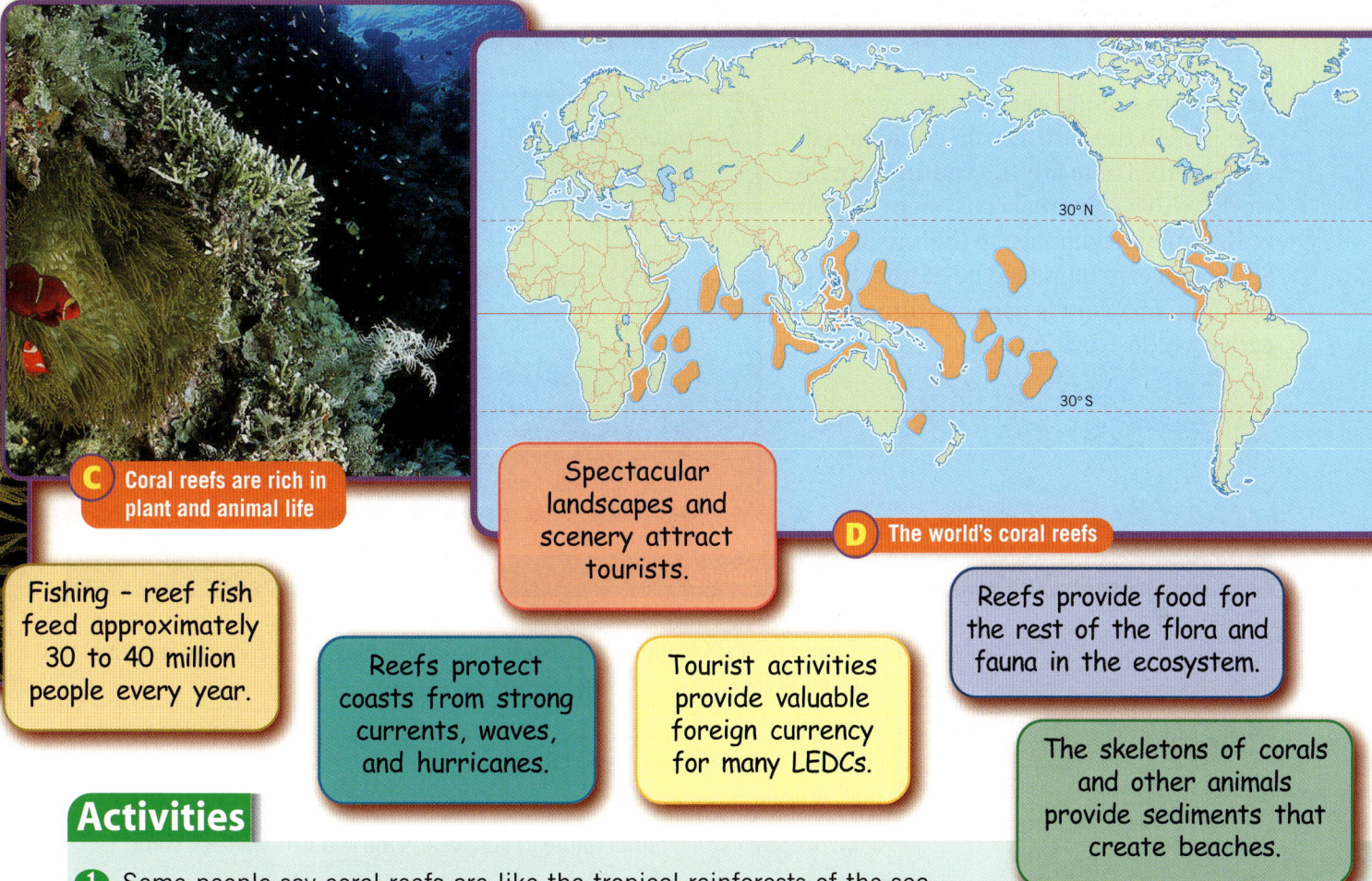

Fishing - reef fish feed approximately 30 to 40 million people every year.

Spectacular landscapes and scenery attract tourists.

Reefs protect coasts from strong currents, waves, and hurricanes.

Tourist activities provide valuable foreign currency for many LEDCs.

Reefs provide food for the rest of the flora and fauna in the ecosystem.

The skeletons of corals and other animals provide sediments that create beaches.

Activities

1 Some people say coral reefs are like the tropical rainforests of the sea.

  a Make a copy of the table below. Then put each of the words and phrases beneath the table in the correct column. The information on pages 75 and 108 may help you.

Coral reefs only	Tropical rainforests only	Both coral reefs and tropical rainforests

- Located within the tropics
- Colourful
- Rich in animal and plant life
- Create spectacular scenery
- Take many years to grow and mature
- Use photosynthesis to make energy
- Are under threat from human activity
- Provide work for local people
- Protect the soil
- Shelter fish
- Easy to find out about in newspapers, magazines, and on TV.

  b Which, if any, did you find difficult to place in your table? Briefly explain your answer.

  c Think of some words and phrases of your own to add to your table.

  d Do you think that 'tropical rainforests of the sea' is a helpful description of coral reefs?

2 Using the Internet and other sources, collect information on different coral reefs around the world. Compare them by completing a table like the one below. You could add columns of your own to this table. You can find a useful website is at http://www.heinemann.co.uk/hotlinks (insert code 1631P) **ICT**

Location of coral reef	Main features / Description of coral reef	Main threats to the coral reef

7 Geography Matters

Coral reefs under threat

As we have seen, coral reefs are very special, but they are also an endangered ecosystem. There are 109 countries in the world with a coral reef ecosystem and 93 of these report damage to their reefs. Some reefs are damaged by nature, but the main problem is people. Human activity is destroying coral.

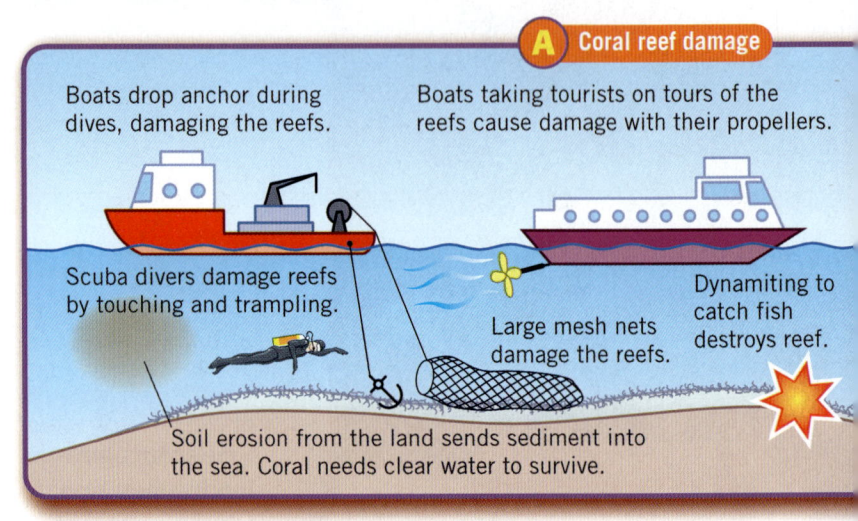

A Coral reef damage

- Boats drop anchor during dives, damaging the reefs.
- Boats taking tourists on tours of the reefs cause damage with their propellers.
- Scuba divers damage reefs by touching and trampling.
- Large mesh nets damage the reefs.
- Dynamiting to catch fish destroys reef.
- Soil erosion from the land sends sediment into the sea. Coral needs clear water to survive.

Natural threat to coral reef	What's the problem?
Storms	Storm waves can destroy fragile coral, and sediment can cover the living plants so they cannot photosynthesise. Hurricanes are getting more common as global warming increases.
Rising sea level	Sea levels have risen nearly 25 cm over the last century, and will contine to rise in future. As the sea level rises, the coral gets deeper. Slow-growing coral needs shallow water to survive.
Warmer sea	Coral needs a certain temperature to survive. As the sea gets warmer, some coral dies.

B Natural threats to coral reefs

Coral reefs – a magnet for tourism

Tourism is the world's fastest growing industry. The sheer beauty of coral reefs attracts tourists to places like the Caribbean. One hundred million people go on holiday to the Caribbean every year, earning 40 per cent of the region's Gross National Product (GNP).

Scuba diving is getting more popular and allows the tourist to get a close look at the colourful coral reefs and their diverse marine life. Unfortunately, it can also damage coral reef ecosystems.

C The Caribbean region

Can the Earth cope?

Tourist activity	Damage caused
Scuba diving	Divers can damage the delicate coral reef ecosystems.
Snorkelling	Inexperienced snorkellers can trample coral with their flippers, by getting too close or resting on the reef. They often do not realise the damage they cause.
Boat trips	Cruises taking visitors out to the reefs are often careless where they drop anchor.
Boat trips	The water movement caused by boats travelling too fast or too close damages coral reefs.
Boat hire	Tourists do not know the local waters and can run aground on a reef.

D Direct impacts of tourism on coral reef ecosystems

Curaçao

E Curaçao

Curaçao may be a tourist paradise, but it is a conservationist's nightmare. Today, few tourists in the Caribbean stop here. But if tourist development is not carefully managed it could become yet another tropical island swamped by hotel chains and wealthy western tourists.

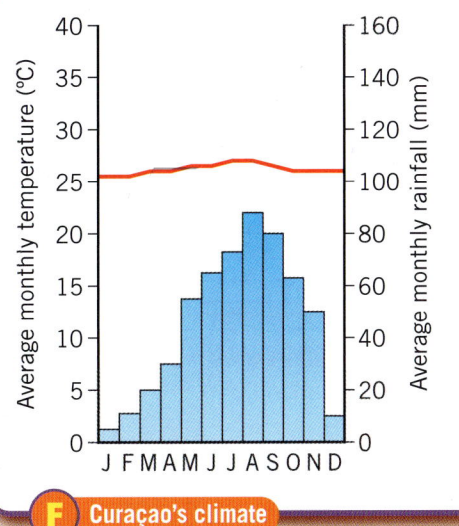

F Curaçao's climate

Activities

1. Imagine that you are planning a holiday to Curaçao. Use the information on these pages and an atlas to help you plan your trip.
   a Describe the location of Curaçao.
   b Use climate graph **F** to write a short description of the climate of Curaçao. Suggest a good time of year to visit the island.
   c Study map **E**. Which part of the island do you think has more tourist development – the east or west coast? Explain your reasons.
   d Write a postcard home describing your time on the island: http://www.heinemann.co.uk/hotlinks (insert code 1631P) will help you add more detail.

2. Table **D** shows the direct impacts tourists can have on coral reefs. Use the following phrases to produce a similar table showing the indirect impacts tourism may have on coral reefs.
   - Solid waste disposal from cruise boats
   - Pollution from coastal tourism development
   - Overfishing the reefs to feed the increasing number of tourists
   - Local rural people looking for work in the tourist industry set up squatter camps on the coast.

3. **ICT idea** Find out more about Curaçao by looking at the websites at:
   http://www.heinemann.co.uk/hotlinks (insert code 1631P)

7 Geography Matters

Review and reflect

In this unit you have studied resources and ecosystems. You have learned how people use and misuse them. You have also learned that people have different opinions about how to solve problems in the future. Overfishing is just one example of the way that people overexploit ecosystems. If we think about future generations, then we need to manage resources in a more sustainable way.

A Our future environment?

"The time is 3:17, the temperature is 58°F and the quality of life is 24 per cent"

B The kids were thrilled after finding sandcastle aids already on the beach

C We caught him in polluted water

Can the Earth cope?

B Development compass rose

Activities

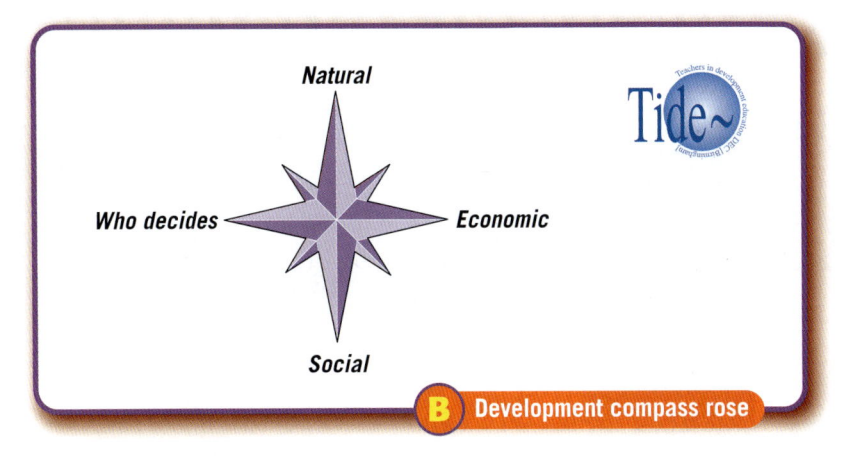

1 a Work in pairs or small groups. Look back through this unit and make a list in rough of all the resource and environmental issues you have studied. Write down:
- what the issue is
- where it is happening
- a few key points about the issue, for example the problem and solution.

b Stick an outline map of the world in the centre of a large piece of paper. Locate all the issues on the map, then neatly annotate (label) on the details about each.

c Discuss which issues:
- have already had an effect on your lives
- might affect young people in other parts of the world
- might affect young people in future.

d Find a way of showing your ideas on your map.

2 Choose one resource or environmental issue from this unit to think about in depth.

a Make a copy of the development compass rose **B** in the centre of a large piece of paper.

b In pairs, discuss the issue, then write around the outside which problems or changes are:
- **N**atural – to do with ecosystems
- **E**conomic – to do with jobs and money
- **S**ocial – to do with people and the way they live
- **W**ho decides – the people who make decisions.

3 Choose one of the cartoons on page 128 that shows a negative future for the world.

a In pairs, discuss what you think it is saying about the future.

b Each design your own cartoon to show a positive future, or the future you would prefer.

c Discuss the main differences between the cartoons.

d Finally, write a summary of your ideas – make sure you include some of these key words from this unit:
- sustainable
- resource
- conservation
- ecosystem.

8 Crime and the local community

A Violence at anti-Capitalism protests, London, 2000

B ITV's The Bill, a popular image of the police

C Peaceful protests in Seattle, USA, 2000

D Graffiti on a train

E CCTV in Oxford

Learn about

Crime happens all over the world – in cities, in towns and in the countryside. Some types of crime affect people much more than others. Views on different types of crime vary from person to person. This unit looks at patterns of criminal activity within local areas. You are going to investigate:

- what crime is and how it is caused
- what people feel about crime
- how crime varies locally and nationally
- how the problem of crime might be solved.

What is crime?

A **crime** is any action or offence that is punishable by law. Crimes include murder, burglary, assault, robbery, sexual assault, shoplifting, joyriding, blackmail and fraud.

Compared with many other countries there is a lot of crime in the UK. However, the 2000 British Crime Survey showed that crime rates are falling. Here are some facts:

- Shoplifting in the UK totalled £1.4 billion in 1996–1997.
- More than one in twenty British homes is burgled every year.
- Half of all violence by strangers is committed by people who have been drinking.
- About 80 per cent of criminals are male.
- Babies under the age of one year are at more risk of being murdered than any other age group.
- Since 1988 burglaries have fallen by 20 per cent and car thefts by 15 per cent.

What are the causes of crime?

This is difficult to answer but here are some facts:

- More criminals are young rather than old.
- There is more theft in rich societies than there is in poor societies.
- Crime rates increase when more people use illegal drugs.
- Crime rates increase when there is more unemployment in the country.

Is all crime recorded?

Most information about crime comes from official police data, but only about a quarter of all crime is reported to the police.

- Some crimes are not reported because people think they are trivial. An example is speeding, although it may lead to accidents and death.
- The young and people from ethnic minorities may be unhappy with the service they get from the police.
- Many violent assaults, sexual attacks and other crimes are not reported because the victim knows the attacker.

Activities

1. Add your own definition of the word *crime* to your word bank.

2. In a group of three or four, list all the different types of crime that you can think of. Look at photos **A** to **E** to get you started.

3. a Copy the table below. It classifies crimes into five different types.

A Theft	B Violent crime	C Damage to property	D Traffic offences	E Drug crimes

   b Put your answers from question **2** into the correct column.

   c Are there any problems? Do some crimes fit into more than one column or no column? Explain why.

4. Crime report

   a Over a two-week period, keep a record of the crimes that are shown in the media. Use these three headings:

   local TV or newspapers   national TV news or newspapers   TV entertainment programmes

   b Does the media affect what we think about crime? Think about which crimes are more serious than others, where crime happens, when it happens and who it affects. Here are some ideas to get you started:

   - 'The way that crime is shown on TV sometimes makes us think that …'
   - 'Certain crimes are reported on the news, so we might think that … whereas some crimes are not reported on the national news, so this makes us think that …'

8 Geography Matters

What do people feel about crime?

Getting Technical

- **Burglary:** entering a building illegally in order to commit a crime
- **Robbery:** stealing from somebody by threatening to use, or using, violence
- **Vehicle theft:** stealing, or trying to steal, a car, van, motorbike, etc. or a part of that vehicle
- **Fraud:** using trickery or cheating to steal something

Are people afraid of crime?

Table **A** shows what crimes different people are most worried about. It compares males and females and people of different ages. It also compares people in London with all people in England and Wales

A Percentages of people who feel very worried about some types of crimes

	London				England and Wales			
	Males aged 16–59	Males aged 60 and over	Females aged 16–59	Females aged 60 and over	Males aged 16–59	Males aged 60 and over	Females aged 16–59	Females aged 60 and over
Burglary	23	21	28	23	18	18	26	25
Mugging	15	19	26	26	12	13	26	26
Theft of car	24	17	23	10	24	19	27	23
Racial attack	10	9	18	11	6	4	12	7

Activities

1. **a** A hypothesis is a statement of what you might expect. Below are some suggestions to get you started. Try to write three hypotheses of your own.

   b Now look at table **A**. Was each of your hypotheses correct? Use table **A** to write an answer for each one.

Hypothesis about:	Hypothesis	Is this correct?
males and females	I would expect males to be just as worried about crime as females	No. Females of all ages were more worried about crime
old and young people		
people in London		
mugging		

2. Study the data in table **A**.

   a Draw a multiple bar graph to show how different groups of people fear theft of a car. The 'How to' box on page 133 will help you.

   b Describe what your graph shows. Then try to explain your findings.

Table **A** shows that people in this country are worried about crime. The crime rate in cities is higher than in rural areas, but many people in rural areas are also very worried about crime. Tables **B** and **C** compare crime rates in Wiltshire with crime rates in London. Wiltshire is a mainly rural area in southern England.

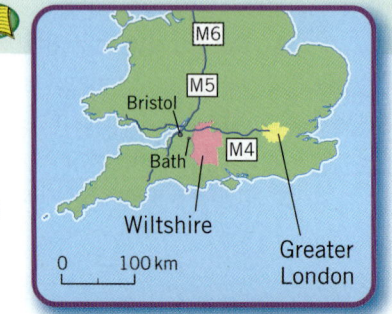

Crime and the local community

Type of crime	Number of offences	% of all crimes
Theft	16 746	44
Burglary	5 718	15
Criminal damage	7 151	19
Violence	4 519	11
Fraud and forgery	2 086	5
Robbery	258	1
Drug offences	1 172	3
Other offences	811	2
Total crimes	38 461	
Total population	593 300	

B Reported crime in Wiltshire, 1999–2000

Type of crime	Number of offences	% of all crimes
Theft	426 235	41
Burglary	129 145	13
Criminal damage	151 590	14
Violence	156 880	15
Fraud and forgery	105 150	9
Robbery	36 317	3
Drug offences	26 233	3
Other offences	20 497	2
Total crimes	1 052 047	
Total population	7 285 000	

C Reported crime in London, 1999–2000

Activity

3 Study the data in table **B**.

a Draw a pie graph to show reported crime in Wiltshire in 1999–2000.

b Describe what your graph shows. The writing frame below will help you.

> In Wiltshire in 1999–2000, the total number of reported crimes was ... The pie graph shows that some crimes made up a large percentage of the total. These include ... Other crimes ... I also notice that ... Overall, the pie graph tells me ...

How to ...

... draw a multiple bar graph

A multiple bar graph is good for showing information divided into groups, such as people worried about car theft in London and in England and Wales.

1 Draw two axes on graph paper. The vertical (y) axis has a number – percentage of people worried. The horizontal (x) axis shows the groups of people.

2 Plot the data for people worried about car theft in London. The bars for males have been done for you. Add two bars for females.

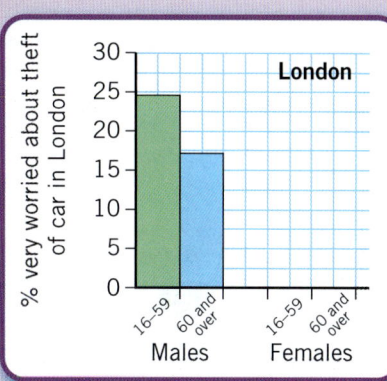

3 Draw a similar multiple bar graph for England and Wales.

How to ...

... draw a pie graph

A pie graph divides up a circle like slices of a pie. It is a good way to show percentages of something, like the different crimes committed in Wiltshire.

1 Use a calculator to turn all the percentages into degrees. For example, theft: 44% or $\frac{44}{100}$:

$\frac{44}{100} \times 360°$ (degrees in a circle) = 158°

2 Draw a circle. Use a protractor to mark 158°.

3 Mark the first segment, then repeat for the other crimes.

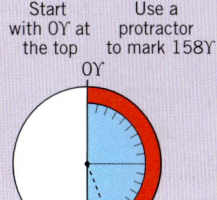

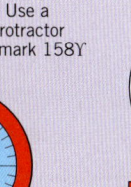

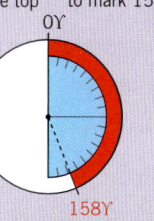

4 Add a key and title to your graph.

8 Geography Matters

Where do people expect crime to happen?

Case Study: Crime in Oxford

A Central ward

B North ward

C West ward

D Blackbird Leys ward

E South ward

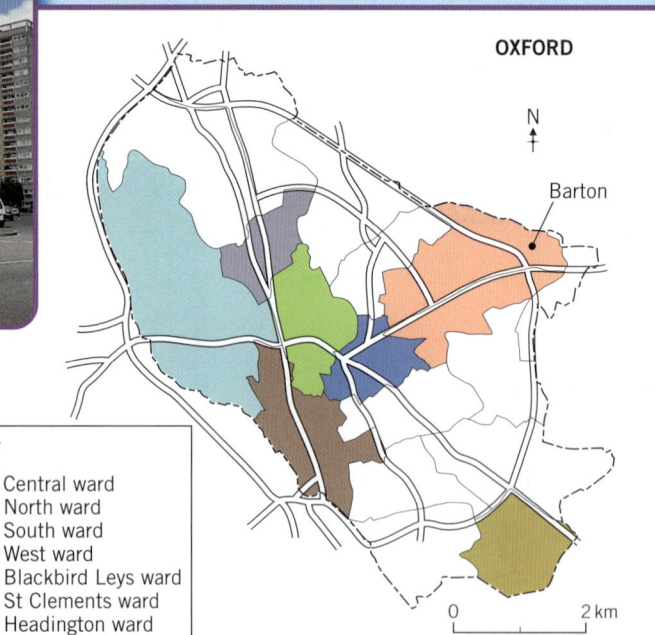

F St Clements ward

G Central ward

OXFORD

Barton

Key
- Central ward
- North ward
- South ward
- West ward
- Blackbird Leys ward
- St Clements ward
- Headington ward

0   2 km

134

Crime and the local community

H Barton, part of Headington ward

Oxford is a medium-sized city with a population of about 115 000 people. It is a good place to study crime because levels of violence and crime are not particularly high. Photographs **A** to **H** show different areas of Oxford. The activities will help you think about your perceptions of crime. Table **I** shows the crime figures for the different **wards**, or districts, of Oxford.

Ward	All crime
Oxford total	25 678
Central	4 671
St Clements	2 185
Quarry	2 005
North	1 706
Blackbird Leys	1 467
Iffley	1 318
Headington	1 179
East	1 093
Temple Cowley	1 078
Wolvercote	978
Marston	957
South	885
Littlemore	811
West	775
Wood Farm	758
Cherwell	752
Marston Parish	495
Risinghurst	295

I Crime figures for Oxford by ward, 1998

Data provided by the Thames Valley Police

Activities

1. Study photographs **A** to **H**.
   a Copy the table below. Grade each picture on a scale of 1–5, where 1 is safe and 5 is unsafe.
   b Put your results together with those of the rest of the class.
   c Which areas do people think are most safe and least safe?
   c Is there any variation between the results for girls and boys?

Photo	Score	Reason
A		

2. Which place do you think is the most likely to have a burglary? Give a reason.

3. Now compare the results from your class's survey with those in **I**.
   a List the areas in order, according to your survey.
   b Now compare them to the order produced by the Thames Valley Police.
      i How do they compare?
      ii Can you think of reasons for any differences that you have noted?

4. **Extension**
   Take photographs of your local area which show contrasting images. Show them to a friend or family member and ask them to score the images as you did for activity **1**. Make a short presentation about people's impression of crime. You could use a digital camera and presentation software. **ICT**

8 Geography Matters

Mapping crime in Oxford

Oxford has a wide mix of housing and standards of living. It ranges from the wealthy areas in north Oxford to housing estates at Barton and Blackbird Leys on the edge of the city where levels of unemployment are high. Map **A** shows the overall pattern of crime in Oxford.

Patterns of crime in Oxford – can we explain them?

Burglary is a big problem in Oxford, but some houses are more likely to get broken into than others.

A Crime in the wards of Oxford

Ward	All crime
Oxford total	25 678
1 Central	4 671
2 St. Clements	2 185
3 Quarry	2 005
4 North	1 706
5 Blackbird Leys	1 467
6 Iffley	1 318
7 Headington	1 179
8 East	1 093
9 Temple Cowley	1 078
10 Wolvercote	978
11 Marston	957
12 South	885
13 Littlemore	811
14 West	775
15 Wood Farm	758
16 Cherwell	752
17 Marston Parish	495
18 Risinghurst	295

Data provided by the Thames Valley Police

B Pattern of burglary in Oxford, 1999

Key
Recorded burglaries
- over 250
- 100–249
- 50–99
- 25–49
- 0–24
- ---- City boundary
- Roads
- Railway
- Rivers

Activity

1 a Look at map **B** and use the words below to copy and complete these sentences:

Some parts of Oxford have more burglaries than others. The area bordering the Cowley Road has 10 per cent of all Oxford's burglaries. In general there are few burglaries in the _____ and _____ of the city. Burglaries are concentrated in the _____ and _____ of Oxford.

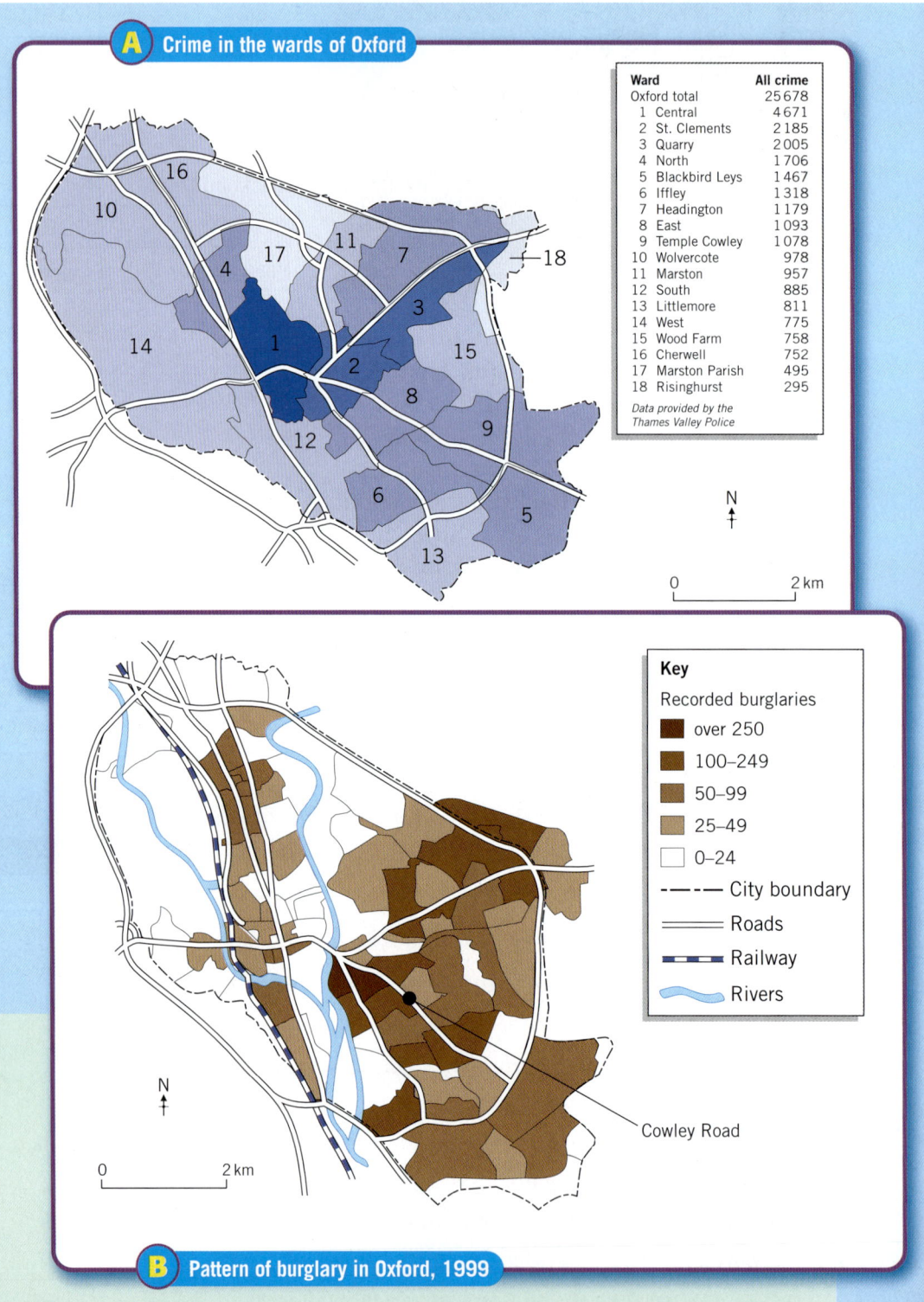

   north   south   east   west   suburbs   centre

b Look back at photos **F** and **H** on page 134. Which houses are more likely to get burgled? Give three reasons for your answer. Do other people agree with your answer?

C Pattern of vehicle theft in Oxford, 1999

Key
Recorded thefts
- over 250
- 151–250
- 101–150
- 51–100
- 0–50
- — · — City boundary
- ══ Roads
- ▬▬ Railway
- ～ Rivers

D This car has been stolen and dumped

Key
Recorded sexual attacks
- Over 5
- 3–4
- 2
- 1
- 0
- — · — City boundary
- ══ Roads
- ▬▬ Railway
- ～ Rivers

Getting Technical

- **Pattern:** where things are
- **Factor:** something that brings about change
- **Process:** how or why things change

E Pattern of sexual attacks in Oxford, 1999

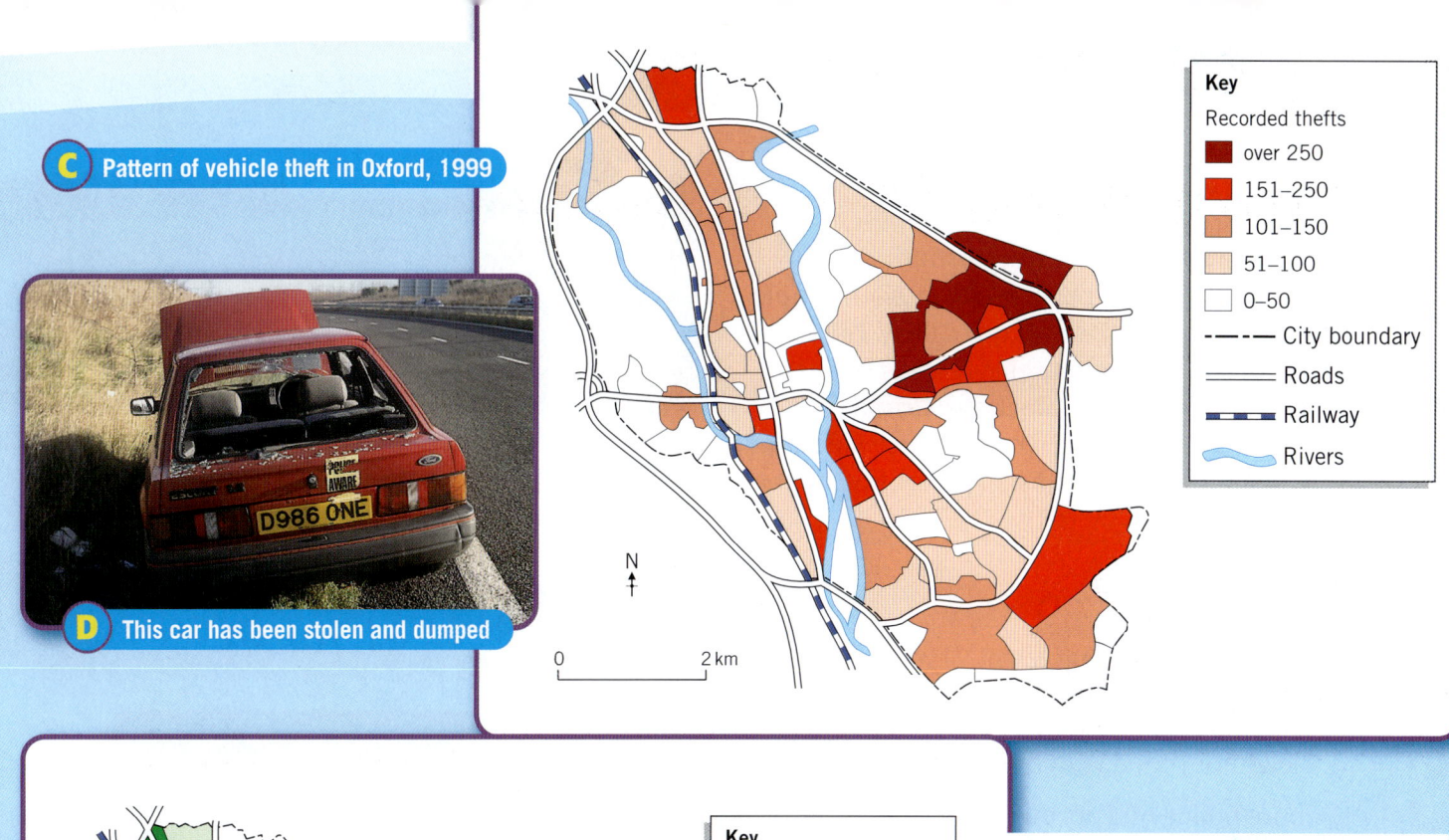

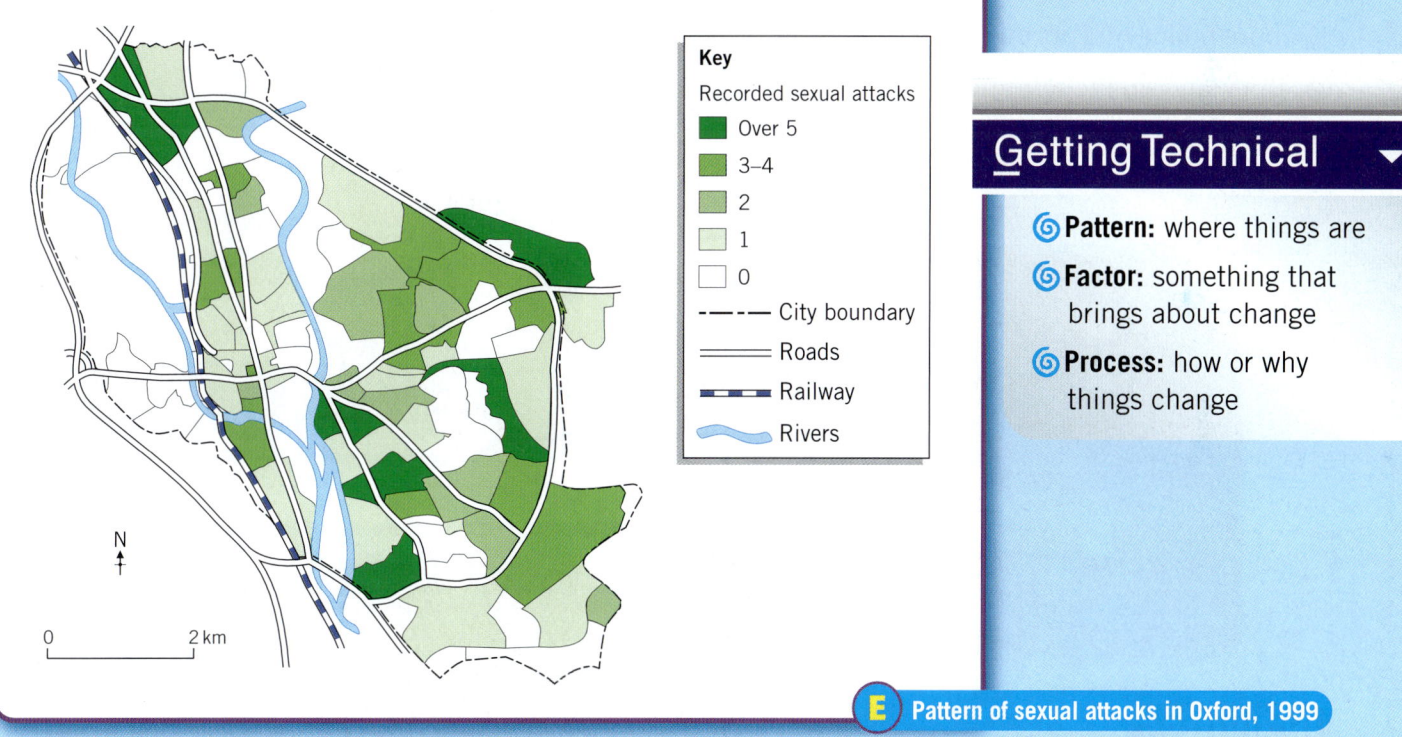

Map **C** shows the pattern of car thefts. Vehicle theft is a serious problem in Oxford. The Blackbird Leys estate has a bad reputation for joy riding. Map **E** shows the pattern of sexual attacks. These are not really concentrated in one location. Some places are obviously more dangerous than others, particularly if there are lots of young, single women living in an area.

Activities

2 Map **C** shows the pattern of vehicle theft.
  a Is this the same pattern as burglaries?
  b Why are more cars stolen from some places than others? Give two reasons. Here are two clues:
   - Car parks
   - Joy riders.

3 a In which part of Oxford would you expect shoplifting to be concentrated? Give two reasons for your answer.
  b How do you think closed-circuit TV cameras (CCTV) will affect the pattern of shoplifting?

8 Geography Matters

Fighting crime

Over half of all burglaries happen during the evening or night. Ten per cent occur when people are away for the weekend or on holiday. Houses with poor security are most likely to get burgled, but flats also have more break-ins. **Crime prevention** schemes can help to reduce different types of crime. Below is a list of prevention methods:

- security guards
- increased use of CCTV
- better street lighting
- security alarms
- Neighbourhood Watch schemes
- more police officers on the beat
- strict laws on the sale and drinking of alcohol in the city centre.

F Reward offer following a theft

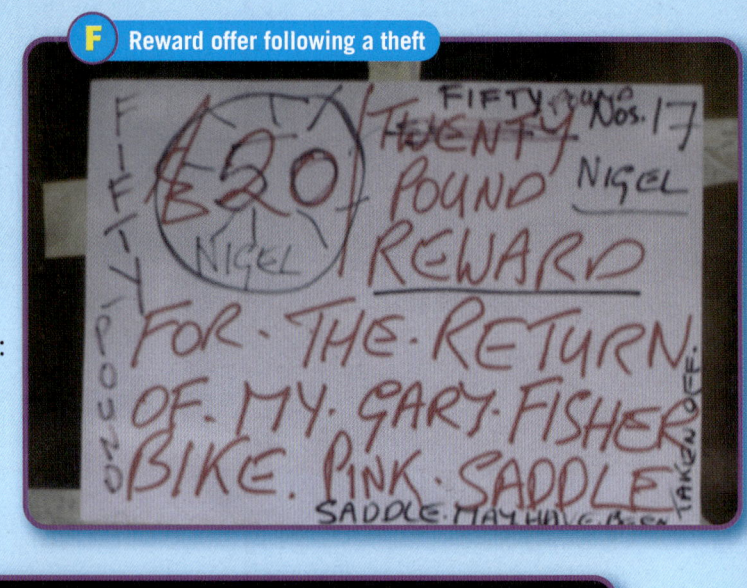

H Security alarms on recent housing developments

G An underpass in Oxford

I Neighbourhood watch schemes help to reduce crime

Activities

1. Look at the list of **crime prevention** methods above. For each one:
   a Say which types of crime it will help stop.
   b Explain how it prevents the crime.

2. Copy and complete the table below.

Crime prevention method	What does it prevent?	How?
security guards	shoplifting	shoplifters think they might get caught

138

Crime and the local community

How to ...

... plot a density map of crime in Oxford

Density maps are sometimes called **choropleth** maps. Map **B** on page 136 is a choropleth map.

1. Decide on six groups, e.g. 0–799, 800–1599, 1600–2399, 2400–3199, 3200–3999 and over 4000 crimes per year.
2. Choose six colours – similar colours or shades are best. Shade the areas with the most crimes with the darkest shade, and shade the areas with the smallest amount of crime with the lightest shade.

Activities

3 **a** Maps **B**, **C** and **E** on pages 136–137 are **density maps**. On a copy of map **A**, plot a density map to show the distribution of total crime in Oxford.

   b Describe and explain the distribution. You could do this by labelling key points from the text around your map.

4 **Extension**

Use the Thames Valley Police website at http://www.heinemann.co.uk/hotlinks to investigate the enquiry question:

What are the Thames Valley Police doing to reduce crime, disorder and fear in the Thames Valley region?

5 Look at photo **G**. How could this area be made safer?

6 The Thames Valley Police website also has a list of **frequently asked questions (FAQs)** about young people and the law. It tells you about your rights, and also what happens to those who commit an offence.

Investigate the Thames Valley Police website or the site of your local force. Use the information to design a leaflet or poster to tell young people about how the law affects them.

7 **a** In groups of three or four, make a list of five questions you might ask about crime.

   b Use the Internet to investigate your questions. The websites listed at http://www.heinemann.co.uk/hotlinks (insert code 1631P) contain information about crime.

8 Geography Matters

Patterns of crime nationwide

Activities

1 Use map **A** and an atlas to investigate the pattern of crime in England and Wales.

a Make lists of areas with the highest and lowest rates of crime. You could set your work out in a table like this:

High crime areas	Low crime areas
London	

b Discuss with a partner which sorts of areas have high crime rates and which have low crime rates. A population density map might help you here. Write notes about the main pattern you notice on the map.

c Finally, look for anything surprising on the map. For example, are there any places you would expect to have a high rate of crime, but which do not?

2 a Discuss with your partner what factors or reasons might explain the pattern you have found. Your work on the rest of this unit should help you with this.

b Share your ideas with another pair or the whole class – try to agree a short list of possible reasons for differences in crime rates.

3 You are now ready to write a short report on patterns of crime in the UK. The writing frame below may help you:

> I am going to describe the main features of …
> One of the main things I noticed …
> Some areas …
> However, …
> The main factors which explain this pattern …
> To summarise …

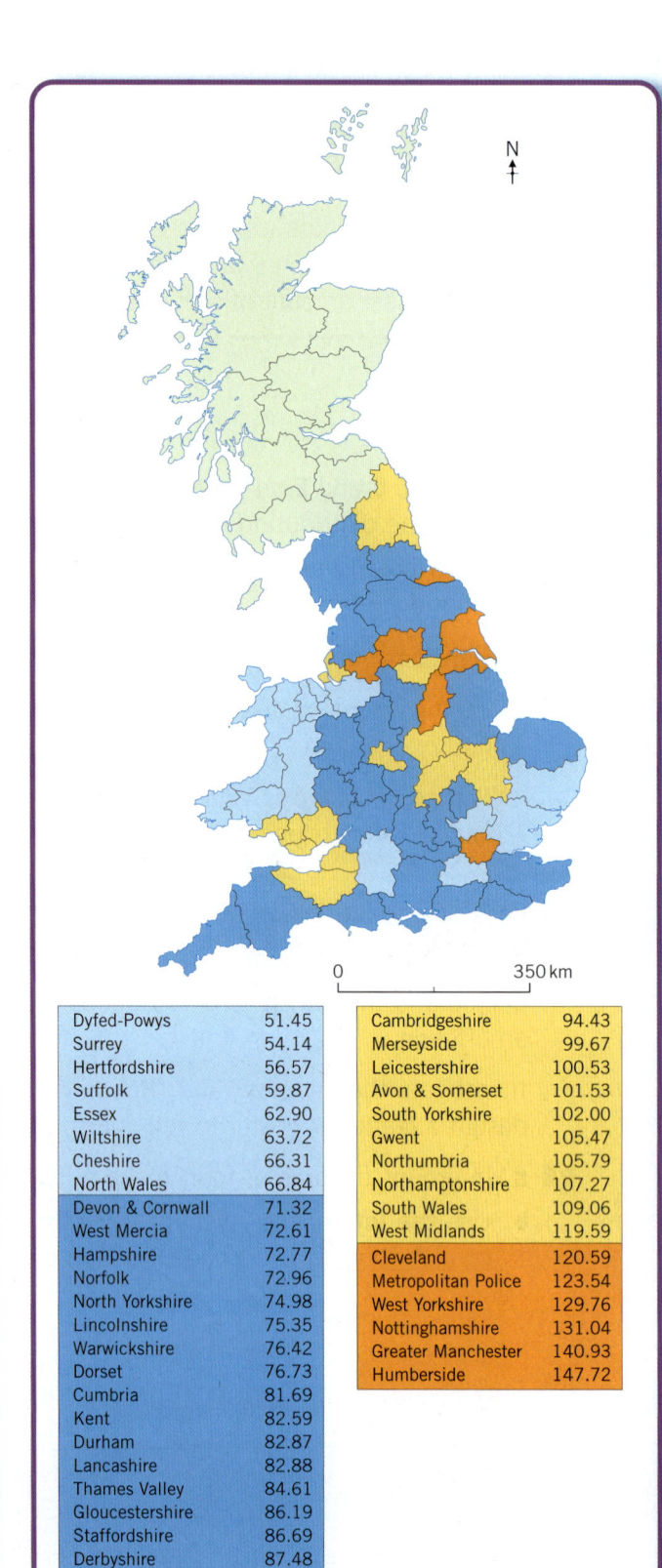

Dyfed-Powys	51.45		Cambridgeshire	94.43
Surrey	54.14		Merseyside	99.67
Hertfordshire	56.57		Leicestershire	100.53
Suffolk	59.87		Avon & Somerset	101.53
Essex	62.90		South Yorkshire	102.00
Wiltshire	63.72		Gwent	105.47
Cheshire	66.31		Northumbria	105.79
North Wales	66.84		Northamptonshire	107.27
Devon & Cornwall	71.32		South Wales	109.06
West Mercia	72.61		West Midlands	119.59
Hampshire	72.77		Cleveland	120.59
Norfolk	72.96		Metropolitan Police	123.54
North Yorkshire	74.98		West Yorkshire	129.76
Lincolnshire	75.35		Nottinghamshire	131.04
Warwickshire	76.42		Greater Manchester	140.93
Dorset	76.73		Humberside	147.72
Cumbria	81.69			
Kent	82.59			
Durham	82.87			
Lancashire	82.88			
Thames Valley	84.61			
Gloucestershire	86.19			
Staffordshire	86.69			
Derbyshire	87.48			
Sussex	87.67			
Bedfordshire	88.86			

A Reported crimes per thousand people in England and Wales

Crime and the local community

Review and reflect

Things you have learned about	Pages	Examples	Geography skills	Key skills
What is crime?	131	UK		
What are the causes of crime?	131	UK		
What do people feel about crime?	132, 133	Wiltshire, London, UK		
Where do people expect crime to happen?	134, 135	Oxford		
Mapping crime in Oxford	136, 137	Oxford		
Patterns of crime nationwide	140	UK		

Activities

1. Make a large copy of the table above.
   a. Complete the fourth column, which reminds you what geographical skills you have used. For example, you may have drawn a map, summarised data, looked at photographs and drawn conclusions, described a pattern and suggested reasons to explain a pattern.

   b. Think again about how you did the activities. You should be able to come up with a list of key skills to put in the fifth column.

2. Look back through this unit to check that you know the meaning of the key words in **bold**. Use them to update your geography word bank.

3. **Extension**

   Conduct a class debate on an issue in crime that your class finds interesting. Use what you have learned about crime from this chapter, but think especially about your local area. For example, you may wish to argue that:

   Young people are not that bad – despite the statistics

   or discuss some other aspects of crime that affect young people. You could ask the Police Community Liaison Officer or Schools Liaison Officer to come along and give a presentation to the class and listen to your points of view.

help!

Your key skills may include:
- communication (language)
- numeracy
- ICT
- working with others
- improving your own learning.

Glossary

Adaptations   special features developed by plants to help them survive in a difficult environment, e.g. very hot and dry conditions.

Altitude   height of the land above sea level.

Arch   a natural rock bridge. It is formed when the sea erodes through a headland.

Atmosphere   the layer of gases surrounding the Earth.

Audience   the people who use a shopping area.

Bedding planes   horizontal cracks between layers of rock.

Calcium carbonate   the chemical that makes up limestone rock.

Cave   a hole beneath the surface or in a cliff. It is formed by the action of water.

Cavern   a large cave.

Chalk   a hard, white sedimentary rock. It is made up of the skeletons of millions of tiny sea animals.

Charcoal   a raw material made of partly burnt wood. It can be used instead of coal to make iron.

Choropleth map   a map using density shading for particular groups. It is also known as a **density map**.

Cirrus   high-level cloud formed of ice crystals.

Clay   a soft, fine sedimentary rock.

Clints   the surface 'slabs' of rock on a limestone pavement.

Community   a group of plants and animals that live closely together.

Conflict   where groups of people have different ideas about how an area should be used. These conflicts can be shown on a **conflict matrix**.

Convection rain   heavy rain formed by the cooling of moist air which has risen from the heated ground or sea.

Crime   an action that breaks the law.

Crude oil   petroleum as it is taken from the ground, before refining.

Cumulonimbus   very tall storm clouds formed when air rises very quickly.

Cumulus   heaped up masses of cloud with bumpy tops.

Density map   see **choropleth map**.

Deposition   when a river or the sea dumps or **deposits** what it is carrying.

Discharge   the volume of water which passes through a river at one point in time. It is measured in cubic metres per second.

Dispersed   scattered.

Drought   a time of low rainfall, often lasting many years.

Dry valleys   valleys formed on permeable rock after the Ice Age. Water now flows under the ground and no river can be seen.

Economic development   the success of a country at producing useful goods.

Equatorial   a type of climate found near the Equator.

Evapotranspiration   evaporation from the soil and other surfaces and water released from plants.

Extensive ranching   cattle farming in which there are only a few cattle per hectare.

Food chain   a cycle that passes nutrients from organism to organism. Plants make food using sunlight and are eaten by animals. Bacteria in the soil break down dead plants and animals into soil nutrients. Plants take these up through their roots and start the cycle again.

Forecast   a weather forecast predicts future weather.

Frequently asked questions (FAQs)   the part of a website that gives answers to the questions people ask most often.

Frontal rain   precipitation caused when warm air is forced to rise over cooler air.

Gradient   slope.

Granite   a very hard igneous rock made of crystals of minerals.

Grykes   gaps between blocks of stone on a *limestone pavement*.

Headlands   hard rocks which are left jutting out into the sea. They are often cliffs.

Hierarchy   a series of geographical features that build up: for example, a small village, a market town, a large town, a city.

Honeypot   a place that attracts large numbers of tourists.

Humidity   the amount of water vapour held in the air. When this is high the weather is **humid**.

Hydro-electric power   a way of generating electricity by using the force of water to turn a turbine.

Hydrological cycle   a never-ending circulation of water. Water evaporates from the sea and land, rises and condenses to form clouds. It then falls back to Earth as precipitation.
Ice ages   periods of time when the land surface was covered in ice due to low temperatures. The last Ice Age in the UK was between 19 000 and 10 000 years ago.
Intensive   farming that produces a lot of crop per hectare.
Isotherm   a line on a map that joins places with the same temperature.
Joints   vertical cracks in rock.
Latitude   distance north or south of the Equator measured in degrees.
Layer shading   using a series of colours to show the height of land on a map.
Limestone   a sedimentary rock formed from calcium and the carbon remains of sea creatures.
Limestone pavements   limestone exposed at the surface to reveal *clints* and *grykes*.
Limestone scars   vertical rock faces that are exposed.
Longshore drift   the transport of material along a beach. It happens when waves hit the beach at an angle.
Lowland   land between 0 and 100 metres above sea level, usually fairly flat.
Marble   a hard metamorphic rock.
Meteorologist   a scientist who studies the weather.
Nutrients   chemicals in the soil used by plants.
Ocean current   a flow of warm or cold water.
Ozone layer   the layer of the upper atmosphere, from about 12 to 50 kilometres above the Earth's surface. It protects the Earth from harmful radiation from the Sun.
Photosynthesis   green plants use the energy of sunlight to convert carbon dioxide and water into glucose which they use for growth. At the same time they release oxygen into the air.
Pillars   formed when stalactites and stalagmites join together.
Plateau   a high flat-topped hill or hilly area.
Porous   rocks with tiny holes in them which hold water are porous.
Prevailing winds   the winds which blow most frequently over an area. They are, described by the compass direction from which they come.
Refined oil   oil in a form that can be used in, for example, homes and cars. It is made by removing the impurities from crude oil.
Relief rain   precipitation caused when air is forced to rise over hills and mountains.
Resurgence   where water emerges at the surface.
Retail goods   goods bought by consumers, often in shops.
Revetment   a barrier placed along the foot of a cliff or sea wall to break the power of the waves before they reach the coast.
Savanna   an area of tropical grassland with tall grasses and a few trees.
Selva   rainforest.
Sink   a place where water disappears underground as it reaches permeable rock.
Spit   a long beach formed by longshore drift. Spits often stretch across the mouths of rivers or where the coast suddenly changes direction.
Spring   a place where water reaches the surface, for example after passing through permeable rock.
Stack   the remains of collapsed arches left when cliffs are worn away.
Stalactites   icicle-shaped deposits of calcium carbonate hanging from a cave roof.
Stalagmites   deposits of calcium carbonate which build up on a cave floor.
Stratus   low clouds forming a layer or 'sheet' across the sky.
Sustainability   using resources wisely today, so that people in the future can still use them. Resources used in this way are **sustainable**.
Swallow hole   a funnel-shaped hole which leads underground.
Temperature   how hot or cold a place is.
Transport   carry. For example, rock fragments that have been eroded are removed or transported by the sea, wind, ice or rivers.
Upland   land over 100 metres above sea level, usually hills or mountains.
Velocity   the speed of a river. It is measured in metres per second.
Ward   a small local area in a town or city.
Water vapour   water when it is a gas.
Weathering   the breakdown of rocks by air, moisture and plants and animals.

Index

Amazonia 75, 80–4, 111

beach management 32
Beachy Head (Sussex) 27–9
biomes 108, 109
Birling Gap (Sussex) 28–9
Birmingham 36–7, 41–2
Brazil 64–9, 85–7, 111
    developments 80–4
    regional differences 70–5

cattle ranching 81
choropleth maps 139
cliffs 22, 23, 24, 27–9
climate 56–63
climate graphs 56–7
clouds 48, 49, 50, 51, 52, 53
coastal deposition 25
coastal erosion 22, 23–4, 27–9, 32
coastal management 18, 30–2
coasts 18, 33
conflict matrices 26, 87
conservation 102–3, 120, 121, 123
contour lines 9, 98, 99
coral reefs 124–7
crime 130–3, 141
    patterns 134–7, 139, 140
crime fighting 138, 139
cross-sections 8–9, 13, 98, 99
Curaçao 127

data collection 11, 17
deforestation 80, 81, 82–3, 84, 106
density maps 139
deposition 5, 21, 25
descriptions 23, 42
development 76–9

ecosystems 106–8, 110–13, 116–27, 128
England, rocks and relief 90–1
environmental issues 66–7, 106, 107, 129
erosion 5, 6–7, 20, 21–2, 23–4, 27–9, 32
Europe 46–7, 51–3, 56–62
explanations 40, 42

field sketches 12
fieldwork investigations 10–17
fishing 120–3, 125
flood protection 30–1
Florida (USA) 32
food chains 112

geographical hierarchies 68
geographical questions 10, 17, 18, 45, 55, 65

geological timescale 91
GNP (Gross National Product) 78, 79
goods 35, 37, 38
graphs 15, 55, 56–7, 133
Gross National Product (GNP) 78, 79

hierarchies, geographical 68
hydrological cycle 49

Ingleborough Hill (Yorkshire) 98–9
Internet shopping 43–4

Karst region (Croatia) 104–5

limestone 19, 88–9, 91, 92–3, 102–5
limestone features 88–9, 94–6, 100–1
location 68
long profiles 6–7, 8, 14

Malham Cove (Yorkshire) 88, 95, 103
marine ecosystems 116–27, 128
mining 84
multiple bar graphs 133

National Parks 97, 102–3
natural resources 106, 110, 114–17, 128–9
North Sea, fishing 122–3
nutrient cycle 112, 113

oceans 116–27, 128
oil industry 118, 119
OS (Ordnance Survey) maps 8–9, 14, 29, 30–1, 98–9, 100–1
overfishing 120, 121, 122–3, 128
Oxford 134–9

perceptions of crime 132–3, 134–5
performance standards 39
photographs 23, 65, 66–7
photosynthesis 112, 113
physical maps 47, 51
pie graphs 133
plants 109, 112, 113
political maps 47
pollution 106–7, 118, 119, 121
Poplar Road (Kings Heath, Birmingham) 41–2
population and resources 107, 114, 115
precipitation 48, 49, 50–1, 60–1
proportional lines 15
proportional maps 114, 115

questions, geographical 10, 17, 18, 45, 55, 65

rain 48, 49, 50–1, 60–1
rainforest 80–4, 111, 113

relief maps 90
resources 106, 110, 114–17, 128–9
river channels 12, 13, 15
river valleys 4, 6–9
rivers 4–5
    erosion 5, 6–7, 20
    investigations 10–17
    long profiles 6–7, 8, 14
roads 80–1
rock types 91
Rondônia (Brazil) 82–3

satellite images 46, 47, 51, 52–3
scattergraphs 55
seas 116–27, 128
shopping 34, 35, 41–4
shopping environments 34, 35, 36–7, 39, 40
shopping hierarchies 37, 38
situation 68
sustainable development 75, 76, 110, 111, 121, 123, 128

temperatures 58–9
tourism 32, 58, 61, 62, 97, 102
    coral reefs 125, 126–7
Towyn (North Wales) 30–1
transport developments 80–1

vegetation 109, 112, 113

waves 20, 22
weather 46, 48, 50–5, 56, 63
weather forecasting 53, 54–5
weather maps 51, 54
weathering 5, 6, 19, 20, 21, 93

Yorkshire Dales 97–104